HOW LIKE A GOD

The LTCB International Library Trust

The LTCB (Long-Term Credit Bank of Japan) International Library Trust, established in July 2000, is the successor to the LTCB International Library Foundation. It carries on the mission that the foundation's founders articulated as follows:

> The world is moving steadily toward a borderless economy and deepening international interdependence. Amid economic globalization, Japan is developing ever-closer ties with nations worldwide through trade, through investment, and through manufacturing and other localized business operations.

> Japan's global activity is drawing attention to its political, economic, and social systems and to the concepts and values that underlie those systems. But the supply of translations of Japanese books about those and other Japan-related subjects has not kept pace with demand.

> The shortage of foreign-language translations of Japanese books about Japanese subjects is attributable largely to the high cost of translating and publishing. To address that issue, the LTCB International Library Foundation funds the translation and the distribution of selected Japanese works about Japan's politics, economy, society, and culture.

International House of Japan, Inc., manages the publishing activities of the LTCB International Library Trust, and Sumitomo Mitsui Trust Bank, Ltd., manages the trust's financial assets.

HOW LIKE A GOD

DEIFICATION IN JAPANESE RELIGION

SATO HIROO

translated by David Noble

Transliteration of Foreign Words

The Hepburn system of romanization is used for Japanese terms, including the names of persons and places. Except in familiar place names, long vowels are indicated by macrons. An apostrophe is used to distinguish syllable-final *n* from *n* at the beginning of a syllable. The spelling of non-Japanese words that have been incorporated into Japanese reflects the way these words are pronounced by Japanese speakers.

The local custom of placing the family name first has been followed for the names of Japanese, Chinese, and Korean persons.

This book originally appeared in Japanese as *Hitogami shinkō no keifu* (Tokyo: Iwata Shoin, 2012). International House of Japan retains the English-language translation rights under contract with Satō Hiroo and through the courtesy of Iwata Shoin.

First English edition published October 2016 by International House of Japan
11-16, Roppongi 5-chōme, Minato-ku, Tokyo 106-0032, Japan
Tel: +81-3-3470-3211   Fax: +81-3-3470-3170
E-mail: ihj@i-house.or.jp
URL: http://www.i-house.or.jp/

Printed in Japan
ISBN 978-4-924971-43-1

Contents

CHAPTER 3

New Deities and the Tumuli   59

CHAPTER 4

Between *Hitogami* and *Mononoke*   81

CHAPTER 5

Escorts to the Other Shore   105

CHAPTER 6

The Undeparted Dead   133

Preface to the English Edition

I AM DELIGHTED AND HONORED THAT this book has been selected for translation in the LTCB International Library series for widespread distribution at home and overseas.

It tells the story of the origins, growth, and transformation of the gods of the Japanese islands over a period spanning more than ten thousand years, from the Jōmon period to the present. The gods of Japan have been the subject of a vast corpus of previous research. And it would be no exaggeration to say that the bulk of it has been devoted to efforts to explicate the *kami* of Shintō, countless traces of which remain even amid the advanced civilization of the present day.

One premise has been common to virtually all of this prior research on the Japanese gods: that these deities can be grasped with descriptions such as "indigenous" or "unique." This almost inevitably gives birth to a perception that to explicate the nature of these gods is to explicate the mentality of the Japanese people and to uncover an essence of Japanese culture that remains fundamentally unaltered with the passage of time.

While this approach has made rich and valuable contributions to our understanding of the Japanese gods, it is impossible to deny that it has also greatly biased research in this field. Defining the Japanese gods as traditional presences who have existed since remote antiquity has meant that research on the gods from a historical perspective is practically nonexistent. This is a serious problem. At the same time, seeing Shintō as something unique to Japan has been a factor in ignoring the diversity of deities inhabiting these islands, as well as discouraging research comparing Japan with other regions of the world.

Given this current state of research, in this book I have attempted to discuss the gods of the Japanese islands in a format as broadly applicable as possible, and one comparable with other regions. My goal is to open the way to comparisons between Shintō and the religions of other countries, while at the same time presenting to the global tradition of theological research—dominated until now by a Eurocentric concentration on the study of the Christian world—new horizons for investigation inspired by the completely different cultural tradition represented by the gods of Japan.

I am not, to be quite honest, confident in how fully I have realized such lofty ambitions. But in addition to the English edition of this book, a Korean translation is presently underway, to be published later this year. It would bring me the greatest happiness if this book would, through these translations, reach people outside of Japan and make some small contribution to the advancement of world scholarship.

The translation, publication, and distribution of this English translation has been sponsored by the LTCB International Library Trust and administered by International House of Japan, and I am grateful to both of these institutions. As managing editor, Saji Yasuo's fine attention to detail has ensured that this English publication is the equal if not the better of the original Japanese edition in almost every respect. And without David Noble's unstinting labor in producing such a fine and readable English translation, this book would never have come into being. I would like to express my deepest appreciation to both of these individuals, and to all the other members of the staff involved in its publication.

Satō Hiroo
May 2016

When Humans Become Gods

I think no one would deny that until quite recently it was the common practice of the Japanese people to take those who once lived amongst us, sharing our joys and sorrows, and after a certain time had passed after their deaths and certain conditions had been met, to enshrine them in accordance with generally established procedures as deities to be celebrated, reverenced, and prayed to.

Yanagita Kunio, "Hito o kami ni matsuru fūshū"

The human quest for the divine

I F WE EXAMINE the history of the human race, we find virtually no tribe or people who were without religion. From well before the dawn of recorded history, people have recognized existences that transcend the human, seeking their presence and heeding their counsel. In this sense, it seems fair to say that religion is one index of what distinguishes human beings from other animals. Even so, why is it that we find this necessary? Why is it that we have continued to seek the divine with such persistence and determination?

1

For believers convinced that their god or gods have always existed, such questions are beside the point, and I do not intend to begin by rejecting opinions premised upon the existence of god(s). But neither will I adopt such a position here. The purpose of this book is to grasp, from an objective and scholarly perspective, the birth and evolution of the gods. In the distant past of this string of islands we now call Japan, something transcendent sprang from the dimly-lit recesses of the human mind,

Figure Intro-1 Why is it that people see the image of the divine in nature? (Sarutahiko Shrine, Nara)

and as it took on more definite shape and form, caused people to bow before it. This book, supported insofar as possible by concrete historical sources, aims to elucidate the process by which this occurred.

This will be an exploration of the true identity of the gods who have been such essential partners to mankind, as well as an interrogation of the inscrutable nature of the human beings who have always found these gods necessary.

The insights of cognitive anthropology

As already noted, wherever one looks in the world—ancient or modern, East or West—no society has existed without gods. Particularly in premodern societies, religion possessed immense significance and function. Because of this, gods have continued to be a crucial theme of study, not only among those who believe in them, but among academic researchers. For medieval theologians and scholars of religion, proof of the existence of God was the central theme. And in modern times, a prodigious volume of research related to gods and deities has accumulated in every academic field, from philosophy and history to literature, art history, architecture, and religious studies.

This book will frequently draw upon the accomplishments of such research. But here I would like to make special note of a methodology that has been influential in recent years in addressing this issue: the discipline of cognitive anthropology.

One might describe the traditional approach of the historical sciences, archaeology included, as one of differentiation and classification. The surface of our planet teems with living creatures, among them human beings, who in turn are divided into many peoples, each with its own history and culture. A comparison of all of these cultures with one another should underline the unique features of each while at the same time yielding certain parameters that could be used for their systematic classification. To uncover the origins and development of these diverse cultures in the recorded history of the past—this methodology forms the mainstream of contemporary historical studies, and especially that of cultural history.

But cognitive anthropology does not follow this methodology. It is not interested in diversity, but in the common cognitive structure shared by *homo sapiens* as a biological species and in the universality of the mental functions achieved by human beings at particular stages in their evolutionary development.

At present, our planet is home to a variety of races and peoples with different colors of skin, speaking different languages. At first glance, one might think that humanity comprises an almost infinite number of variations, even at a single point in time. Yet if we consider human beings as a single species, transcending racial and regional variation, we should find a remarkable commonality among all of us. With regard to our basic sensory and cognitive faculties—vision, hearing, the capacity for language acquisition—racial categorizations are essentially meaningless. This is why people of different races can compete equally under uniform conditions and rules in the Olympics or in scientific competitions of various kinds.

It is this commonality of cognitive structure at the species level that is emphasized by the discipline of cognitive archaeology. With regard to the gods and deities that are the subject of this book, we have archaeological evidence from around thirty to forty thousand years ago, in different places around the globe, of the depiction of things which did not exist or were not of immediate utility for daily life—such as figurines or cave paintings of a man with the upper body of a lion. And we find widespread evidence dating to more than ten thousand years ago of funeral rites being practiced. These phenomena are linked to a perception of existences transcending the human and might be called the original template of religious thought.

Cognitive archaeology tells us that these cognitive faculties have their origin in revolutionary changes in the structure of consciousness occurring about sixty thousand years ago in the brains of the modern human species (*homo sapiens sapiens*). It was as a result of this "big bang" in human consciousness that people seem to have acquired the capacity to conceive of the divine. All subsequent complex developments of human society have their origins in this epochal event.[1]

The basic approach of cognitive anthropology is to decipher the operations of mind of ancient humans by examining their sites and relics from the perspective of cognitive development, while at the same time attempting to extrapolate from this to elucidate human cognitive structure itself.

In his *Cahiers Sauvages* series, published by Kōdansha, and especially in the volumes *Kuma kara ō e* (From Bears to Kings, 2002) and *Kami no hatsumei* (The Invention of the Gods, 2003), noted anthropologist Nakazawa Shin'ichi applies the findings of cognitive anthropology to propose new and stimulating hypotheses concerning the birth of the gods. The work of cognitive archaeologist Matsumoto Naoko, who in her detailed reading of changes in Jōmon pottery and figurines and settlement sites has discovered the birth and development of the concept of the supernatural, has also shattered my previous conceptions of what archaeology is about.[2]

A perspective on the divine

I would like as much as possible to integrate the most recent developments in the field of cognitive anthropology into this book, and keep an eye on the latest theory and findings in a variety of academic fields outside the cognitive sciences as well. Yet I will not be basing my discussion on the premise that human beings possess a universal cognitive structure. Instead, I would like to assemble the materials I have close at hand, without utilizing any particular theory or methodology, and, through a close examination of individual sources, pursue from my own perspective the birth and development of the gods in these islands of Japan.

To avoid misunderstanding, I should state clearly that my reason for not adopting a method premised on the idea that human beings share a common cognitive capacity is not because I doubt this proposition. Quite the contrary, I believe it is undeniable that human beings possess a specific—and universal—cognitive makeup. Not only in prehistoric times but throughout recorded human history, humans, regardless of ethnicity and region, have created astonishingly similar cultures. As recent research in linguistics has shown, the human brain does not start as a blank slate. Just as animals possess innate sets of survival instincts, human beings are equipped with certain capacities that might be described as preinstalled firmware.

Although few contemporary historians would agree, I am convinced that what might be described as historical "laws" definitely exist. I believe that it is the interaction between the universality of the cognitive system possessed by human beings, and the diversity of environmental factors shaping its development, that give rise to both the similarities and unique aspects of the history of different regions.

Of course, the ultimate goal of this book is not to discover such laws of history. Frankly, that is a task that far exceeds my abilities. Rather, my aim is first of all to use my own eyes to pursue, as meticulously as possible, the traces left by the birth and development of the gods of the Japanese archipelago, setting aside all preconceptions and focusing on the sources available to me.

Naturally this voyage of exploration, devoid of maps or compass, is likely to be a circuitous and uncertain one. Placing a priority on primary source materials is well and good, but even this has its limitations; there will be many places where leaps are necessary to clear the gaps and fissures between sources. Especially in dealing with prehistory, the question of how complete an image can be constructed from an assemblage of fragmentary data will be a determining factor in the success or failure of my efforts.

Even if my labors are rewarded and I manage to sketch an overall picture, it is not likely to be anything that could be described as meticulous and complete in every detail. A professional shipwright uses precise plans to build a boat; by comparison, mine will be a humble handmade craft patched together from various bits, and without a keel. Perhaps it will capsize and sink as soon as it is launched.

Fully aware of this risk, I will take heart from the courage of the Jōmon people of prehistoric Japan who set out to sea on their log rafts, and boldly take up this great theme of the birth and evolution of the gods of the Japanese archipelago.

Gods and "human gods"

The problem of the divine has been a crucial area of inquiry for the human sciences in their pursuit of what it is to be human. Innumerable methodological approaches and perspectives exist, and there is a danger that a casual entry into this subject will quickly lose direction and focus. This book, then, will proceed from a single perspective: the phenomenon of *hitogami*, or actual historical personages who have been deified—human beings who have become gods.

It is likely that many, if not most Japanese almost immediately associate the idea of humans becoming deities with Yasukuni Shrine—where 2.46 million men and women who fell in Japan's internal and external conflicts from the Boshin Civil War of 1868–69 through World War II are enshrined as deities (*kami*). Shrines venerating the war dead exist all over Japan, but none comes close to rivaling Yasukuni Shrine—a nationally administered shrine with special official status until the end of World War II—in scale or in the number of dead enshrined there. Nationally administered facilities memorializing those who have given their lives in service to the nation in time of war exist in many countries, of course, but Yasukuni Shrine is certainly highly unusual in enshrining them all as deities.

Precisely because of the uniqueness of this form of veneration, Yasukuni Shrine has repeatedly become the subject of controversy—as represented most visibly by the fierce disputes that roil the East Asian nations

Figure Intro-2 Torii at the entrance to the Yasukuni Shrine in Tokyo

every year on August 15, the anniversary of the end of World War II, when Japanese cabinet ministers pay official visits to the shrine.

Yasukuni Shrine can clearly be seen as a case of belief in "human gods" (*hitogami*), or the deification of human beings. But what are the origins of this belief? The official answer of Yasukuni Shrine itself is provided in the following statement:

> From antiquity the Japanese people have believed that the spirits of the dead reside forever in this land, watching over and protecting their descendants. . . . The Japanese have long thought of the spirits of people who have performed significant services, not just for their families but to the local and national communities as tutelary deities (divine spirits) of the region or

nation, and have venerated them accordingly. Yasukuni Shrine and other "shrines for the protection of the nation" (*gokoku jinja*) throughout the country may be said to be examples of this unique aspect of Japanese culture.[3]

Many contemporary researchers and experts would agree that the notion that the spirits of the dead abide in this world to protect the lives of their descendants is grounded in traditional Japanese thought. The majority of the currently popular commentaries on Japanese culture are variations on this theme. It was Yanagita Kunio, founder of Japanese folklore studies, who laid the foundations for this theory, arguing that in traditional Japanese belief the spirits of the dead returned to the mountains to become *kami*, deities watching benevolently over later generations.[4] The quotation from Yanagita cited at the beginning of this chapter is a succinct expression of this view, and Yasukuni Shrine itself is asserting that its enshrinement of the spirits of the war dead is grounded in these traditional forms of Japanese belief.

If this belief that our ancestors become gods who watch over their descendants is a unique aspect of Japanese culture, when did it take shape? When Yasukuni Shrine asserts that such beliefs have existed "from antiquity," this inevitably raises the question of precisely when that was.

Scholars have generally expressed two different answers regarding this question. The first has to do with the belief in *goryō*, or vengeful spirits, that developed in the Heian period (794–1185). During the early Heian period, the spirits of the dead were increasingly believed to be invisibly active in human affairs, and among them the spirits of defeated political leaders such as Prince Sawara (posthumously awarded the title of emperor—as Emperor Sudō—even though he never reigned), Prince Iyo, and Sugawara no Michizane, Minister of the Right, came to be regarded (and feared) as possessing immense supernatural powers. Eventually all of them were enshrined as *kami*, and in the process transformed into beneficent beings who could bestow blessings on the people who venerated them. Many experts locate the origins of the belief in *hitogami*, or deified humans, in this tradition of *goryō*.

8

Another view locates this in the cult of *gimin*, or peasant martyrs, that arose later during the Edo period (1603–1867), when it became a widespread practice throughout Japan to venerate as *kami* individuals who were perceived as having sacrificed themselves to relieve the sufferings of their people. Sakura Sōgorō, a legendary village headman from a domain in what is now Chiba Prefecture, is a famous example. In contrast to the *goryō* mentioned above, the *gimin* included many commoners without any special political rank or power. There are some who argue that the roots of the belief system expressed by Yasukuni Shrine—in which all people, regardless of social status, rank, or position, have the potential to be enshrined as *kami*—may be found in this *gimin* tradition.

The diversity of *hitogami* beliefs

I have just introduced two dominant theories of the origins of the transformation of humans into gods in, respectively, the *goryō* beliefs of the Heian period or the Edo-period *gimin* tradition. Certainly both offer examples of the transformation of human beings into deities. But it makes me uncomfortable when attempts are made to directly connect these examples with the modern creation of Yasukuni Shrine.

First of all, this discomfort stems from a suspicion that the veneration of human beings as gods predates the Heian period. As I shall argue in detail later, the funerary rites associated with the keyhole-shaped tomb mounds (*zenpō kōenfun*) that began to appear in the third century can be read as a clear intent to elevate the deceased to the status of gods. And in fact, it is my belief that the origins of these customs can be traced back to the Jōmon period (ca 10,000–300 BCE).

A second doubt arises in terms of whether *hitogami* beliefs in different periods of Japanese history are actually similar or equivalent in content. Both the *goryō* and *gimin* traditions do involve the deification of human beings, and thus can be subsumed under the term "*hitogami* beliefs." Everywhere in the Japanese islands there are a number of other traditions that can be seen as venerating humans as gods, using terms such as *arahitogami*, *ikigami*, and *sokushinbutsu* that suggest living gods or buddhas. However, if we carefully examine the content

9

of these beliefs, we find that there are so many variations on this theme that it is almost impossible to group them all under a single rubric such as "*hitogami* beliefs."

How attuned has the existing scholarly literature been to the content and variability of these beliefs? Has it not tended to avoid detailed examination of the process and systems by which humans were transformed into gods, contenting itself instead with sweeping statements regarding *hitogami* as being "a unique aspect of Japanese culture"?

Yanagita Kunio himself regarded the custom of venerating humans as deities as a universal practice throughout the Japanese archipelago, but also wrote that it is quite difficult to point to a "consistent Japanese temperament" uniting past and present.[5] Taking this cue, in the field of folklore studies there have been ongoing attempts to explicate and categorize the various transformations of *hitogami* beliefs.

Hori Ichirō followed up on Yanagita's discussion of *hitogami* beliefs by classifying them into two types—*ujigami-gata* (ancestral gods) and *hitogami-gata* (human gods)—and examining their different characteristics. *Ujigami* were shared by a particular hereditary and/or regional community, serving as a symbol of the unity of that community, so they tended to be objects of an exclusive and exclusionary worship. In contrast, *hitogami* were identified as individuals and had a more inclusive nature, reflecting an aspiration to a broader network of faith transcending local communities.[6] Miyata Noboru has explicated *hitogami* beliefs in early modern Japan with a typology of four functional types: deities which (1) foster subservience to authority, (2) aid in exorcism of evil spirits, (3) respond to the desire for relief from material want, or (4) act as saviors of the world.[7] Komatsu Kazuhiko, in turn, has argued that the deepest strata of the belief in human deification are to be found in the so-called *tatarigami* (malevolent deities who will cause harm if not worshipped and placated)—and that the benevolent forms of deified humans, revered for the extraordinary good deeds they performed while still living (whom he terms *kenshōgami*, or meritorious deities), are a development out of this earlier tradition.[8]

These are all valuable studies, and it goes without saying that they are an important rebuke to the tendency to tidy up the issue of

10

hitogami with an appeal to Japanese uniqueness. Even so, I believe that there is still a diversity and richness inherent in Japan's *hitogami* beliefs that have yet to be fully grasped by existing terminology and classifications. In particular, we lack proper chronological studies surveying the transformations in *hitogami* beliefs over time. The time has come for a broad-based but thoroughgoing attempt, setting aside all preconceptions, to trace the temporal current of *hitogami* beliefs through the use of available historical sources and a review of the research literature that has accumulated in relevant fields.

The aims of this book

As such an attempt, the first goal of this book will be to elucidate the process by which the *hitogami* came into being in these islands, tracing it back to as distant an era as possible. Then I will examine the variations that the concept of deified humans underwent down through the ages until it finally flowed into the "loyal spirits" (*chūkon*) ideal of modern times, situating it within its historical and cultural context. I will then look beyond the Japanese islands in an attempt to determine in broad outline how unique the Japanese belief in deified humans actually is, by comparison to a variety of foreign examples of human beings who have undergone some form of supernatural transformation.

As a result of this investigation, this book will demonstrate how deeply intertwined the discovery of the gods and the advent of defied humans are in the Japanese islands, and from this perspective I intend to offer a hypothesis regarding the appearance of the concept of the gods and its evolution. By shedding light on such issues, I believe I will also be able to offer new materials and new perspectives that may deepen and advance discussion of the uniqueness of the Japanese *kami* as well as the debate surrounding Yasukuni Shrine. I also think it may provide a new orientation for the discourse on the religiosity of the Japanese that is so often represented by the question of why the Japanese are so indifferent to religion.

Finally, I could not be happier if this book manages to transcend the little realm of these islands and contributes to research in pursuit of the divine in the wider world outside Japan.

CHAPTER 1

The Birth of the Imperial Spirits

1. "Imperial Spirits" as Divine Beings

Pursuing the origins of *hitogami*

W HEN WAS IT that human beings first began to perceive in certain other humans the image of something transcending the human—the visage of the divine? In his essay on this subject, Yanagita Kunio took as a representative example the cult of Hachiman, which dates back to the beginning of the Heian period (794–1185).[1] The origins of this cult are to be found in the deification of the spirit of Emperor Ōjin (late fourth to early fifth century), although subsequently the phenomenon of deifying the spirit of an individual who had died harboring some deep resentment and venerating him as Hachiman could be observed in many regions of Japan. Yanagita saw this Hachiman cult as the prototype for Japanese beliefs in *hitogami*.

As noted in the Introduction, it has become a commonplace of scholarship since Yanagita to initiate any discussion of the origins of the *hitogami* phenomenon by citing Heian-period beliefs in vengeful spirits (*goryō*). This may be taken as representative of the general consensus among contemporary scholars that the origin of *hitogami* beliefs is to be found in the veneration of malevolent deities (*tatarigami*) that appears to have arisen throughout the Japanese islands during the

Heian period. But is this understanding actually correct? I would like to begin my investigation with a reexamination of this established theory.

As I have already indicated, most contemporary research on *hito-gami* adopts two basic premises: (1) that *hitogami* beliefs originated during the Heian period and (2) that malevolent deities (*tatarigami*) were the origin of the *hitogami*. Overturning this established view naturally requires the substantiation of two principal counterarguments: (1) that the origins of *hitogami* beliefs predate the Heian period, and (2) that the *hitogami* developed, not out of the *tatarigami*, but from a different lineage of deities. The strategy to be adopted is also obvious. I must attempt to discover—dating as early as possible—concrete examples of *hitogami* that were not associated with so-called malevolent deities.

But do such examples actually exist? As the first response to this question, I would like to take up the issue of the "imperial spirit" (*ten-nōrei*). Something we might describe as the imperial spirit makes frequent appearances in Japan's first official historical chronicle, *Nihon shoki*, completed in Yōrō 4 (720), and its sequel *Shoku Nihongi* of

Figure 1-1 The Kashihara Shrine, where the "imperial spirit" of Emperor Jinmu is enshrined.

Enryaku 16 (797). For example, in the *Nihon shoki*, Prince Yamato Takeru reports to Emperor Keikō his success in subduing the Kumaso tribes by "trusting in the Emperor's Divine Spirit" (*mitama no fuyu*). It is also recorded that in the early years of her sixty-nine-yearlong regency, the Empress Consort Jingū, mother of Emperor Ōjin, decided to lead an expeditionary force against the Korean state of Silla, saying "I, having received the instructions of the gods of Heaven and Earth, and trusting in the Spirits of the Imperial ancestors, floating across the deep blue sea, intend in person to chastise the West."[2] And an imperial edict (*senmyō*) contained in the *Shoku Nihongi*, dated the fourth month of Tempyō Shōhō 1 (749), celebrates the production of gold from a mine in the province of Mutsu, attributing its discovery to the benevolent powers of buddhas, deities of the heavens and earth, and the "spirits of the emperors" (*tennō ga mitama*).

The language of these historical sources may differ somewhat, but it is beyond question that by the eighth century those associated with the imperial court imagined the supernatural existence of an imperial spirit or spirits (*mitama*) who might lend support to its current endeavors.

Orikuchi Shinobu and the "imperial spirit"

One scholar who focused his attention on the imperial *mitama* was the famous folklorist Orikuchi Shinobu. Many will no doubt remember the enthronement ceremony that took place in 1990 marking the era change from Shōwa to Heisei and proclaiming at home and abroad the accession of the new emperor. Enthronement rituals upon the accession of a sovereign are common throughout the world—past and present, East and West—and this Japanese ceremony was no exception. But from ancient times, in addition to this enthronement ceremony, another accession ritual has been practiced in Japan: the Daijōsai.

The enthronement ceremony (*sokui no rei*) was conducted in the daytime, in a public venue, with honored guests invited from all over the world, and it was broadcast on television. In contrast, the Daijōsai is conducted in a special purpose-built compound, before a small and very select audience, in the hours before dawn on a specific day (*u no hi*) of the eleventh month in the traditional astrological cycle.

Neither the purpose nor the overall content of the ceremony have been publicly revealed. Despite being a major ritual on a par with the enthronement ceremony itself, the Daijōsai is very much a private affair of the imperial household and proceeds in strictest secrecy—to the extent that when it was last conducted in 1990, there was debate over whether the expenses for it should be paid out of public funds.

Why does Japan conduct two separate accession ceremonies? Many scholars have turned their attention to the Daijōsai, sensing that the answer to this question might also provide clues to the mysteries of the Japanese imperial system and its remarkable longevity, virtually unparalleled among the world's monarchies.

The first question is what exactly the nature of this secret ceremony actually might be. Over the years, a variety of opinions have been published on this subject. Among them, one of the most persuasive is that the Daijōsai should be understood as a ritual of transmission of the "imperial spirit." It was Orikuchi Shinobu who first proposed this idea.

> In antiquity, the body of the Emperor was regarded as the vessel of his spirit. The Emperor's body was spoken of as *sume-mima no mikoto*—"the flesh of His Majesty," an honorific formed around the word *mima*, which originally meant flesh or corporeal body....
>
> Into this honored flesh the spirit of the imperial ancestors (*tennōrei*) enters, and at that moment the Emperor becomes a superior being.[3]

Here Orikuchi describes the body of the emperor as a vessel—one that is presumably empty prior to the imperial accession. And no matter how precisely the orthodox protocol for the accession is observed, secular ceremonies alone are insufficient to create an emperor. In order to truly succeed to the imperial throne, that empty vessel must go through the process of being filled with the spirit of the imperial ancestors and thus embodying a sacral authority unavailable to ordinary mortals.

So the Daijōsai is a ritual in which the new emperor embodies the spirit of his ancestors. By entering the body of the new emperor in the course of this rite, the imperial spirit transforms the emperor into a sacred being. This is the reason that the Daijōsai must accompany the other ceremonies of imperial enthronement. But what exactly is this "imperial spirit"? Orikuchi interpreted it as the *manā* (spirit or soul) of the sun goddess Amaterasu Ōmikami as inherited through the generations of emperors who were her descendants. The imperial spirit would depart the corpse of a deceased emperor and take up residence in the body of the new emperor in the course of the Daijōsai ceremony. It was then that the new emperor would be transformed into a being possessing an authority and power equivalent to that of his divine ancestress, Amaterasu.

Due to the existence of this system, no matter how many generations passed, the sacred authority of the imperial house embodied by each emperor could be passed down without any alteration or degradation. In Orikuchi's words, "the flesh might change, but with the entry of this spirit, the emperor achieved identity with his predecessors."

The deified emperor

Orikuchi's hypothesis regarding the sacred authority of the emperor—with the mystical image it evoked with the term "imperial spirit" (*tennōrei*) and its highly original interpretation of the Daijōsai—exerted immense influence over later scholars of the emperor system. In archaeological circles, the standard interpretation is now that the rituals enacted at the so-called keyhole-shaped tombs (*zenpō kōenfun*) of late Japanese prehistory were rites of inheritance of the spirits of the "great kings" (*ōkimi*) for whom they were built. For example, the following passage by Terasawa Kaoru is clearly premised upon Orikuchi:

> I think that the rituals of spirit inheritance of the early Kofun-period chieftains ("great kings") later developed into the inheritance of the imperial spirit (*tennōrei*), eventually forming the core of the original Daijōsai ritual. In his "Daijōsai no hongi," the great folklorist Orikuchi Shinobu argues that the true significance of the Daijōsai resides in the ritual in which the new emperor lies upon the *shinza* [a specially prepared couch or bed] wrapped in the *madoko-ofusuma* [a ritual coverlet] and

inherits the imperial spirit from the deceased emperor—a ritual that may have achieved its complete form concurrently with the establishment of the keyhole tombs.[4]

Considerable research has been published based on Orikuchi's hypothesis of the Daijōsai as a ritual of inheritance of the imperial spirit, elaborating upon it by uncovering and reinterpreting related historical source materials. For example, Emperor Chūkyō died before he was able to perform the Daijōsai and was frequently referred to as a "half-emperor"—focusing attention on the Daijōsai as a crucial element in the making of an emperor.

On the other hand, a rebuttal of the Orikuchi hypothesis has also been attempted, primarily by historians working with textual sources. The grounds for this critique are quite simple. By interpreting examples of the term "imperial spirit" as they appear in the historical literature, it is possible to isolate several distinct variations on this theme. Some sources use the term "imperial spirit" to express the sacral authority possessed by the reigning emperor. But some historians assert that the central concept of the spirits or souls of the imperial ancestors is as a kind of composite being protecting the reigning emperor, and that there is no way this can be understood as the *manā* (spirit or soul) of the sun goddess Amaterasu Ōmikami as inherited through the generations of emperors descended from her.[5] This criticism, based on meticulous textual analysis, is highly persuasive, and thus the interpretation of the "imperial spirit" as a collective spirit of the imperial ancestors has become widely accepted among textual historians.

It is impossible to deny that the the concept of "imperial spirit" (or spirits) requires further investigation. And it is true that the concept is not consistent across historical sources. But as we have also seen from the examples cited above, the imperial spirit was unquestionably seen as a presence which, along with the deities of heaven and earth, protected the imperial throne. This is a completely different order of being from the vengeful spirits of the Heian period; while comprised of the spirits or souls of the dead who had once lived in this world, the imperial spirit was also seen as an equivalent presence to the established gods of heaven and earth. For the people who compiled the *Nihon shoki* and the *Shoku Nihongi*, the "imperial spirit" was unquestionably a deity.

The Jinshin Disturbance (Jinshin no Ran) of 672 was a successional dispute pitting Prince Ōtomo (Emperor Tenji's son and designated heir), against Prince Ōama (Emperor Tenji's younger brother; later Emperor Tenmu). The *Nihon shoki* tells us that following an oracular pronouncement, Prince Ōama sent a representative named Kome to visit the tomb of Emperor Jinmu and make offerings there of horses and weapons. Clearly Emperor Jinmu is seen here as a supernatural guardian.[6] This passage suggests that behind the focus in the *Nihon shoki* on the "imperial spirit" was Emperor Tenmu's understanding that he had achieved victory in the Jinshin Disturbance through the miraculous intervention of the spirit of Emperor Jinmu.

Imperial spirits as guardians

It is possible to confirm from other passages in historical sources that the imperial spirit(s) were seen as equivalent to deities. For example, in the intercalary second month of the tenth year of the reign of Emperor Bidatsu (581), there were disturbances on the northern frontier by the Ezo people. The emperor summoned their chiefs and, standing on the banks of the Hatsuse River and facing Mount Mimoro, had them swear an oath of loyalty that concluded, "If we break this oath, may all the Gods of Heaven and Earth, and also the spirits of the Emperors, destroy our race."[7] Here we can see no functional distinction whatsoever between the gods of heaven and earth and the spirits of the imperial ancestors.

Similarly, on the twenty-ninth day of the fifth month of the third year of Jingo Keiun (769), Empress Shōtoku issued an edict, recorded in the *Shoku Nihongi*, which declared the court lady Agata no Inukai no Aneme guilty of conspiring to cast a spell upon the empress and replace her on the throne with the son of Prince Shioyaki; a sentence of death was commuted to one of exile. The fact that this treason had been foiled before it could come to fruition was attributed by the edict to "the power of the miraculous divine authority of Rushana Nyorai; of the Sutra of Golden Light; of the bodhisattva Kanzeon; of guardian deities including Brahma, Indra, and the Four Wisdom Kings; as well as the protective power and aid benevolently bestowed ever since the creation of our august land by the spirits of the imperial ancestors and the gods of heaven and earth."

The Rushana Nyorai (Vairocana Buddha) mentioned here is the Great Buddha of the temple Tōdaiji in Nara, whose eye-opening ceremony was conducted in Tempyō Shōhō 4 (752). The Sutra of Golden Light (Suvarṇaprabhāsa Sūtra) was a sutra venerated in the Nara period (710–794) as a protector of the nation. The provincial temples (*kokubunji*) established concurrently with Tōdaiji were officially titled as Temples for Protection of the State by the Four Heavenly Kings Golden Light Sutra. The bodhi-sattva Kanzeon (Kannon) was believed to reside in the "pure land" or paradise of Potalaka, but because mention of this deity follows immediately on that of the Great Buddha of Tōdaiji, this probably refers not to that otherworldly presence but to a specific Kannon image like the Fukūkenjaku Kannon that is the main image of the Sangatsudō subtemple of Tōdaiji. Similarly, it is highly likely that the reference to the guardian deities Brahma, Indra, and the Four Wisdom Kings is not to heavenly guardians in the abstract, but to the very concrete images of these deities installed in the temples of Nara. The "gods of heaven and earth" are Japan's own indigenous *kami*, and the "spirits of the imperial ancestors" are just that: the souls of generations of deceased emperors. It goes without saying that all of these deities have different origins and characters. But as we see here, they were all venerated as beings of the same class.

Figure 1-2 Statue of Tamonten, one of the Four Wisdom Kings (Hōryūji)

The great Edo-period (1603–1867) scholar of National Learning Motoori Norinaga wrote as follows concerning the nature of the "gods" or *kami*:

> Beginning with the myriad heavenly and earthly deities seen in the ancient texts, the word *kami* also refers to the spirits residing in and venerated at shrines, as well as those human beings, birds and beasts, plants and trees, oceans and mountains which possess exceptional and unusual powers or virtues making them worthy of reverence.[8]

While this is difficult to understand from a modern perspective, for people of the eighth century the image of the Great Buddha, the text of a sutra, and the indigenous gods of Japan could all be perceived as sacred presences (*kami*, deities) possessed of unusual and sacral authority. The moral tales recounted in the *Nihon ryōiki* (Record of Miraculous Events in Japan), an early ninth-century collection, also feature Buddhist images, sutras, and Japanese deities as essentially equivalent levels of being. In these texts the generations of "spirits of the imperial ancestors" are understood as beings of essentially the same category as the various and sundry other deities, including the traditional *kami* of heaven and earth.

As we can see from the preceding discussion, by the Nara period the spirits or souls of past—but once actually living—emperors were believed, along with a variety of traditional deities, to reside in special locales either within or surrounding the palace or capital, where they continued to offer protection and assistance to the reigning emperor. These imperial spirits, including those such as Emperor Jinmu and Emperor Ōjin, who were clearly perceived as individual deities, were not the souls of resentful losers in the political battles of the day. There is a well-defined line separating these imperial spirits from the vengeful spirits of the following Heian period.

Thus, the origins of venerating humans as gods can be traced back at least as far as the concept of imperial spirits as it arose during the Nara period (710–794). And these spirits are clearly different in nature from the vengeful spirits frequently alluded to as the first examples of "human gods" (*hitogami*).

2. "Living Gods" (*Akitsukami*)

The imperial mystique

Having come to this point, new questions emerge. First of all, are these imperial spirits (*tennōrei*) we encounter in the eighth century really the earliest verifiable examples of *hitogami* in the Japanese islands? And second, why is it that the concept of *hitogami* seems to mature in this period and emerge in the form of these imperial spirits? Let's begin by addressing this second question—the background for the emergence of the *tennōrei*.

After Prince Ōama's victory in the succession dispute following the death of Emperor Tenji which is known as the Jinshin Disturbance of 672, he ascended the throne as Emperor Tenmu, moving the imperial capital from Ōtsu to Asuka Kiyomihara and initiating a series of institutional reforms. The overarching goal of the new institutional framework constructed by Emperor Tenmu and his wife and successor, Empress Jitō, was to firmly establish the emperor as sole representative of the state and make this position absolute. It is believed that it was during this period that the term "emperor" (*tennō*) replaced "great king" (*ōkimi*) in referring to the head of state. Defeated in the Battle of Hakusukinoe (663) by the combined forces of Tang China and the Korean state of Silla and forced to relinquish its ambitions on the Korean peninsula, the nascent Yamato court reflected on this experience and set itself the task of constructing a unified state, under the authority of the emperor, that would be powerful enough to compete with its continental neighbors.

The investment of the emperor with transcendent power had repercussions that reached the realm of the gods as well. There was a reorganization of the lineage of the various deities into a hierarchy that situated at its apex Amaterasu Ōmikami, regarded as the divine progenitrix of the imperial line. In order to express the splendid isolation of the emperor from his subjects, his ancestress Amaterasu must be worshipped as a supreme goddess, and the successive generations of emperors be positioned as her descendants, locating them within the lineage of gods inhabiting the Japanese islands from time immemorial.

But it was not just that the emperors were regarded as descendants of a divine lineage. The reigning sovereign was also elevated to the status of a deity—an *akitsukami*, or "living god."[9]

Ōkimi wa	Our great Sovereign
Kami ni shi maseba	Is a very god indeed:
Amakumo no	See how high amidst
Ikazuchi no ue ni	The clouds of heaven she now dwells
Iori seru kamo	Encamped upon the thunder![10]

This poem is presumed to have been composed by Kakinomoto no Hitomaru on the occasion of a visit by the Empress Jitō (some say Emperor Tenmu) to Ikazuchi-no-oka ("Thunder Hill") near Asuka. The poem praises the majesty of the empress, metaphorically turning her ascent of the hill into an image of the sovereign as a god dwelling amid the thunderclouds. A number of similar poems paying homage to the emperor as a deity may be found in the *Man'yōshū*, the earliest extant collection of Japanese poetry.

One need only begin reading the *Kojiki* or *Nihon shoki* to realize that the deities (*kami*) depicted in these chronicles were not limited to a particular bloodline such as that of the imperial ancestors. In the mythical age of the gods, everyone was a god. In the *Nihon shoki*, Ninigi no Mikoto, great-grandson of Amaterasu, is to descend from heaven to take possession of the Central Land of Reed Plains that will become Japan: "But in that Land there were numerous Deities which shone with a luster like that of fireflies, and evil Deities which buzzed like flies. There were also trees and herbs all of which could speak."[11] In the seventh century, each of the major clans revered its ancestors as specific divinities of the age of the gods, and so in this sense everyone in that era was a descendant of gods. And not only human beings—animals and plants had once been deities as well, and capable of speech.

But by the time we get to the *Man'yōshū*, the meaning of the concept of *kami*—god or deity—has clearly changed. The qualitative

difference between the *kami* and ordinary human beings is emphasized. An ideological manipulation was being performed, in which
the transcendent nature of the gods was absolutized at the same time the
emperor was being established as sole sovereign.

In his accession edict upon assuming the imperial throne, contained in the *Shoku Nihongi*, Emperor Monmu is described as "the
heavenly sovereign [*tennō*] who rules the Great Land of Eight Islands
as a manifest god."[12] This self-proclamation of the emperor as a sacred
being (a manifest or living god) upon accession to the throne would
become a standard trope in the accession edicts to follow. As a result,
by the end of the seventh century the emperors would succeed in elevating themselves into transcendent beings clearly differentiated from
the common run of humanity. Premised upon this development of the
emperor into a living god, the Daijōsai ceremony was created to impart
greater reality to the emperor = god script by providing the theatrical
setting for the emperor's transformation into a deity.

Establishment of the imperial mausolea

This policy pursued during the reigns of Emperor Tenmu and
Empress Jitō of elevating the sovereign into a transcendent being was
symbolized by the establishment of an imperial mausolea system (*ryōbosei*). This system, created as the centralized imperial state (*ritsuryō
kokka*) was in the process of formation, attempted to prohibit further
construction of tumulus-style graves—previously widespread among
the ruling elite—except for individuals of prescribed rank and status.
Even among those for whom the construction of such mausolea was
permitted, the size of the tomb and other features were to be strictly
determined by rank and social position, in a hierarchy whose apex was
the emperor. Another goal of this system was to achieve a tangible,
visible imperial lineage unbroken since the age of the gods by clearly
establishing the gravesites and mausolea of the generations of emperors
since Emperor Jinmu.[13]

As already noted, the principal support for the elevation of imperial
authority during the reigns of Emperor Tenmu and Empress Jitō was
the idea that the emperors were direct lineal descendants of Amaterasu

Ōmikami. However, this process required the lineage to be traced without break from the most recent generations back to the most remote past—no mean feat. It is generally accepted by modern historians that the first emperor, Jinmu, and the "eight undocumented monarchs" from the second emperor, Suizei, down to the ninth emperor, Kaika, are essentially legendary or fictive beings created when the ancient chronicles were compiled (though some of them may have been modeled on actual historical figures). And it is believed that, in order to lend credibility to this fictive lineage, specific tumuli were identified as burial sites of the early legendary emperors.

If this were the case, how was it that presumably nonexistent graves came to be identified as imperial tombs? In this regard, archaeologist Imao Fumiaki makes an extremely interesting observation concerning the construction of Aramashi no Miyako (Fujiwarakyō), the capital that Empress Jitō constructed in Asuka. Within the area selected for the capital there were numerous tumuli from the Kofun period (circa fourth to seventh century). The majority of them were seen as obstacles to the construction of the new capital and were simply leveled to make way for it. A few, however, were preserved, and it is Imao's hypothesis that a select group of the tumuli within the precincts of the capital was appropriated by the emerging Japanese state to represent the tombs of the early emperors, regardless of whoever had actually been buried there originally.[14]

The *Nihon shoki* and *Kojiki* chronicle a single imperial lineage originating with Amaterasu and continuing unbroken since the time of Emperor Jinmu. This was the foundation of imperial authority and power. In order to give credibility to this lineage, the early imperial state in its formative period posited a collection of particularly impressive tumuli as the graves of the imperial ancestors—regardless of the actual personages entombed there. At the same time, the other tumuli in the area of the capital were unceremoniously razed as having no utilitarian value. The result was an imposing range of tumuli visible from within the precincts of the newly constructed imperial palace giving visible representation to a lineage of emperors stretching back unbroken to distant antiquity—a sacred lineage, a lineage of gods—and thus imbued with newly symbolic presence.

Tumuli as divine residences

The state, having attached new significance to the tumuli as imperial tombs (*ryō*, *misasagi*), also provided a new interpretation of the generations of ancestral spirits now thought to reside there: they were now defined as guardian deities protecting the reigning emperor. The "imperial spirits" (*tennōrei*) appearing in the texts of the *Nihon shoki* and *Shoku Nihongi* arose in this political context of the late seventh century, when the first written legal codes (*ritsuryō*), modeled on those of China, were being implemented to define the institutional structure of the emerging imperial state.

The imperial mausolea designated by the process described above were defined as sacred precincts which ordinary people were not permitted to enter, tended and guarded by a specially designated caste, the *ryōko* (as prescribed in the *Sōsō-ryō* [Funeral and Burial Code]). In addition, "worship of the entombed spirits" (*ryōrei o matsuru*) was cited as the most important of the official duties of the *misasagi no tsukasa* (commissioner of imperial mausolea), who was charged with overseeing all affairs related to the imperial tombs (as prescribed in the *Shikin-ryō* [Personnel Code]). On the other hand, lesser members of the imperial house, from imperial consorts on down, as well as other members of the court nobility, were to be interred not in *misasagi* (mausolea for the emperors), but in graves (*haka*), which were excluded from the official management reserved for the tombs of the emperors. The common people were, as a general rule, no longer permitted to make and maintain graves. So the funerary system became, along with the ceremony of accession (*sokuirei*) and the Daijōsai that were also established during the reign of Empress Jitō, an institution which functioned to elevate the emperor to a status transcending all others, sacralizing him as both a descendant of gods and as a manifest or living god (*akitsukami*) in his own right.

Following the official designation of the mausolea of generations of emperors, the state established a system in which official envoys or messengers (*nosaki no tsukai*; *hōhei no tsukai*) were periodically sent to bear offerings to the imperial mausolea. The establishment of this official system of venerating the imperial tombs was clearly intended to demonstrate that imperial spirits resided there forever, keeping a watchful eye over the affairs of the nation and protecting it from harm.

This was also the time when the traditional *kami*, who had previously had no fixed abode, began to be conceived of as permanently inhabiting specific shrines (see chapter 3.3). Prior to this, *kami* were believed to be summoned by prayer to alight temporarily in a *yorishiro* (an object used during religious rituals to provide them with a physical space to inhabit), and to depart when the ritual was ended. But from the late seventh century onward, as the *kami* began to receive regular veneration and offerings from official messengers dispatched for that purpose, the concept began to take root that the *kami* continually resided in shrines dedicated to them, protecting the emperor.

Thus, as the *ritsuryō* state began to take shape, both the spirits of the imperial ancestors and the traditional *kami* began to be posited as deities serving as guardians of the nation.

3. Mountains: The Abode of the Gods

Malevolent deities return to the mountains

We may assume that behind the designation of ancient burial tumuli as imperial mausolea (*sanryō*, lit., "mountain tombs"), and as the abode of the spirits of the imperial ancestors, lay a belief common at the time that the most imposing and finely shaped mountains or hills to be seen from one's home or village were in fact the home of the gods. Miwayama in Nara, and Katsuragisan, frequented by the deity Hitokotonushi no Kami, were representative examples of specific mountains regarded as abodes of the gods (*kamunabi*).In the entry for the district of Tsukuba in *Hitachi no kuni fudoki*, an ancient gazetteer for the province of Hitachi, a legend is related in which the deity Mioya no Mikoto went on a round of the abodes of the gods who were his progeny, and reaching Mount Fuji at dusk, asked the god of the mountain if he might spend the night there. But the mountain deity refused, saying that he was observing the fast for Niinamesai, the harvest festival, and could not entertain guests. So Mioya no Mikoto went to Mount Tsukuba, where he was welcomed with open arms. The gazetteer relates that this is the reason why the summit of Mount Fuji remains cold and inhospitable to mankind throughout the year, while Mount Tsukuba should enjoy abundance and many visitors.[15] The gazetteer also makes note of a variety of deities inhabiting other mountains.

In *Fujisanki*, an account of the famous mountain by Miyako no Yoshika, it is written that on the fifth day of the eleventh month of Jōgan 17 (875), people celebrating a festival in the foothills of the mountain witnessed "a pair of beautiful women dressed in white" dancing at the summit. Villages and ritual sites were often located so as to have a view of a landscape dominated by a *kamunabi yama*—a divine mountain abode—in the distance. It is assumed that such choices were becoming common during the Yayoi period (ca 300 BCE–300 CE), as agricultural land was developed and permanent settlements established.

The reason the gods inhabited the mountains was first and foremost because they were places of purity. The entry for Kuji district in *Hitachi no kuni fudoki*, for instance, tells of how a god came to be enshrined at the summit of Kabire no Takamine. This god had been a malevolent deity and was disturbing the local people. They implored it to leave, saying, "Where you are now, farmers have houses nearby, and day and night the area is polluted. Thus you should not remain here. Move instead to a pure realm high on the mountain and reside there." And in the *Engi shiki*, an early tenth-century compilation of governmental regulations and ceremonial procedures, there is a prayer (*norito*) for "banishing malevolent deities" that encourages them to leave the precincts of the palace where they are wreaking mischief and move instead to "a pure place amid mountains and rivers."

The *kami* were thought of as beings who loved cleanliness and purity, and therefore, when it was thought that some deity was exerting a malevolent influence, the first thing to suspect was that it or its place of residence had somehow become polluted. The *Nihon shoki* relates that when Emperor Nintoku was on a hunting expedition to Awajishima, the god Izanagi, who lived there, was greatly offended by the fresh tattoos of some of the emperor's entourage, saying through a medium, "I cannot endure the stench of blood." An entry in the *Shoku*

Nihongi for the twenty-ninth day of the seventh month of Enryaku 1 (782) records an incident in which officials of the court participated in religious rites while dressed in mourning, thus intermingling auspicious matters (ceremonies for the gods) with inauspicious matters (death and mourning) and offending the gods, from the deities of Ise on down, who showed their displeasure in a variety of ways. It was particularly necessary to keep the *kami* from direct contact with any of the pollutions associated with the daily life of human beings—including death, blood, and excrement.

Since the mountains were regarded as a pure land in which the gods dwelled, they also from very early times became a place for ascetics seeking to gain supernatural powers. One exemplar of this was En no Gyōja (En the Ascetic), portrayed in the *Nihon ryōiki* (Volume I, Tale 28) as being able to fly through the heavens and employ spirits and *kami* at his command. We should note that the powers achieved by such ascetic practitioners as En no Gyōja emanated from their purity of mind and body. It was believed that by entering the sacred space of the mountain fastnesses, and leading a life far from that of the mundane world, these ascetics succeeded in purifying body and mind to the point that they could acquire immense supernatural powers rivaling those of the gods.

Purified spirits

We have just established that "purity" is the keyword in thinking about the *kami* of ancient Japan. The reason the gods made their abode in the mountains was because the mountains were a place of purity.

Yanagita Kunio wrote in "Senzo no hanashi" (About Our Ancestors, 1945), that in the Japanese islands it has been believed since antiquity that the souls of the dead went to abide in the mountains, and ever since this theory has been hugely influential in folklore and religious studies. Yanagita's observation has inspired numerous subsequent studies uncovering local ceremonies and practices welcoming the dead home from the mountains during the midsummer festival of *obon*, such as the clearing of grass and weeds from paths leading to graveyards (*bonmichi*) so the souls of the dead may find easier passage.

In his analysis of the elegies (*banka*) of the *Man'yōshū*, Hori Ichirō points out that in many of these poems the spirits of the dead ascend to conceal themselves in a high place, usually in nearby hills or mountains, and cites as the context for this the existence of a general notion that the dead went to abide there.[16] The Yanagita/Hori thesis won many supporters, and at this point the idea that in Japan the dead were traditionally believed to reside in the mountains has become generally accepted. However, at least as far as the ancient texts are concerned, it is almost impossible to find passages clearly stating this notion. Instead, an overwhelming number of texts write of the mountains as the abode of the *kami*.[17]

In antiquity, death meant a state in which the soul or spirit (*tama*) became detached from the physical body. The flesh and bones of the deceased, from which the soul had departed, were nothing more than a withered husk—and what concerned people was what had become of the *tama*. Immediately after death the recently departed soul possessed a destructive power that might harm the living, and the task of the funerary rituals of antiquity such as the *mogari* (wake or mourning period) was to soften and avert this malevolent force. This was thought to be accomplished by purifying the spirit of the deceased. In the various rites to pacify the souls of the dead we can see a parallel to appeasing the wrath of the gods through purification.

After being purified through various rituals, the dead souls would depart for the realm of the dead to join the spirits of the ancestors. In the *Kojiki* and *Nihon shoki*, this land of the dead, Yomi no Kuni, is described as being at the end of a slope called Yomotsu Hirasaka. In the *Izumo fudoki* entry for the district of Izumo we find stories relating to Yomi no Saka (the slope of Yomi) and Yomi no Ana (the cave of Yomi), on the seacoast in the district of Uka no Sato. In ancient times the realm of the dead was not restricted to the mountains; caves, seacoasts, offshore islands, and ravines were also believed to house them. In Aoba Ward of the city of Sendai, at the foot of a hilly area known as Mogasaki, numerous ancient tunnel tombs or burial caverns known as *yokoana* have been preserved, including the Dainenjiyama tomb cluster. It is believed that from the sixth to the eighth century more than a thousand dead were interred here.[18] Thus, neither documentary nor archaeological evidence supports the idea that the dead all departed to reside in the mountains.

It seems that in ancient times, before the custom of pilgrimage to ancestral graves (*haka-mairi*) became established, the sense was not so strong that the spirits of the dead attached themselves to the place where they were buried. The Heian-period poet Izumi Shikibu, active at the end of the tenth century, composed the following poem on Ōmisoka, the last night of the old year:

> It is said the dead return this night, but you do not.
> Is my dwelling-place so devoid of spirit?[19]

The folk belief that the spirits of the dead returned from wherever they resided to visit loved ones on the last night of the year was widespread in ancient society. There are numerous other poems in the classical literature of the Heian period that allude to this. Even in the tenth century, the dead were still not thought to reside permanently in any particular location, and could not be easily summoned up, no matter how badly the living might wish to see them.

Among the souls or spirits of the dead, only a select few were believed to have attained the degree of purity and special power that would single them out for treatment as *kami*. Or, conversely, we might say that in order for a soul to be able to take up residence in the mountains, it must first become a god.

Imperial tombs conceived as mountains

If we reconsider the policies of the early imperial state in light of the understanding that spirits of the dead who have attained the status of *kami* would ultimately abide at the summit of mountains, we discover some very interesting things.

As we have seen, at the end of the seventh century it became state policy to designate certain particularly impressive tomb mounds constructed during the Kofun period as imperial mausoleea, regardless of the identity of the personages actually buried there. So designated, these tumuli were then officially assigned guards and custodians (*ryōko*) and became the object of periodic rituals and offerings. This system functioned to make the populace aware that the imperial spirits being offered such veneration and service were permanent residents of these tumuli.

Significantly, under the administrative code (*ryōsei*) of the time, the imperial mausolea were called *sanryō* ("mountain tombs") and an official known as *yamatsukuri no tsukasa* ("commissioner of mountain-building") had clearly defined responsibilities concerning their construction and maintenance. It is possible to read in this a mechanism for the artificial creation of mountain tombs as abodes for the defied imperial spirits, grounded in the common belief that mountains were in fact where the gods resided. In the Heian period, the imperial spirits venerated in these tumuli would frequently cause rumbling noises or wreak other forms of havoc when they felt their space to have been violated in some way. An entry in the *Shoku Nihon kōki* for Jōwa 8.10.15 (841) relates that the cutting down of trees at the Kashiwabara no Misasagi (the tomb of Emperor Kanmu) provoked a curse that caused physical distress to the reigning emperor, Ninmyō, who dispatched messengers to chant sutras at Kanmu's tomb.

The curses (*tatari*) of the imperial tombs have frequently been interpreted as the activity of ghosts or souls of the dead (*shiryō*). However, in ancient times such curses tended to be regarded as characteristic of *kami*. In the *Nihon shoki*, it is written that when the Empress Saimei moved her capital to Asakura, trees from the Asakura Shrine were cut down in order to build the palace, incurring the wrath of the gods and producing a variety of unusual phenomena including the appearance of foxfires (*onibi*) and an epidemic of illnesses. In Jōwa 14 (847), the *sumai no tsukasa* (an official charged with overseeing sumo matches in the imperial presence) cut down a *tsuki* tree that stood in front of the district office of Kadono to make a large drum, inciting the wrath of the gods, which was appeased by donating the drum to the Matsuo Shrine. This process—the cutting of trees, divine anger and punishment, contrition and appeasement—is exactly the same as that associated with the imperial tombs. The imperial mausolea were seen as equivalent in nature to traditional shrines.

To repeat, in ancient times, the mountains—and especially their summits—were regarded as the purest places in this world and the abode of the gods. They were believed to be a place where only exceptional human souls or spirits, of a purity rivaling that of the gods, could abide. And in the period of the early *ritsuryō* state, the imperial tombs (*sanryō*) were identified as mountains, where it was believed that the imperial spirits actually resided as *kami*.

Origins of the imperial spirits

Up to now I have been addressing one of the two questions raised earlier—that of why, in the eighth century, the spirits of the imperial ancestors came to be conceived of as *kami*. But now let us shift our attention to the second question: whether or not these imperial spirits were the earliest examples in the Japanese islands of *hitogami*, humans transformed into gods.

In fact, the spirits of the emperors were not the only human souls to be made the object of veneration and supplication. According to the *Shoku Nihongi*, in the eighth month of Tempyō Jingo 1 (765), Empress Shōtoku issued an edict citing, as evidence for Prince Wake's involvement in an attempted coup, a document in which he prayed for the assistance of his "ancestral spirits" (*sakitama*). In the ninth month of Tempyō 2 (730), gifts from the state of Balhae on the Korean peninsula were offered at six imperial tombs and at the grave of Fujiwara no Fuhito. In the tenth month of Tempyō Shōhō 7 (755), imperial messengers were dispatched with offerings to the mausolea of Emperor Tenji and his successors as well as to the grave of Fujiwara no Fuhito. And the tumulus grave of Fujiwara no Kamatari (fig. 1-3) at the summit of Tōnomine was known for producing miraculous signs and portents warning people of future events.[20]

It is likely that the image of the progenitors of a clan as protectors of their descendants was a common one, even before the rise to prominence of the imperial spirits toward the end of the seventh century. In the *Kojiki* and *Nihon shoki*, the origins of the major clans are traced back to founding ancestors in the age of the gods. And it was

Figure 1-3 Fujiwara no Kamatari's grave stands at the summit of Tōnomine.

a commonly shared social paradigm that just as Amaterasu Ōmikami protected her descendant Emperor Jinmu, divine progenitors protected the interests of the descendants of other clans.

The *ritsuryō* state, based on this ancestral paradigm, secured a locus of residence for the spirits of the imperial ancestors by assigning specific tumulus graves to specific emperors, imparting a powerful reality to their existence. Then, by skillful manipulation of the sources used in official chronicles such as the *Nihon shoki*, the functions of these ancestral spirits were elevated to equal or surpass those of the traditional *kami*—the goal being to institutionally establish the imperial ancestors as divinities. At the same time, the implementation of the system of imperial mausolea (*ryōbosei*) established a hierarchical framework of regulations for veneration of the ancestors of the imperial family and other powerful clans, and effectively closed the door to the spirits of the dead of other clans being elevated to similar divine status.

Official acknowledgement was also made of the exceptional status of Fujiwara no Kamatari and his son Fujiwara no Fuhito, founding ancestors of the powerful court family, who were already perceived as *kami* by the society at large. However, four days after an imperial messenger was dispatched to the grave of Fujiwara no Fuhito, as mentioned above, an imperial edict was issued (and recorded in the *Shoku Nihongi*) addressing the practice of "creating shrines to worship the spirits of the dead" in Aki and Suō provinces, and forbidding such practices. This is an exceptionally revealing example of how the elevation of certain privileged spirits to be worshipped as *kami* was simultaneously accompanied by the prohibition of similar veneration of any other spirits of the dead. But if the spirits of the emperors were not the earliest examples of the deification of human beings (*hitogami*), then how far back in time can we trace the elevation of a specific historical personage into a god?

In considering this question, we must begin by looking back as far as possible into antiquity and attempting to understand what sort of beings the *kami* of the Japanese islands were, and how they came to acquire that sacred status. But written historical sources can only take us so far. We must view this question from a broader perspective, incorporating insofar as possible the fruits of research in related fields such as archaeology.

Let us begin by stepping back in time to more than ten thousand years ago, when human activity begins to leave its first prominent traces in the Japanese archipelago. I would like to consider the mechanism by which *hitogami* first came into being and the significance of the imperial spirits within the broad context and lengthy span of time extending from approximately ten thousand years ago until the end of the seventh century, when the imperial spirits first gain prominence.

Continental concepts of ancestors

Before doing so, there is another issue I would like to address: a comparitive look at concepts of deified humans on the Chinese mainland and the Korean peninsula. The seventh century was an era in which Japan was in close communication with continental Asia, especially Korea, including military clashes. Large numbers of people traveled back and forth between Japan and the continent, for a variety of purposes. Indeed, the *ritsuryō* system of government the imperial court was adopting was based on Chinese-style penal (*ritsu*) and adminis-trative (*ryō*) codes. We may assume that the Japanese archipelago was immensely influenced by its continental neighbors in terms of thought and worldview.

During the Shang (Yin) dynasty, which ruled in northern China during the second millenium BCE, the legitimacy and authority of the Shang kings were bolstered by tracing their ancestry back to legendary emperors. The spirits of deceased former kings were believed to ascend to heaven and join the ranks of the heavenly imperial ancestors, and maintaining the connection with these deified ancestors was essential in confirming the position of the reigning sovereign. This was recog-nized as a familial, blood connection between transcendent heavenly beings and earthly rulers, and thus has similarities to what we have seen thus far of the concept of the emperor in Japan during the forma-tive period of the *ritsuryō* state.

However, when the Shang were overthrown and supplanted by the Western Zhou dynasty about 1100 BCE, there was a major change in the conception of the relationship between the sovereign and the transcendent powers of heaven. This took the form of the "mandate of heaven," in which the earthly sovereign was seen as having received a directive from the emperor of heaven to rule the earth in his stead. As a result, the notion of an *a priori* blood relationship between transcen-dental heavenly beings (former sovereigns) and the earthly ruler was broken. All one needed to become emperor was to receive the mandate of heaven; conversely, the loss of this mandate meant a ruler's down-fall. This notion of imperial legitimacy became established, and later would be systematized by Confucian concepts such as *geming*, signify-ing a regime change through a transfer in the mandate of heaven.

Did this mean that veneration of ancestors by the reigning emperor had become completely irrelevant to ruling the state? No, not at all. From the time that the concept of the emperor of heaven had become established in ancient China, the sovereign's most important acts were the sacrificial rites (*jiaosi*) for the veneration of heaven. And of almost equal importance were the rites that the reigning emperor would con-duct at the tombs of his ancestors (*zongmiao*).

But what relationship was there between the rites of heaven (*jiaosi*) and the rites for the imperial ancestors? After the concept became established of an emperor of heaven conferring his mandate upon an earthly sovereign, the souls of the former kings or emperors were believed to ascend to heaven where they served at the side of the heavenly emperor. The mandate of heaven was not conferred by the emperor of heaven directly upon the earthly sovereign, it was believed, but transmitted indirectly through the spirits of the earthly ruler's ancestors. Thus worship at the imperial tombs was, along with the sacrifices to heaven, seen as a principal ritual duty of the sovereign, and from the Later (Eastern) Han dynasty (25–220 CE) onward these two sets of important rites began to be referred to by a single term: *jiaomiao*.[21]

At the end of the seventh century in Japan, efforts proceeded to deify the emperors and the generations of their ancestors as *kami*, but in China the idea of a direct blood relationship between the earthly emperor and the transcendent figure of the emperor of heaven had already been lost; China had entered an age in which the relationship between the two had become fraught with greater tension.

CHAPTER 2

From Dead Souls to Deities

1. Dawn of the Gods

Neanderthals and modern humans

W HEN WAS IT that the people living in the Japanese archipelago first became conscious of the presence of deities—beings that transcended humankind? In recent years, the birth of the gods has been most actively pursued in the field of cognitive archaeology, as touched upon in the introductory chapter.

Physical anthropology tells us that the direct ancestors of modern human beings (*homo sapiens sapiens*) first appeared in Africa 100,000 to 200,000 years ago. Until that time, other human groups had been lords of the earth—the Neanderthals and other hominids. And from that time onward, until perhaps 20,000 to 30,000 years ago, *homo sapiens sapiens* continued to coexist with these other members of the human family.

It has been said that, apart from being a bit trimmer, *homo sapiens* did not differ that greatly in physical appearance from *homo neanderthalensis*. In fact, as far as cranial capacity is concerned, Neanderthals had somewhat larger brains. But in terms of the way the brain functions, it is safe to say that *homo sapiens* made a crucial leap forward.

39

What made the difference? To address this point, I will borrow the metaphor—often employed by evolutionary psychologists—of the Swiss Army knife. As you know, a Swiss Army knife is actually a small toolkit that may include a variety of implements: a knife, a spoon, a saw, a can opener, etc. Psychologists tell us that the human brain resembles this, because within it there are a number of cognitive domains (or modules) supporting a diversity of intelligences: a natural history intelligence, functioning to interpret natural phenomena and animal behavior; a social intelligence, functioning to convey thought and intention; a technical intelligence, supporting the capacity to make things based on mental images, and so on.

But Neanderthals and proto-modern humans did not have the capacity to integrate these independent modules with one another. At best, they could only bring them into play one at a time as needed, like the various tools of a Swiss Army knife. But about 30,000 to 60,000 years ago a "Big Bang" occurred within the brains of *homo sapiens*. Circuits connecting the various modules in parallel switched on, and the result was the flourishing of a new type of intelligence characterized by "cognitive fluidity."

The origins of anthropomorphism

Borrowing the theories of Steven Mithen, one of the pioneers in the field of cognitive archaeology, let's examine these ideas more closely, while touching on some specific examples.[1]

Hunting was the most important means of obtaining food for both Neanderthals and *homo sapiens*. But there was a major difference in how they pursued this essential activity. Neanderthal hunting was opportunistic—they would hunt prey when they saw it. In this sense they were not that different from a lion or any other carnivore. In contrast, from sometime a bit past the peak of the last Ice Age (approximately 18,000 years ago), the hunting methods of *homo sapiens* clearly began to focus upon specific prey and, because of this, to observe the behavioral patterns of these animals and to use more sophisticated strategies for hunting them, such as ambushes. Supply caches were established, and a complex division of labor in the hunt was also employed.

What was the source of this development in hunting styles? We may hypothesize that it was the cognitive fluidity with which *homo sapiens* was equipped. We might say, in terms of the isolated modules described earlier, that the practice of hunting and gathering as members of a group involves the social module, while the capacity to classify different animals and recognize specific prey belongs to the natural history module. Neanderthals also possessed these cognitive abilities. What they lacked was the ability to integrate them. If they came upon a herd of gazelles, they could recognize them as prey and might even act as a group to hunt them; what they could not do was adopt a group strategy in advance, such as ambush, lying in wait to attack a herd.

Unlike the Neanderthals, *homo sapiens* were able to determine their prey in advance, predict its behavior, lie in wait in a specific place for a specific type of animal, and use appropriate hunting techniques to capture and kill it. What permitted this was anthropomorphism—the attribution of human mental traits to animals. If animals had minds like people, then their behavior was not random, but guided by certain patterns based on a self-aware will. And it is plausible that it was this form of thinking that enabled tactics such as ambushes.

Seeing animals and humans as equivalent or similar beings is not something that could come from either the social intelligence or the natural history intelligence operating in isolation. This capacity could arise only when the barriers between awareness of other humans (social intelligence) and awareness of animals (natural history intelligence) were removed and a mind that could move fluidly between the two was born. An anthropomorphic conception of animals required a mind that had the cognitive fluidity to transcend the limitations of the Swiss Army knife.

The power to see the unseen

This cognitive fluidity gave human beings another important trait: the ability to imagine things that did not actually exist.

There is a famous figurine, discovered in southern Germany, with a human body but the head of a lion. Carved out of ivory, it is believed to be well over 30,000 years old. In Europe, beginning about 40,000 years ago, carved ivory figures of animals and cave paintings representing both human and animal forms were created in large numbers. This was the birth of the most ancient artworks made by human beings. And it is noteworthy that this period also saw an outpouring of articles of personal adornment such as beads and pendants, and burials began to be accompanied by various grave goods.

This "cultural explosion," according to Mithen, would have been impossible without the development of a cognitively fluid mind capable of forming connections among the various domains of intelligence. The lion-man does not exist in the real world—it is a being that can only be formed within the human mind. Nor is it something that could have possibly been born out of one of the isolated modules of the brain. Personal ornaments and grave goods were also "embellishments" unnecessary for meeting the demands of daily life, and can be thought of as arising in a similar way. In many aspects of life we see evidence that cognitive faculties cutting across several domains were developing rapidly during this period.

Having come this far, the discovery of the gods was imminent. Or rather, the spate of art objects suddenly born of the advent of a more fluid intelligence, and transcending literal representation, should probably be seen as a phenomenon inseparable from the birth of the divine. Images such as the lion-man are unquestionable evidence that the people who made them had discovered something transcending the beings of the natural world. Grave goods are another indication they did not see the dead as merely inanimate corpses; one can sense the consciousness of some form of supernatural presence. In this way, humankind came to perceive, amid the phenomena of their natural environment, an invisible transcendent power.

Representing transcendence

Thus far, I have been introducing hypotheses concerning the birth of the divine of cognitive archaeologists such as Steven Mithen. However, as stimulating as they are, I do not propose to premise my consideration of the birth of the gods in the Japanese islands directly upon these ideas. As I said in the introduction, I want to stick as closely as possible to concrete source materials and to seek with my own eyes the traces left by the passage of the gods upon this archipelago.

Prior to World War II, the orthodox archaeological wisdom was that there had been no human habitation in the Japanese archipelago prior to the neolithic peoples who arrived bearing the cord-patterned (jōmon) pottery that gives the Japanese neolithic its name—the Jōmon period (10,000–300 BCE). What overturned this, providing evidence of the existence of a paleolithic culture in Japan, was the discovery by Aizawa Tadahiro of paleolithic remains at a site in Iwajuku in Gunma Prefecture in 1949.[2] Many sites and stone tools have since been discovered that provide incontrovertible evidence of human habitation reaching back into paleolithic times. Even so, it is difficult to use existing evidence to see very far into the minds of the people of that era in the Japanese islands.

If we examine their stone tools, these were obviously made for practical purposes but also display design elements transcending simple utility. For example, large stone spear points of the Mikoshiba type, dating from the late paleolithic period, have been worked into symmetrical forms so delicate that they were easily breakable and not really suited to practical use.[3] It would appear that the creation of a stone tool that had a beautifully balanced form had become an end in itself. This concern with design has become, for cognitive archaeologists, something of an index for the birth of the divine, and suggests that certain stone tools were being regarded in a way that transcended their primary nature as objects for practical use.

At a turning point more than ten thousand years ago, the Japanese archipelago suddenly arrived at a new stage of cultural development. This was the beginning of the Jōmon period. The concern with design observed as early as paleolithic times is much more notable in the stone tools and ceramics of the this period. It is unclear how the *kaen doki* (flame-ware pottery) of the middle Jōmon was used, but it is obvious that it had already completely departed from utilitarian constraints.

At the same time, during the Jōmon period more direct expressions of the transcendent begin. Many researchers have noted that the images of snakes (vipers), boars, and frogs that figure so frequently in the motifs of Jōmon pottery are not naturalistic depictions of animals, but instead symbols of sacred beings. And the *dogū*, or earthenware figurines, that were produced in such prodigious numbers during the Jōmon period are certainly an expression of transcendence.

An autonomous realm of the dead

Progress in the archaeological approach to funerary customs has presented us with a number of interesting findings concerning the Jōmon concept of death. Particularly noteworthy is that late Jōmon settlements clearly separated the dwellings of the living from the burial places of the dead.

Jōmon settlements took the form of a circular arrangement of dwellings around a central plaza. And occupying the center of the plaza were graves. This structure—a graveyard surrounded by the homes of the living—was the prototype of the Jōmon settlement. Yet about 4,000 years ago, as the late Jōmon period commenced, changes in this pattern began to occur. Graveyards began to escape the confines of the settlements and take shape as a locale independent from everyday

Figure 2-1 Ōyu Stone Circles (Kazuno, Akita Prefecture)

dwelling places. The stone circles (*kanjō resseki*) found in large numbers in eastern Japan typify this. Even among specialists opinions differ concerning how to interpret this phenomenon. But most of them would agree that it indicates a clear demarcation between the world of the living and the world of the dead.[4]

Thus, to a certain stage, Jōmon people had seen the dead simply as members of the community who had ceased activity. There was no clear assumption of a personality distinct from the body of the deceased that might continue in some way after death. Just as young people became full-fledged members of the community by undergoing certain rites of passage, the dead, after a ritual—a funeral—marking their separation from the community, were buried in the central plaza of their village, continuing to share the space in which they had once lived. Infants or small children might be buried within the dwelling or in another nearby place, or interred in urns resembling the mother's womb, which suggests that there may have been a belief that the dead could return as newborn babies.[5] The living and the dead shared the same locus of everyday activity, the same world, and breathed the same air.

In contrast, when the graveyards were removed from the villages, it is likely that this meant a general sense had spread among the people that a realm of the dead existed that was quite different in nature from the world of the living. Just as the living gathered together in communities to conduct their daily lives, the dead possessed their own independent realm in which they pursued an autonomous existence. The graveyards or burial sites then became a place where periodic rituals were enacted venerating the dead who resided there—the spirits of the ancestors—and people came to share an image of ancestral spirits residing in the burial grounds as objects of ritual worship.

However, at this stage the ancestral spirits to be venerated remained an anonymous collective of the souls of the dead interred in the burial ground; no specific individuals had yet distinguished themselves as more important than the rest. For ancestral spirits to become deities—like the spirits of the emperors of the early Japanese state or the spirits of individuals such as Fujiwara no Kamatari—individual souls had to escape from the collective and evolve into beings superior to the others.

From ancestral spirits to gods

What was the process by which certain souls of the dead ascended to the status of gods? As a prerequisite for considering this question, we must first ascertain how "gods" were understood in Jōmon culture. When the people of the Japanese islands first felt the presence of spiritual powers transcending the everyday world—i.e., gods or deities— what was it that inspired such feelings? As with people elsewhere in the world, we may assume that it was natural phenomena surpassing the capacity of humans to understand and control. The gods make frequent appearances in the earliest extant written documents of the Japanese archipelago—the chronicles *Kojiki* and *Nihon shoki* and the *fudoki*, or provincial gazetteers. The vast majority of them are the result of humans sensing the operations of the divine in the natural phenomena surrounding them.

For the Jōmon people, phenomena such as the drama of the transits of the sun and moon, thunder and lightning, and the emergence of young shoots from seed were all the workings of deities. The process of gestation and birth—akin to the creation of something from nothing— was also an event surpassing human understanding. The superhuman capacities possessed by certain animals were seen as godlike, and the awe-inspiring forms of towering crags and great trees were regarded as possessing extraordinary powers.

Initially the gods were seen as identical with the phenomena or things perceived as godlike. The young green shoots of the reeds were gods. Sharks, deer, swans—each was individually conceived of as a deity. The snakes and boars depicted on Jōmon pottery were also gods. Eventually the concept of the divine shifted to a new level: from a perception of deities as immanent in or identical to certain specific things or phenomena, to a conception of them as a primal force underlying and causing various phenomena. In other words, the gods began to be conceived as more abstract identities, separate from the specific objects or phenomena that inspired the sense of a divine presence.

The endings *chi* and *mi* appended to the names of certain deities, such as Kagutsuchi 火神 (fire god) or Yamatsumi 山神 (mountain god), and the word *tama* 魂 are indicative of this. *Tama* was used in plant-related compounds such as *inadama* (rice spirit) and *kodama* (tree spirit), but the spirit or soul of humans and animals was also expressed by the word *tama*. The *tama* had already become an entity on a different plane of existence from its host; while it might exert influence over the being in which it resided, it was not confined by the individual characteristics of its host.

Of course, even after the birth of this new conception of the divine, the tendency to perceive certain phenomena as deities did not immediately disappear. The god that legendary hero Prince Yamatotakeru encountered atop Ibukiyama in the *Kojiki* took the form of a white boar, and in the section of *Hitachi no kuni fudoki* (Gazetteer of the Province of Hitachi) dealing with Namegata county, the malevolent deities known as Yato no Kami make their appearance as snakes. However, it is certain that with the development of ritual and ceremonial practices, the concept of divinity became progressively more generalized and abstract.

As noted, in the late Jōmon period burial sites began to be separated from residences, and the dead to occupy an autonomous world of their own. It was precisely at this time that earthenware figurines began to be made which depicted obviously non-human forms—the *shakōki dogū*, which have enormous oval eyes with horizontal slits, resembling snow-goggles; and others with large, heart-shaped faces. The advent of these highly abstract figurines might be considered an index of the growth of a concept of the divine that was increasingly removed from concrete objects and phenomena. Some stone circle sites have yielded prodigious amounts of these figurines and other ritual implements. The image of beings that transcended the human, and of another world invisible to the eyes, seems to have rapidly pervaded Jōmon culture at a certain point in time.

2. Jōmon Gods and Yayoi Gods

Undepictable gods

The abstraction of the divine proceeded even more vigorously with the entry into the Yayoi period (ca. 300 BCE–300 CE). One of the most

47

striking differences between the Jōmon and Yayoi periods was the disappearance of the *dogū*. These earthenware figurines, the characteristic expression of the transcendent during Jōmon times, were produced in great quantities throughout the period—but we see almost no examples from the Yayoi period. Nor is this limited to the *dogū*. The Yayoi period is one which lacks religious images in the broad sense of concrete representations of sacred beings.

This being the case, how were gods represented in the Yayoi period? By depicting not the form of the gods themselves, but symbols or images associated with them. Yayoi pottery and bronze bells (*dōtaku*) were decorated with a variety of images and motifs. But in none of them do we see anything that might be thought of as direct representations of deities. Instead of gods, what appear are images of shamans worshipping the gods. Either that or images of buildings elevated on piers (*takayuka-shiki*) that suggest places of ritual or worship, and trees that may have served as the *yorishiro* (dwelling places) for gods.

Tatsumi Kazuhiro interprets the motif to the right of the structure depicted at the top of fig. 2-2 to be an image of a god descending to that building.[6] And Terasawa Kaoru argues that the faces depicted on the bronze bells with "evil-eye" design (*jashimon*) and on Yayoi pottery with human features are representations of ancestral spirits, or gods.[7] While these interpretations cannot be completely denied, conversely it is also true that there is no evidence that conclusively supports them. And even if we provisionally accept these to be representations of ancestral spirits or deities, they are in no way typical of the period. In fact, the desire to see these as representations of deities is an indicator of how rare such depictions are in the Yayoi period.

From the Yayoi period into the Kofun period, large numbers of earthenware funerary sculptures called *haniwa* were produced, many of them depicting human beings in a variety of guises. Most represented servants of the deceased king pursuing various trades: scribes, warriors, falconers, peasants. And there are numerous surviving *haniwa* that appear to depict shamans praying to the deities. But among all these images, there are none which would seem to be depictions of the gods themselves. The bronze bells that are the characteristic relic of the Yayoi period are also in themselves not a representation of the sacred but instruments to be used in ritual and worship.

So we have people worshipping gods, and the implements used in that worship—but the gods themselves are nowhere to be seen. There is no direct representation of sacred beings as there is in the Jōmon *dogū*. The Yayoi period was one in which the gods erased their presence.

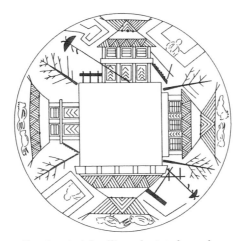

Figure 2-2 Yayoi-period dwellings depicted on a bronze mirror
(from Tatsumi Kazuhiro, 1992)

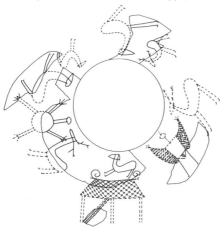

Figure 2-3 Motif on an earthenware vessel
(from Tatsumi Kazuhiro, 1992)

The role of the shaman

We may assume that this absence of direct representation is associated with the abstraction of the divine discussed earlier. The Jōmon period was one in which the gods were still understood as inseparably linked to specific phenomena and objects. The sun and the moon, snakes and boars, were all gods themselves. Pregnancy, birth, and other events were seen as individual examples of the workings of the gods. Even the *dogū* figurines were fundamentally complete in and of themselves; their sacral nature did not require confirmation by a higher power or the assumption of an invisible *tama* or spirit inhabiting them.

However, from the late Jōmon period onward, a perception of the divine not as specific individual phenomena or things but as a power lying behind them and giving rise to inexplicable phenomena gradually became the norm. Because the transcendent presence known as *tama* was invisible, it could not be given sculptural or pictorial form. Instead, we find images of shamans praying to the gods, or of shrines and trees that served either as symbols of the gods or as their *yorishiro*, the objects that give them a physical habitation.

In the Yayoi period, *mokugū*, or carved wooden figurines resembling the *kokeshi* dolls of later times, began to be created. They should probably be understood not as embodiments of a transcendent being like the Jōmon *dogū*, but as *yorishiro*. Sticklike, without clearly defined facial features, the external appearance of the *mokugū* suggests that it is more appropriate to see them as temporary lodging places for the gods rather than as a representation of the gods themselves.

Taking this concept of invisible deities as our basic premise, from the Yayoi period into the Kofun period the typical form of worship of the deities became a process in which a god was first summoned to inhabit a *yorishiro* such as a tree or rock outcropping, prayed to, and then, at the conclusion of the ceremony, expected to depart. Typical sites for this mode of worship, which did not require established shrine buildings, have been found at Okinoshima (Fukuoka Prefecture), Miwayama (Nara Prefecture), and Tenpaku Iwakura (Shizuoka Prefecture).

Surrounding Miwayama are a number of ritual sites looking upward toward the mountain and its foothills. Rather than establishing permanent fixed locations for the worship of the mountain, temporary installations were created at spots with a good view of the mountain, from which the mountain gods might be summoned with supplication and prayer. The Tenpaku Iwakura site is located atop a cone-shaped hill surrounded on three sides by the river Jingūjigawa, where there is a towering pair of boulders more than 5 meters in height. Beginning in the early Kofun period, this was a site for rituals summoning gods to these rocky thrones and then bidding them farewell.[8]

Prior to the Kofun period, the gods were not subjects for worship at a distance (*yōhai*). They were within conversational reach; people could supplicate them, receive their instructions, speak with them—and this was the fundamental form that worship took.

What happened to the *dogū*?

I have just been discussing the shift in the conception of the divine between the Jōmon and Yayoi periods. Of course, it is not easy to draw a clear line of demarcation between the two periods in this regard.

In the late Jōmon period highly abstract *dogū* begin to be produced, but at the same time we see the appearance of the so-called *gasshō dogū*, realistic figures with their hands together in an attitude of prayer. What the scholar of religion Isomae Jun'ichi has named *kussetsuzō dogū* (earthenware figures with bent limbs) are of this type.[9] The purpose for which such figures were created is unclear,

Figure 2-4 A *gasshō dogū* (Collection of Hachinohe, Aomori Prefecture).

but it has been suggested that they may be a direct depiction of a posture for worship in collective rituals.[10]

If *dogū* of this type do in fact depict the posture of prayer, this leads us to another important point. If *dogū* had previously been expressions of the transcendent and thus objects of worship themselves, here they have become representations of a form with which to address a transcendent being. In other words, these figures presuppose a more transcendent or sacred presence—a god or deity—distinct from the *dogū* itself. We may infer that this is a development connected with the transition from a stage at which the deities were tied to specific objects or phenomena to one in which they were perceived as an invisible power working behind and giving rise to individual phenomena.

During the transition from the Jōmon to Yayoi periods, another type of *dogū* began to be made—"container-type" *dogū* with hollow torsos, thought to have been used as funerary urns as human remains have been found in some of them. What appear to be pairs of male and female figurines have also been unearthed in considerable numbers from collective burial sites. Harada Masayuki sees this as evidence that the *dogū* which in Jōmon culture had served the realm of festival were transformed in the Yayoi period into implements serving the realm of the funeral.[11]

Here as well, we may see a process in which Jōmon pottery, and specifically the *dogū*, in response to the spread of the concept of invisible deities and the rise of new forms of belief and practice oriented toward them, ceased in their original function as the object of ritual and worship, and were transformed into ritual or funerary implements.

The origins of faith in the gods of heaven and earth

If we accept the hypothesis just outlined regarding the evolution of the divine from the late Jōmon into the Yayoi period, then it is clear that we must make major revisions to the common understanding of the gods of Japan. Even today, we frequently hear that Shintō is a "uniquely Japanese" folk religion inherited from time immemorial. If asked exactly when is meant by "time immemorial," the answer will probably be the Yayoi period and the beginnings of a society based on rice cultivation. Ninigi no Mikoto, the grandson of the sun goddess Amaterasu Ōmikami, who descended to earth to rule over Japan, was a personification of the *inadama*, or spirit of the rice plants, and among the Japanese gods there are many others deeply associated with rice. Rice plants are an indispensable part of Shintō ritual, including the Niinamesai, an annual rite in which the emperor makes an offering of newly harvested rice to the deities of heaven and earth. Thus the view stressing the connection between the Japanese gods and rice, and interpreting Shintō within the traditions of a culture based on rice cultivation and evolving since the Yayoi period.

In recent years, another hypothesis has become increasingly influential: one which seeks the origins of Japanese culture and its gods in the Jōmon period. Nelly Naumann, in her *Yama no kami* (Mountain Gods), criticizes Yanagita Kunio for linking the mountain gods with the religious beliefs and practices of agricultural communities, arguing that these deities were originally worshipped by pre-agricultural hunters and gatherers.[12] Her assertion that the Japanese gods were rooted not in Yayoi culture, but in the hunter-gatherer society of the Jōmon, and her criticism of single-minded interpretations of mountain deities in terms of ancestor worship, have had great value. We should also not overlook her suggestion that the mountain gods of slash-and-burn agriculturalists should be positioned somewhere between the mountain gods of hunters and gatherers and those of settled rice agriculturalists.

Even in the wake of Naumann's critique, Yanagita's theory of an alternating cycle between mountain gods (*yama no kami*) and the gods of the fields (*ta no kami*) continued to predominate, but Naumann's perspective, with later revisions, has been established with the support of Japanese ethnologists such as Sasaki Kōmei.[13]

Actually, this shift in focus to a period predating Yayoi culture began in the 1980s, when Umehara Takeshi and others drew attention to Jōmon culture as the prototype of Japanese culture. According to Umehara, what has defined Japanese culture down to the present is not the agricultural culture of the Yayoi period, but the hunting and gathering culture of the Jōmon, which preceded it and which endured for a considerably longer period of time. Its philosophy of the cycles of life and of *wa*, or harmony, would shape the foundations of Japanese culture for ages to come. He argues that today, when advanced industrial society appears to be reaching a dead end, we should pay fresh attention to the wisdom of the Jōmon people.[14]

Yet using examples of extant folk customs to link the origins of worship of mountain gods, or rituals conducted at *iwakura* (the rock formations into which these gods were invited to descend), to Jōmon culture requires a bit of a leap—both logically and in terms of the handling of source materials. It is also difficult to find clear and objective grounds for a methodology based on drawing a sharp demarcation between Jōmon and Yayoi cultures and discriminating between them according to a typology of their religious beliefs and practices. Our first order of business should not be to extrapolate about past eras from later source materials and examples, but to base our methodology on a strict use of source materials from the eras in question to reconstruct the characteristics of these past societies and cultures. At present we have an incomparably richer base of archaeological knowledge regarding the Jōmon and Yayoi periods than ever before, making such an approach even more important.

To sum up, approximately 4,000 years ago, with the beginning of the late Jōmon period, the concept of the divine took a great leap forward. The gods were separated from concrete objects and phenomena, and became progressively abstract. This eventually resulted, in the Yayoi period, in widespread societal acceptance of the idea of invisible gods. The concept of the gods in the Japanese islands, while deeply connected to changes in social structure related to the transition from hunting and gathering to settled rice-paddy cultivation, also displayed elements of continuity that transcended such chronology.

3. Memorialized Spirits

Spirits into gods

As we have seen, conceiving of immortal spirits as independent of mortal flesh was intimately related to the development, from the late Jōmon into the Yayoi period, of the concept of deities as invisible and transcendent beings. As the concept of invisible gods became more widespread, it seems likely that spirits, or *tama*, took on an increased aura of transcendence.

But even if *kami* (gods) and *tama* (spirits) began to be regarded as equivalent in nature, it was not the case that all human spirits were unconditionally accepted as deities. The *tama* of an ordinary person, after leaving the body and being pacified and purified by funerary rites, was fated to gradually fade from the memory of others with the passage of time. Transformation into the sort of spirit—or god—that could exert influence for generations over masses of people would have to await the emergence of individuals able to leave their mark on history or occupy a position of sufficient distinction that their memory would be inscribed in the minds of all the members of the larger community. The first figures that come to mind as meeting such conditions are chieftains or priests, great figures who might be considered the progenitors of a clan or community.

In the *Kojiki* and *Nihon shoki*, there are various passages in which a particular clan is described as descended from a certain animal and as possessing an admixture of that animal's bloodline. Hoori no Mikoto, for instance, dives to the bottom of the sea in search of a lost fishhook and visits the sea-god's palace, where he meets and marries Toyotama-hime, the sea-god's daughter, whose true form is that of "a sea-monster eight fathoms in length" (*yahiro no wanizame*). The child the two conceive is Ugayafukiaezu, father of the first Japanese emperor, Jinmu. The blood of animals thus pulses in the imperial lineage.

Similarly, according to the *Kojiki*, Ikutamayori-hime was visited by Ōmononushi no kami, the deity of the mountain Miwayama, and became pregnant. The god's true form was that of a snake, and the child she conceived inherited the powers of that deity, and this was the beginning of the lineage of the clan descended from Ikutamayori-hime. Other tales abound. "On Taking a Fox as a Wife and Producing a Child," a story from the first volume of the *Nihon ryōiki* (Record of Miraculous Events in Japan), relates how the Kitsune no Atai family of Mino province came to inherit the bloodline of a fox (*kitsune*), and with it produce generations who were possessed of great strength and unusual fleetness of foot.

In this concept of progenitors or founding ancestors who were children of *kami* and inherited the powers of animals we can see the emergence of clan gods (personified deities) out of a fusion of nature gods with ancestral spirits.

The advent of royal graves

The chieftains of the Yayoi period initially possessed an extremely strong shamanic character, serving as intermediaries between the gods and humans. In the reign of the Emperor Sujin, when Ōmononushi no kami, deity of Miwayama, demanded worship, it was his child Ōtataneko who was appointed as head priest. In Yayoi society, worship rituals for the gods (*kami matsuri*) were a key element in the maintenance of the community, so it was only natural that shamans, who conducted these rituals, held considerable authority and prestige. The frequent depictions of shamans in Yayoi art and *haniwa* figurines reflect this situation.

On the other hand, in the middle Yayoi period the authority of secular powerholders seems to have gained relative dominance over that of religious figures. The context for this was created by warfare and international contacts aimed at the unification of tribes and clans and the consolidation of a nation-state. An unending series of armed conflicts and active political negotiations required clan chieftains to possess a highly developed political judgment and the capacity for swift and effective military response. As a result, the power of secular chieftains with the requisite political and military abilities rapidly increased. Thus, beginning about 200 BCE in northern Kyushu, we begin to see the advent of what could be described as "royal tombs" characterized by large assemblages of bronze vessels.[15]

At about the beginning of the Christian era, the northern Kyushu region was the scene of active conquest and incorporation by powerful clans of more peripheral and weaker ones. These powerful clans gradually evolved into minor states, which were eventually united under a more centralized power. This state began to offer tribute to royal courts of China. The development of such states then began to spread to other parts of the Japanese archipelago.

As the unification of clans progressed and the area controlled by the resulting states expanded, the status of the king or monarch was increasingly enhanced. And as it grew, the impact of his presence on the people surrounding him grew as well. By the late Yayoi period, many such living individuals appeared—not distant clan founders from the depths of myth—who were able to impress their memory in the minds of generations to come. The most dramatic evidence of this is the massive tomb mounds that began to be constructed throughout western Japan beginning in the second century BCE. We may assume that this is the process by which the "memorialized dead" were raised out of the anonymous mass of their fellows and into history.

CHAPTER 3

New Deities and the Tumuli

1. The Hashihaka Tomb Mound

The emergence of keyhole-shaped tombs

IN THE MIDDLE of the third century CE, an epoch-making event occurred at the perimeter of the Nara Basin in central Japan—the construction of a massive *zenpō kōenfun* (keyhole-shaped tomb mound) known as Hashihaka. The Hashihaka tomb mound was certainly not the first of the keyhole tombs, but it was on an incomparably grander scale than its predecessors, measuring more than 280 meters in overall length. With the completion of the Hashihaka tomb, the curtain opened on the Kofun (Tumulus) period[1] in the Japanese islands, which would last for some three centuries.

Hashihaka is located at the southeastern edge of the Nara Basin, near what is now Makimuku station in the city of Sakurai in Nara Prefecture—in an area known from antiquity as "Yamato."

> Yamato is the crest of the land—
> In the close-folded
> Green-fence
> Mountains it is hidden:
> Yamato, the beautiful.[2]

Figure 3-1 Hashihaka (at right, tree-covered), with Miwayama looming in the background

So, in the *Kojiki*, sang the legendary warrior-hero Prince Yamato-takeru, fallen fatally ill in the midst of a military campaign and longing for his homeland. For many Japanese, the land in the vicinity of Hashihaka, nestled on three sides into the greenly wooded slopes of the surrounding hills like a courtyard garden, remains a primal and deeply nostalgic vision of the ancestral landscape.

The history of the Nara Basin goes back a long way. According to the *Nihon shoki*, Japan's first emperor, Jinmu, led a lengthy military expedition from Hyūga in Kyushu to the Nara region, where he enthroned himself at Kashihara and formally commenced his reign. This was in the year 660 BCE. For hundreds of years after this, until the construction of the capital of Heijōkyō in the early eighth century, almost all of the emperors established their palaces in this part of the Nara Basin.

The majority of postwar historians have adopted a skeptical attitude regarding the actual existence of Jinmu and the early generations of his imperial successors. On the other hand, the narratives of the historical chronicles have established in the minds of the Japanese people an image of Nara as occupying a position of centrality in the Japanese archipelago from the depths of antiquity. In the third century, gigantic keyhole-style tombs (of which the Hashihaka tumulus is the representative example) began to be constructed in the Nara region before they appeared in other areas, a development thought to have been premised upon an accumulation of technical and cultural knowledge developed during the Yayoi period (ca 300 BCE–300 CE).

But eventually doubts surfaced regarding this generally accepted scenario based on evidence that, at least through the Yayoi period, the Nara Basin was not a particularly developed region. Bronze artifacts such as vessels and mirrors represented the cutting edge of Yayoi-period culture, but only comparatively poor examples of these were found in excavations in the Nara Basin. Clearly, the region was operating at a level inferior to that of northern Kyushu or to neighboring regions like Ōmi or Kibi. Iron tools were also slow to reach this area. In the Yayoi period, far from being a cultural center of the Japanese islands, the region centered on the Nara Basin was a sparsely populated backwater.[3]

The keyhole tumuli of the third century—and particularly the Hashihaka *kofun*—were massive monuments that appeared quite suddenly in what were at the time remote and undeveloped areas. The archaeological evidence of this backwardness completely overturned the view of the Kinai region—Yamato and its vicinity—as the most advanced area in the Japanese archipelago, with construction of the tumuli and the birth of the Yamato court as extensions of developments that had already taken place there during the Yayoi period.

But if this was the case, who built the Hashihaka *kofun*? And why build it in Makimuku? What was their intent? At the very least we may assume that the tomb was intended to express the absolute superiority of the individual interred there over all the other members of the community. So it is a quite interesting phenomenon from the perspective of the development of the concept of *hitogami*—deified humans. With such issues in mind, let us now attempt to survey the spiritual world of the people who built the keyhole tombs.

The roots of the keyhole tombs

The cluster of keyhole-shaped tomb mounds that began to be built in the vicinity of Makimuku during the third century—and especially the largest of them, the Hashihaka tumulus—are representative early examples of this type of *kofun*. In both form and scale, they are distinctly different from the tomb mounds which preceded them.

What led to the sudden appearance of these massive and uniquely shaped *kofun*? Historians and archaeologists have accumulated a mass of research in the effort to answer this riddle. Perhaps the first answer that occurs to almost anyone contemplating this question is to hypothesize that the Nara Basin was suddenly invaded and occupied by outsiders who were the bearers of the culture that produced such tombs. For a time, the so-called "horse-rider theory" offered an appealing framework for such an argument—and attracted much debate—by positing that a culture of equestrian warriors from mainland Asia invaded the Japanese islands and established a dynasty of conquest.[4] Another intriguing conjecture is based on the idea that Emperor Jinmu was indeed a historical figure who engaged in a campaign of conquest that took him from his home base in Kyushu, the most highly developed region in the Yayoi period, into the Nara region, where he eventually established a new capital.

But such theories of conquest from outside the region all contain a crucial problem: the fact that previous burial systems of the keyhole-tumulus type are not to be found anywhere else—not in Japan, not on the Korean peninsula, not in China. So researchers have turned away from what looks to be a futile search for earlier examples of keyhole-type tombs to concentrate on delving into the origins of the Hashihaka tumulus in an attempt to discover if there are any earlier burial practices and systems with similar elements. In particular, attention has been drawn to the Kibi region in what is present-day Okayama Prefecture, which is known for having possessed a unique local culture from ancient times.

Keyhole tombs frequently had arrangements of *haniwa* arrayed at several levels following the contour lines of the tomb mound. The most common of these earthenware relics were simple cylinders, which in addition to their decorative function served to prevent erosion of the soil from the face of the mound. It has been noted that one type of these *haniwa* cylinders, resembling ceremonial vessel stands (*tokushu kidai-gata haniwa*), have their origins in earthenware vessels used in tumuli in Kibi, where large-scale tomb mounds began to be constructed during the late Yayoi period.[5] Among them, the Tatetsuki *kofun* (in what is now the city of Kurashiki) is a circular tomb (*enfun*) with rectangular projections at opposite ends that have led some scholars to see it as a prototype for the keyhole-style *kofun*. The area is rich in archaeological remains, and flourished culturally in advance of the Nara region. The keyhole-style tomb building that commenced with the Hashihaka site clearly draws on the Kibi tradition.

Yet pointing out this genealogy linking the Hashihaka tumulus to the Kibi tomb mounds cannot provide us with an adequate explanation of it. The Makimuku area where the Hashihaka tumulus is sited shows evidence of large numbers of cultural artifacts from regions other than Kibi; excavations there have yielded pottery of a wide variety of types and styles ranging geographically from western Japan through the Tōkai region. The keyhole-style tumuli were thus the product of an entirely new civilization, apparently arising from a fusion and recombination of traditions and technologies introduced from a number of different regions.[6]

We may posit that the principal architects of this development were people newly settled in the Nara region. We know that simultaneous to the construction of the keyhole-shaped tomb mounds, large-scale, planned urban development was taking place, including the digging of canals and the construction of a system of roads. But it seems likely that this group of settlers was not limited to people from a specific region, given the disparate elements comprising the Makimuku archaeological sites. Nor is there any evidence of conflict with previous residents in the process of settling in the area. The new arrivals appear to have deliberately chosen to establish themselves in Makimuku as a sparsely populated and undeveloped area where they could settle peacefully, with good access to water, at the foot of Mount Miwa (Miwayama). Then, in cooperation with the indigenous people of the area, they embarked upon an ambitious program of city and tomb building that was a compendium of the most advanced technology of their time.

The entombed wife of a god

What brought about these developments? One likely factor was the rise of minor states and movement toward unification that began in northern Kyushu in advance of other regions of the Japanese archipelago. From the middle of the Yayoi period onward, in what are today known as the Fukuoka and Sawara plains extending along the shores of Hakata Bay, funeral mounds that could appropriately be termed royal graves began to be constructed and stocked with rich supplies of burial goods. A number of such minor kingships were unified by more powerful states whose rulers began to pay tribute to the ruling dynasties of China. In the year 57 the king of a state called Na sent a tribute envoy to the Latter Han Dynasty, and in 107 a ruler named Suishō of the kingdom of Wa sent a tribute of 160 slaves.

Eventually an advanced confederation from northern Kyushu, led by a powerful state such as Na, began to expand its territorial reach and influence eastward along the shores of the Seto Inland Sea. The resulting tensions touched off a period of warfare, described in a section of the *Wei zhi* (Chronicle of the Kingdom of Wei) as "great disturbances in the land of Wa," during which settlements were constructed throughout regions bordering on the Inland Sea; they appear to have been strategically sited on high ground for defensive purposes.

In the latter half of the second century, following this period of conflict, large-scale tomb mounds of distinctive appearance began to be seen throughout western Japan. In Kibi, for example, many large tumuli appeared from the late Yayoi period onward, including the aforementioned Tatetsuki *kofun* in Kurashiki that some regard as the prototype for the keyhole-style tombs. In the Izumo region, a type of square tumuli with projecting corners was built in considerable numbers from the late second century. And in the Kinki region, low square tomb mounds surrounded by a ditch or moat began to be constructed at increasingly greater scale and spread throughout the area.

The largest of these tombs might reach dozens of meters in length, demonstrating the exceptional power and authority of the personages interred within. One senses how an extraordinary era of warfare worked to elevate the position of leadership attained by these regional kings.

The northern Kyushu confederation, which appeared earlier than in other regions, enjoyed a geographic advantage that permitted it to virtually monopolize the import of advanced culture, technologies, and materials such as iron from the Korean peninsula. A further advantage over other regions was the political legitimacy conferred upon it through recognition by the Chinese dynasty of the time, the Latter Han.

Radical measures were necessary if the supremacy of the Kyushu forces was to be broken. And so other powerful regions that wished to compete with the Kyushu confederation cooperated to form the new state of Yamato. The arrival in Makimuku of settlers from other regions of western Japan, and the construction of a new capital and prodigious keyhole-shaped tombs for its rulers, can all be viewed in this historical context.

As the first ruler of the new state which took shape in this way it would only be fitting to select a personage whom all of the regions could support without dissent, rather than one of the established regional kings—a ruler able to transcend the interests and intrigues of politics. If one considers the importance of the role played in the community by the shamans in worshipping and communicating with the gods from the Yayoi period onward, then the likelihood of an extraordinarily gifted spiritual medium assuming the position of ruler seems quite high.

In the *Nihon shoki*, the individual interred in the Hashihaka tumulus is identified as Yamato-toto-bi-momoso-hime no Mikoto, the wife of Ōmononushi no Kami, the deity of Miwayama. According to the chronicle, "this tomb was built by men in the daytime, and by gods at night," with lines of people passing the stones hand to hand across the plain from Mount Ōsaka.[7] This hand-to-hand relay suggests the nature of this tomb, built to symbolize the cooperative efforts of disparate clans and tribes. The tradition that the wife of a god was buried there supports the idea that the founding ruler of Yamato was believed to be able to converse with the gods.

In addition, if we consider recent archaeological findings that place the date of construction of the Hashihaka tumulus in the middle of the third century, then it is quite possible that the tomb is that of Himiko, "queen of the state of Yamatai." In the year 239, Himiko sent a tribute mission to the court of Emperor Ming of the Wei, and received in return the title "Queen of Wa Friendly to Wei." This act clearly recognized the importance of diplomacy in competing with the states of northern Kyushu. This effort on the part of Yamato to seize the diplomatic initiative appears to have been successful, for in the fourth century the center of power in contacts with the Korean peninsula shifted to the region around Yamato and away from northern Kyushu. During the same period, the remote island of Okinoshima, floating in the Genkai Sea between Kyushu and the Korean peninsula, became the site of ritual practices initiated by the Yamato state, not the states of northern Kyushu.[8]

In the late third century, keyhole-style tumuli began to be constructed in Kyushu as well. The wave of political reorganization emanating from Yamato had begun to spread throughout the Japanese archipelago, making inroads even in northern Kyushu, the former center of power and culture.

2. Why Were the Immense Tomb Mounds Constructed?

Toward a new type of deity

Even if we accept the hypothesis that settlers from disparate regions needed some sort of symbol to assist their consolidation into a community, why did this take the form of immense burial tumuli? In order to answer this question we must turn our attention away from the keyhole-shaped tombs themselves, and examine what we know of the communities predating that period.

We know from sites such as Sannai Maruyama in Aomori Prefecture that human settlements were well distributed throughout the Japanese archipelago during the Jōmon period. As these settlements grew in scale, some system for organizing their growing populations became essential. The key was a presence transcending the human—the *kami*, or gods.

It is also evident that in the course of the Jōmon period the earthenware figurines known as *dogū* gradually increased in size. One explanation that has been advanced is that these implements, once used for familial worship rituals, later came to be employed in larger ritual practices involving the entire community.[9]

We also observe that in the late Jōmon period burial sites throughout the Japanese islands became separated from dwelling places, and stone circles were constructed as sites for funerary and other ritual observances. From certain of the stone circle ruins, large numbers of *dogū* and other ritual implements have been unearthed. The concept of superhuman beings (gods) progressed rapidly from the late Jōmon period onward. People lived their lives in the presence of these gods, marking various occasions with ritual observances and worship.

Throughout the early Jōmon period, the gods were understood as identical with objects or phenomena perceived as divine. As we saw in Chapter 2, an animal or an earthenware figurine believed to possess special powers was itself regarded as a deity. But in the transition from the late Jōmon period into the Yayoi period, the concept of the divine was taken to the next level: rather than seeing specific beings or phenomena as gods, the gods came to be conceived as a presence and creative force underlying and giving rise to individual phenomena. The divine came to be separated from the phenomena perceived as embodying it and understood as a more abstract presence, called *tama* or *kami*.

In the Yayoi period, direct expression of the form of supernatural beings, as in the *dogū* of the Jōmon period, ceased. Instead, deities manifested themselves indirectly, through intermediaries such as the shamans or trees or other objects that served as *yorishiro*, temporary abodes of the gods. During this period ritual implements such as bronze bells also proliferated. We may conjecture that as the concept of invisible gods matured, the concept of the divine itself grew steadily more universalized and abstract.

In the minor states and kingships that began to develop in the middle of the Yayoi period, this concept of the gods and the worship of them no doubt played an indispensable role in maintaining the social order. Monopolizing the right to act as an intermediary for the will of the gods was the foundation of political power, and shamans who could communicate with the gods possessed great authority. As minor states were unified into larger regional polities, their former clan gods and genius loci became inadequate to serve as the gods to be revered and worshipped by these larger groupings. As the areas controlled by larger states expanded and more diverse groups were drawn into their spheres of influence, the necessity of maintaining a stable political and social order required gods that possessed a more universal and powerful authority able to subsume that of the other deities. The people who gathered at Makimuku, at the foot of Miwayama, were looking for precisely this new type of deity.

Tumuli as dwelling places of gods

How were gods to be created that might be shared among members of a community coming from diverse places of origin? The answer that eventually emerged was to elevate to the status of a god a personage whom all the members of the community shared as a living memory. And it is conceivable that the keyhole-shaped tumulus was a mechanism for giving birth to this new form of deity.

As we have already described, the concept of *kami* or gods was established, at the latest, during the course of the Jōmon period in the Japanese islands. The noble forms of the mountain ranges that people looked up to from their villages were from antiquity believed to be the abode of the gods. The reason the gods dwelt there was that the mountains were a place of purity, and it was only rare individual spirits of the dead who attained a degree of purity and spiritual power sufficient to be allowed to dwell as *kami* in the mountains.

By the end of the seventh century the emerging imperial state had designated as the graves of the successive generations of emperors particularly impressive tumuli (with mounds reminiscent of the mountains) that had been constructed during the Kofun period. As is clearly suggested by the imperial graves being known as *sanryō*, or "mountain tombs," this was a mechanism for artificially creating a residence—in the form of a mountain—as the dwelling place for an imperial spirit to be revered as a *kami*, in accordance with the prevailing beliefs of the era, which held that the mountains were the abode of the gods.

How do the rituals and worship centering on the keyhole-shaped tumuli fit into this genealogy of concepts of the divine? Standing at one of these sites, one immediately feels the rounded rear portion of the immense tumulus to be a mountain, precisely what the people of the late seventh to tenth centuries saw when they spoke of them as "mountain tombs" and regarded them as the abode of deified imperial spirits conceived as tutelary gods. Ōba Iwao has noted the correspondence between the keyhole-shaped tumuli and mountains in relation to the perception of the people of antiquity that "the world after death existed in the purity of the mountains."[10]

The new state which established its capital at Makimuku in the third century required a powerful deity, transcending previous clan and ancestral gods, in order to unite the disparate peoples that comprised it. It seems reasonable to conclude that, from the beginning, the keyhole-shaped tumuli were an effort to create artificial mountains that could serve as the abode of deities possessing sufficient authority and power to be shared by all the people of the polity.

This hypothesis is supported by the formal similarities between the rites conducted at the keyhole-shaped tumuli and those offered to the gods at other locations. From the late Yayoi into the Kofun period, specific locales in the mountains or on smaller islands were chosen as sacred spaces where rock outcroppings, trees, and other natural features were used as *yorishiro*, the temporary dwelling places to which the gods might be invited to be worshipped. Such sites came to be called *iwakura* or *iwasaka*, and there are place-names throughout Japan that remind us of this custom.

Indeed, archaeologists have noted the commonality of both the forms of ritual practice and the ritual implements employed at Okinoshima and at the keyhole tumuli.[11] The same is true of Miwayama.[12] The same order of beings (i.e., *kami*) was being worshipped at all these sites. Moreover, as if in response to the construction of the keyhole tumuli and the establishment of the rituals surrounding them, in the Kinai region large numbers of the bronze bells (*dōtaku*) that had been an important ritual implement up to that time were deliberately destroyed.

What was enshrined in the keyhole tumuli?

So what were these *kami* enshrined in the keyhole tumuli? Given the fact that it was human remains interred in the rounded portion of these tomb mounds, lavishly accompanied by a variety of burial goods, it seems natural to conclude that what was being reverenced was the spirit of the deceased.

The people who assembled in Yamato raised up a monarch as symbol of their new state. It was desirable for this personage to be a religious figure, transcending various and conflicting political interests. But precisely because charismatic rule is dependent on an individual human personality, it is unstable. And, in fact, after the death of Himiko, the struggle over political sovereignty resulted in civil war. As the state of Yamato grew more assertive in diplomacy and military affairs, secular power-holders made their presence increasingly felt, and it was inevitable that political conflicts would intensify among the ruling elite. To overcome this situation, it was essential to construct a stable and enduring system of rule that was not dependent upon the special charisma of figures such as Himiko. The creation of a transcendental presence that could become the symbol of the polity as a whole became the most urgent task facing the Yamato kingdom.

The attempt to elevate an actual, individual human beings to the status of a god had already taken place during the Yayoi period. In the middle Yayoi period, large graves were made for chieftains in various regions. In the San'in region and in Okayama (Kibi), from the late Yayoi period the chieftains' tombs began to be separated from communal burial grounds and built, not only on a larger scale, but at sites along mountain ridges or summits that commanded a view of the surrounding landscape.[13] This was a visible expression of the idea that the world of the dead was divided along a vertical axis according to a hierarchy of status, a phenomenon reflecting the process by which minor states were forming and secular power was becoming concentrated in the hands of specific individuals. From this we can also see that these powerful individuals continued to be treated as extraordinary beings even after death.[14]

It is unclear whether at this stage the chieftains interred in these graves were perceived as being at the same level as the established *kami*. Yet in terms of a hierarchical cosmology that placed the chieftains at the apex, even in the world of the dead, the thinking of the people of this era appears to have been progressing in a direction quite similar to that of the builders of the keyhole tombs. Experiments with building tomb mounds at the summit of mountains should also be noted. Directly influenced by the tumuli of Kibi, the Makimuku tumulus cluster—and especially the Hashihaka tumulus situated at its apex— arose out of these developments of the late Yayoi period. It was not only larger in scale than all previous tomb mounds, but also clearly intended to elevate the deceased ruler to the status of a deity.

The tomb mounds as man-made mountains

However, another issue arises here, as archaeologists have pointed out that there is no evidence of ongoing ritual observances at the tumuli after they were constructed. If the beings thought to reside in the tombs were in fact deities, then why were regular rituals not conducted at the *kofun*? And why did burial mounds continue to be created for the chieftains, one after another?

Sites for religious rituals at Okinoshima and Miwayama contemporaneous with the keyhole tumuli had no large permanent shrine buildings; the *kami* were summoned on each occasion, invited to occupy a rock outcropping or a tree as a *yorishiro*, and worshipped there. The *kami* had neither visible form nor permanent habitation. Some *kami* were also worshipped at the village level, but they did not find fixed abode in a shrine either. The *kami* visited the village only during specific periods when they were being worshipped; when the time of ritual and worship was over, they would depart.

The necessary catalyst for itinerant deities taking up permanent residence in specific shrines were the official rites of worship initiated by the *ritsuryō* state.[15] During the latter half of the seventh century the formation of a centralized imperial state began, and with it construction of a permanent capital as the emperor's residence. These developments were accompanied by a reorganization of the world of the gods into a hierarchy of deities with Amaterasu Ōmikami, ancestral goddess of the imperial line, positioned at its apex. The process of designating specific *kofun* as the tombs of earlier generations of emperors was a way of rationalizing the imperial lineage, a policy inextricably interwoven with this reshuffling of the gods.

The *kami*, from Amaterasu on down, were now newly posited as the protector gods of the sovereign power, acting to maintain it from permanent stations at Ise and in the vicinity of the imperial palace. In return, splendid shrines were built for these gods, where they were offered regular rituals of worship. Professional priests were appointed, and food and other offerings conducted on a daily basis.

This domestication of the *kami*—the establishment of permanent shrines—was not accomplished at one stroke as a result of a specific political or social impetus; we may assume it progressed more gradually, at a number of different levels. Hirose Kazuo has argued that already, by the latter half of the Yayoi period, "people who had begun to feel the comings and goings of the *kami* to be an inconvenience . . . hit upon the idea of shutting them up in shrines surrounded by moats and fences."[16] However, it would not be until a somewhat later time that this notion came to be generally shared.

Amidst this movement toward the domestication of the gods, toward the end of the seventh century the idea became established—primarily with regard to the official shrines with deep connections to the sovereign power—that gods would take up permanent residence in a shrine and offer protection to specific individuals associated with it. The image of imperial spirits inhabiting the *sanryō* ("mountain tombs") and giving protection to the reigning emperor was a part of this system for creating new *kami* who would serve as guardians of the state.

The era of the keyhole tombs, which began in the third century, was one in which the concept of *kami* residing in a specific locale had still not become generally accepted. There might be a vague notion of *kami* existing in a particular mountainous area, but generally speaking their specific whereabouts were unknown and mere mortals could not choose when or where they might encounter a god. Nor were the spirits, or *tama*— once having departed the flesh—something that could be coaxed to take up permanent residence in a specific locale by any means known to ordinary men.

As discussed in connection with the poem of Izumi Shikibu cited in the third section of Chapter 1, even in the society of the tenth century the idea that the dead took up fixed residence in a specific place was still not generally shared. And we are looking at a period some six hundred years before this. No matter how impressive a tomb mound one might build, in a society in which ideas of wandering spirits and traveling deities still had the upper hand, it was probably no simple thing to get the spirit of the deceased to take up residence in it.

The towering tomb mounds, reaching towards the heavens, were man-made mountains. For the ancient people who lived in these islands, it was the mountains that were the proper abode of the gods. The people who built Hashihaka created a mountain in the midst of the plains in an attempt to artificially construct an abode where a spirit or god might be induced to stay. At the apex of the rounded rear portion of a keyhole tomb a burial chamber would be created—doubly and triply sealed as if to prevent the entombed spirit from escaping—while above it a *haniwa* in the form of a house would be placed to serve as a *yorishiro* for the spirit. Later, pillars or trees would sometimes serve as *yorishiro*.

Mitsuhashi Tadashi has pointed out that religious rituals involving the placement of pillars at keyhole tumuli were widely practiced and appear to have had great significance attached to them.[17] It is likely that such pillars and trees were fundamentally mechanisms for inducing the *kami* to stay at the mound.

3. Forms of Ritual at the Tomb Mounds

Ongoing rituals

The issue that we must now address is the assertion that there were no continuing ritual observances at the *kofun*. For if this were the case, does it not suggest that this great experiment—the creation of powerful guardian deities and the construction of artificial mountains in which to contain their power—was in the end a complete failure? I do not think so. Instead, I suspect that in the period of the keyhole tombs, the spirits of the chieftains interred there continued to be venerated in other ways.

As already mentioned, the typical mode by which the *kami* were worshipped during the Kofun period was to invite them to descend to earth at a specific place for the duration of the ritual. The place of ritual had to be one in which the summoned god and the human supplicant could speak to one another. This form of ritual continued into historic times. A passage in the *Nihon shoki* relates that after the destruction of the rebellious Sōga clan, Emperor Kōtoku assembled his ministers of state "under the great *tsuki* tree" and made them swear an oath of fidelity to the emperor.[18] This indicates that even after the Kofun period, state-level rituals were conducted in plazas where there were sacred trees that could serve as *yorishiro* which the deities could be invited to inhabit for the duration of the ritual.[19]

What, then, of the *kannabiyama*, mountains where the gods were thought to dwell? In the case of Miwayama, a shrine exists today—Ōmiwa Shrine—that venerates the mountain itself as the body of the deity. However, this veneration of the mountains themselves as gods, or cults of mountain worship, did not become widespread until early modern times. The mountains were places where the gods dwelt—not gods in their own right. And even when the deities residing in the mountains were worshipped, the construction of large-scale shrines at fixed locations such as Ōmiwa Shrine only took place from the Nara period (710–794) onward. When Emperor Bidatsu (r. 572–585) summoned the chieftains of the Emishi and made them swear an oath of fealty, standing on the banks of the river Hatsuse and facing Mount Mimoro, their oath was directed not to the mountain but to the gods who resided there.[20] Religious rituals in the mountains during the Kofun period, as may be surmised from the various worship sites that have been found dotting the lower slopes of Miwayama, were not addressed to the mountain itself; rather, they took the form of inviting the deities to temporarily inhabit a specific locale where a rock outcropping or other natural feature might serve as a *yorishiro*.

Let us turn now to a consideration of the rituals observed at the keyhole tumuli. Extrapolating from what we have seen so far of the ritual practices of the Kofun period, it seems unlikely that the deities

Figure 3-2 An *iwakura* (rock serving as a *yorishiro*) at Shinobuyama in the city of Fukushima

residing in the tombs would be worshipped at fixed or permanent facilities. Today, a *torii*, or shrine gate, stands before the front portion of the Hashihaka tumulus, marking it as a place of pilgrimage and worship, but the first appearance of such features at the tumuli was in the Heian period (794–1185), and they did not become common until after the renovations of imperial tombs implemented during the Bunkyū era (1861–64), in the final years of the Tokugawa shogunate. With the exception of the Kofun and Ritsuryō periods, prior to the Bunkyū era the imperial tumuli were not venerated with direct ritual observance.[21]

If so, then where were rituals conducted for the deities enshrined in the tumuli? It is probably safe to assume that, in line with the customary form of rituals of this period, they took place in some type of central communal space, where a sacred tree or grove might provide a *yorishiro* for the deity, or in some other place with a vista of the tumulus, at which the important officials of the state might assemble to invite the spirit of the deceased ruler from its residence in the tomb

mound. The construction of the immense keyhole tombs did not necessarily have an immediate impact on the forms of communal ritual
practice. It was merely that the deities to be worshipped had shifted
from the previous clan and family gods to the spirits of sovereigns
regarded as the founders and progenitors of the emerging state.

The Tōmizuka *kofun* in Wakabayashi-ku in the city of Sendai,
Miyagi Prefecture, is an early Kofun-period keyhole tumulus surrounded by a number of sites from which large quantities of earthenware vessels (*hajiki*) and stone implements have been recovered.[22]
From the types of pottery unearthed and the absence of any permanent
ritual structures, these are believed to be typical Kofun-period sites of
worship. From this we can see that for quite a long time after the tumulus was constructed, ritual observances associated with it continued to
be conducted in the vicinity of the tomb.

In addition, at the Ishizuka tomb in Makimuku, in the narrow neck
between the rectangular front portion of the mound and the circular
rear portion, a plain wooden pillar has been discovered that is believed

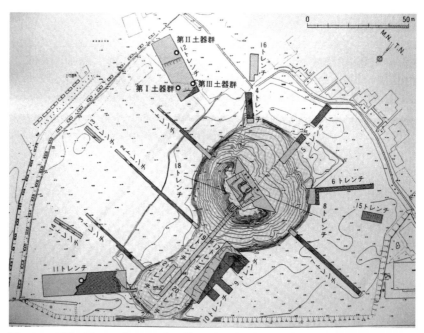

Figure 3-3 The Tōmizuka tumulus (from *Sendaishi*, supplementary volume 2)

to have been used in rituals.[23] It was probably used as a *yorishiro* for summoning and binding the deity resident in the tumulus.

Just as the *kofun* themselves took a variety of forms, the rituals and ceremonials associated with them must have been diverse. Keyhole tombs frequently display a square platform or terrace projecting from the mound itself into the surrounding moat. It has been established that *haniwa* in the shape of houses and human figures were neatly arrayed upon these projections. The purpose of these platforms is still debated, but it is highly likely that they were used as a ritual space into which to invite for worship the deities residing in the tumuli. The *haniwa* in the form of a house placed at the center of such spaces served as the *yorishiro* for the deity being worshiped. But no remains have been found of any permanent or enduring structures at these sites.

The keyhole tumulus system

The construction of enormous *kofun* reached its peak in the fifth century. Clearly the intention was to elevate the personages interred within to the status of *kami*, with the tomb mounds themselves the abode of these deities. However, constrained by the concept of gods and spirits (*kami* and *tama*) that then prevailed, this effort failed to establish any widespread perception of such spiritual presences as lodging permanently in a specific site. Such general acceptance would require the existence of a liturgy and protocol for properly worshipping the spirits of the chieftains interred within the tumuli as deities—forms of ritual observance that at this stage were still under development.

As the system for creating gods out of ancestors was still a work in progress, it did not achieve success with the first generation or two of chieftains—it required repetition and sustained practice to take hold. And it was necessary to keep building bigger and bigger tomb mounds (sacred mountains), counterbalancing the immaturity of the system with an impressive visual display of the transcendent nature of those whose bones were interred within.

Beginning in the late Yayoi period, tumuli for clan chieftains began to be built at a larger scale in almost every region, and the burial sites began to be positioned to literally occupy higher ground—the summits of hills or mountains—in what was clearly an effort to elevate the spirit of the chieftain into a transcendent being. The form of the keyhole tombs perfected in the Kinai region operated both to generate and to bind such deities—and thus was smoothly adopted by communities in other regions which were also seeking to elevate the spirits of their chieftains to transcendent status. The Yamato court, itself a kind of coalition government, did not seek to prohibit such imitation, but instead chose to extend its influence throughout the archipelago by encouraging the diffusion and adoption of the keyhole-style tombs. Thus innumerable copies of such tombs were created throughout the Japanese islands, varying in scale and quality with the size of the groups and the power of their chieftains. What Tsude Hiroshi has dubbed "the keyhole-tomb system"—a social order based on relationships of mutual recognition among these chieftains—came into being as a result.[24]

As keyhole tombs came to be built throughout the Japanese archipelago, the tumuli of the Yamato kingdom inevitably grew even more immense in an effort to preserve their distinctiveness and superiority to those of other regions. Prior to the establishment of the legal and institutional framework of the *ritsuryō* system—the system of centralized government modeled on the institutions of Tang China—and as yet unable to monopolize the claim of being descended from gods, the proto-emperors of the Yamato court, called "great kings," or *ōkimi*, had no other means to assert their authority than to construct tumuli so massive as to overawe any competitors. This was no doubt the reason why individual rulers chose to mobilize all the human and material resources at their command to construct the grandest possible tumuli.

The decline of Kofun culture

Beginning with the reign of Suiko (r. 593–628), the Yamato court experimented in various ways with stabilizing the position and status of the "great kings" and establishing a system of court ranks and etiquette. Then, from the reigns of Emperor Tenmu (r. 672–686) and Empress Jitō (r. 686–697) onward, the rapid development of legal, governmental, and religious institutions marked a crucial turning point with regard to the status of the sovereign. The emperor was not merely the apex of the secular social hierarchy, but possessor of a sacred status passed down through the bloodline of successive generations of deified imperial ancestors. And now the emperor was himself a living god (*akitsukami*).

At the same time, as a descendant of gods, the emperor was protected by the other deities of heaven and earth and by the deified spirits of his imperial ancestors. The position of sovereign ruling over all the islands of Japan had been transformed and integrated into a system of deities transcending secular society. And implementation of the system of imperial mausolea (*ryōbosei*) bolstered the unique status of the imperial house as rulers who were gods and descendants of gods from time immemorial.

Having reached this stage, the efforts of generations of rulers in building massive burial tumuli to certify their own authority—and to use that authority and power as a step toward divinity— were no longer necessary. These massive construction projects that had sapped the wealth and power of each successive ruler had lost their significance. About the middle of the seventh century, the keyhole tombs ceased to be built, replaced by octagonal mounds reserved exclusively for the "great kings." The reforms of the era of Emperor Tenmu and Empress Jitō were advancing the differentiation of the Yamato rulers from lesser kings and chieftains. The rulers had been transformed into beings venerated as gods, not as an extension of their own power and authority, but mediated through an external circuit grounded in the history of these islands since the age of the gods.

Elsewhere in East Asia—the mausoleum of China's first emperor Qin Shi Huang, or the royal tombs of the Three Kingdoms period in the Korean peninsula, for example—there have been periods in which massive tombs and mausolea were constructed. Qin Shi Huang was the first ruler to unify central China, and the Three Kingdoms period in Korea was one of considerable strife and military tension. In the Han dynasty which followed the Qin, the institutions of national rule were more highly developed, and the status of the ruler institutionalized in written law and court protocol and ceremony—thus the construction of gigantic tombs came to an end. After the Korean peninsula was unified by the kingdom of Silla, royal tombs whose major attribute was their scale also ceased to be built.

As Tsude Hiroshi has pointed out, the construction of large-scale royal tombs and mausolea venerating the ruler as a god is a phenomenon, often seen in the early stages of state formation, that disappears after ruling institutions based on a state bureaucracy and written law become firmly established.[25] At the point when the status of the ruler has been subsumed into the system of rule and established as an organ of the state, the kind of monument that reflects the individuality of the sovereign and emphasizes his power loses its raison d'être.

Moreover, regardless of locale, the era of gigantic royal tombs is one in which no religion has yet taken root which is capable of relativizing the secular world. With the diffusion of universal religions such as Buddhism, the ruler is stripped of his privileged position to become yet another suffering human in need of salvation—and the construction of a magnificent tomb completely loses its significance. In Egypt as well, the pyramids housing deceased rulers as divinities began to shrink during the same period that the temples to the sun god grew to increasingly monumental size.

CHAPTER 4

Between *Hitogami* and *Mononoke*

1. Dead Souls Running Rampant

Our revulsion toward corpses

TODAY MANY REGARD a dead person as an eerie or ominous presence. Certainly no one wishes to live with a corpse. The human race has long regarded the dead—and particularly their physical presence—as something to be abhorred. But why is it that people came to abhor the dead? When did this begin? Animals do not display revulsion for dead bodies. Nor do primates. I recall seeing a film of a female monkey continuing to care for her dead child. Such revulsion seems a uniquely human phenomenon.

One source of this abhorrence is undoubtably the powerful smell and grotesque appearance of a corpse. But the feeling of fear we have toward the dead clearly transcends mere physical revulsion. If anything, as we see in ghost stories from past and present, East and West, it is the invisible presence that outlasts the extinction of the flesh—the spirits of the dead—that appears to be the primal source of our dread.

If this is the case, then the fear and awe inspired by the spirits of the dead are predicated on a widely shared concept within human society of a continuance of the personality beyond death. In Japan, this occurred sometime during the Jōmon period (10,000–300 BCE).

As discussed in Chapter 1, it is during the late Jōmon period that we observe burial sites being clearly separated from dwelling places. But there is no documentary evidence at this stage to confirm that this separation was related to a fear of the spirits of the dead. Certain burial customs of the Jōmon period, such as flexed burials (*kussō*) and burials involving the dead person embracing a stone (*hōsekisō*), have been pointed to as efforts to prevent the spirits of the dead from working mischief in this world. On the other hand, we see many cases in which Jōmon people buried their dead near or even inside their dwellings, which has led some observers to conclude that they regarded the dead as intimate and familiar presences.

Beginning in the Yayoi period (300 BCE–300 CE), we have historical records in the form of Chinese documentary sources describing the customs and way of life in the Japanese islands. The third-century *Wei zhi* (History of the Kingdom of Wei) contains a famous section (known as the "Gishi wajinden" in Japanese) dealing with the Japanese state known as Yamatai-koku. It describes the funeral customs as follows:

> When a person dies, they prepare a single coffin, without an outer one. They cover the graves with earth to make a mound. When death occurs, mourning is observed for more than ten days, during which period they do not eat meat. The head mourners wail and lament, while friends sing, dance, and drink liquor.[1]

This indicates that a vigil or wake (*mogari*) was practiced as part of the funeral rites, but it is unclear whether its purpose was to bid farewell to a loved one or to appease a potentially malevolent spirit.

Nor can we clearly read the concept of malevolent spirits in the rituals associated with the *kofun*, whose intent is believed to be the veneration of the deceased as a *kami*. In the prehistoric Japanese islands, as we can see in the chapter of the *Kojiki* devoted to Izanagi's descent into the underworld—Yomi no Kuni—to see his dead wife, there might be feelings of vague fear and revulsion toward dead bodies, but there was no idea that the spirit of a dead person might exercise malevolent powers. The spirits of exceptional individuals—chieftains and emperors—might distinguish themselves from the anonymous masses of the dead, but by being perceived as deities, not as evil spirits. The first definitive appearance of malevolent spirits would have to wait until the eighth century or later—when, during the course of the Nara period (710–794), there was a greater accumulation of written records in the Japanese islands.

Lineage of evil spirits

The first clear appearance of the concept of spirits of the dead visiting calamity upon the living is to be found in the *Shoku Nihongi*, an official chronicle compiled at the end of the eighth century. An entry from Tempyō 18 (746) recording the death of monk Genbō recounts rumors that "he had been stricken by the spirit of Fujiwara no Hirotsugu." In other words, Genbō's death was attributed to an act of malice by the spirit of a man who had led an unsuccessful revolt to remove Genbō and Kibi no Makibi from influential positions at the imperial court, and who was executed in Kyushu after the revolt failed.

In the seventh month of Tempyō Hōji 1 (757), an edict by Empress Kōken ordered the suppression of a treasonous plot by Tachibana no Naramaro and his associates; it also warned the people against engaging in disruptive speech and action and attributing that to "departed spirits" (*bōkon*). From this we can see that there was a rash of rumors at the time that were attempting to attribute various manifestation of unrest to the spirit of Naramaro, who was killed after his revolt failed.

The *Nihon ryōiki* (Record of Miraculous Events in Japan), compiled at the beginning of the Heian period (794–1185), records that in Jinki 6 (729), Prince Nagaya was accused of plotting a rebellion and committed suicide. The emperor ordered Nagaya's bones exiled to Tosa on the island of Shikoku, where many subsequently died of disease. The local people then petitioned the officials, saying "The prince's spirit will cause all of the common people in this province to die!" In another story from this collection, recounted as an event of the reign of Emperor Bidatsu (r. 572–585), a young acolyte who would later become the dharma master Dōjō of Gangōji subdues a malevolent ghost.

A later historical work, the twelfth-century *Mizukagami*, has an entry describing an event said to have occurred in Tempyō Hōji 9 (765): "The deposed emperor Awaji [Emperor Junnin] placed a curse upon the land, causing drought and high winds, social disorder, and the deaths of many people from starvation." It would appear that the Nara period witnessed a growing tendency to connect social calamities with the activity of the spirits of specific deceased individuals.

The state initially responded to this, as we have seen in the example of Empress Kōken's edict of 757, with attempts to prohibit as "malicious speech" (*oyozuregoto*) any talk connecting spirits of the dead with unusual events or incidents. Such rumors focusing on defeated political figures were an implicit critique of the government that had protected itself by eliminating them—certainly an undesirable state of affairs from the perspective of the ruling regime. Maintaining a monopoly on communication with the other world, through oracles, magic, ritual, and the like, was an important basis of state power in ancient times. If people began to think they could freely interpret the wishes and intentions of the dead, this could lead directly to a loss of authority on the part of the state.

By the end of the Nara period, however, the antics of numerous angry spirits born out of the incessant power struggles of the time could no longer be suppressed by authoritarian prohibitions. Since the state could not insert a gag in everyone's mouths, it would be forced to choose a different approach.

Spirits enshrined in imperial tombs

The entry in the *Shoku Nihongi* for Hōki 3.8.18 (772) tells us that an imperial envoy was sent to conduct the reinterment of the "deposed emperor" (Junnin), that sixty priests and monks had been assembled to perform a Buddhist service, and that two monks had been dispatched to the gravesite itself to conduct Buddhist purifying rituals. In the third month of Hōki 9 (778), Junnin's grave was officially ranked as an imperial tomb (*sanryō*) and caretakers assigned to it. Emperor Junnin, forcibly deposed by the retired Empress Kōken and later buried in a nondescript grave, was finally receiving the treatment appropriate to a former emperor.

Similarly, in the twelfth month of Hōki 8 (777), the remains of Imperial Princess Ikami, formerly wife of Emperor Kōnin, who had been deposed from the rank of empress and put to death, were reinterred and her grave accorded official honors. Later, it would be treated as a *sanryō* and equivalent to an imperial tomb. Hōki 8–9 (777–778) were years in which Emperor Kōnin's crown prince suffered from an extended illness, with his recovery uncertain. The imperial court, believing one source of this to be the influence of its defeated (and deceased) political opponents, sought to restore the honor of imperial family members who had been branded as traitors by declaring their graves to be *sanryō* and giving them the honors accorded to imperial tombs.

Certainly these measures were intended to dispel the enmity of personages who had died harboring great resentment, but something more was involved. As noted in Chapter 1, from the late seventh century onward, the spirits of the emperors residing in the *sanryō* had come to be seen as deities in the broad sense, along with the traditional gods and buddhas. Because of this, the treatment of a grave as an imperial tomb meant the veneration of the spirit interred there as a deity in the same manner as the spirit of an emperor. Prince Sawara, who had been Emperor Kanmu's crown prince, fell from power and died in disgrace, but was posthumously awarded the title of Emperor Sudō.[2]

As a result of such measures, the malicious action of spirits of the dead came to be perceived in the same way as the *tatari* of gods of more established pedigree. This meant that the departed spirits were not working their evil in some completely unpredictable manner; they were instead beings that could be controlled and managed with reference to the procedural manual traditionally applied to cases of *tatari*.

The entry in *Nihon kiryaku* (Outline Record of Japan) for Enryaku 11.6.10 (792) reports that the illness of the crown prince was believed to be due to "a *tatari* by Emperor Sudō" and that an imperial emissary was dispatched to Sudō's grave in the province of Awaji in an effort to appease his spirit. An entry in this same chronicle for Taidō 4.7.3 (809) says that a lingering drought was also attributed to a *tatari*, and in this case an emissary was sent to Yoshino Sanryō (the tomb of Imperial Princess Ikami) to clean and tend the gravesite and have Buddhist sutras chanted by monks. The typical method for dealing with the curse of a deity was to eliminate the source of the curse and pacify the deity with Buddhist rituals, and now these methods were being applied to the departed spirits of Prince Sawara and Princess Ikami, branded as traitors to the throne.

These were no longer merely spirits of the dead; they were full-fledged *kami*. Now a number of members of the imperial family who had departed the political scene under charges of treason, through the process just described, came to join the ranks of the gods, in company with the other imperial spirits.

Secret activities of spirits of the dead

Even so, why did the spirits of the dead become such a focus as the Nara period unfolded? As may be seen from the examples cited so far, the gravest problem for which the spirits of the dead were seen as responsible was illness. This capacity of dead souls to harm the living, however, was in itself seen as evil.

Before the spirits of the dead appeared on the scene, sickness was thought to result from a curse of the gods (*kami no tatari*). In the *Kojiki* (Record of Ancient Matters), Japan's earliest historical chronicle, compiled at the beginning of the eighth century, it is recorded that in the reign of the Emperor Sujin a great plague spread throughout the land, threatening to exterminate the entire population. At a loss, the emperor prayed to the gods, and in a dream the deity Ōmononushi appeared to him and declared that the plague was the result of his own curse upon the people, which could be relieved and the land put at peace if a man named Ōtataneko was summoned and made to pray to Ōmononushi. This was done, the plague subsided, and the people returned to a peaceful existence.

But illness was not the only thing visited upon humans by the gods. As far as the people of antiquity were concerned, virtually all of the phenomena of this world were the work of gods surpassing human

understanding. And human beings had no option other than uncondi-
tional submission to the will of the gods.

Tatari was a means for the *kami* to express their will. Ōmononushi
brought a plague upon the people in order to convey to them his wishes.
This may have had the unfortunate result of causing large numbers of
innocent people to lose their lives, but Ōmononushi did not act initially
out of malicious intent. He was simply trying to draw attention to himself and realize his desires.

In ancient times, *tatari* was an inherent attribute of all deities. It
was a divine power that transcended all distinctions between good and
evil. According to Orikuchi Shinobu, before it came to be used as a
term for calamities visited upon humanity by the gods, the word *tatari*
signified "the manifestation of divine intent."[3]

Whenever the *kami* wanted human beings to do something, they
first commanded their attention by means of a *tatari*. In other words,
as Orikuchi says, *tatari* was a phenomenon produced by the gods when
they wished to convey some intention or desire to humankind. In
ancient times there was a belief, adopted from the Asian mainland, in a
specific plague god—*eyaminokami* or *ekijin*—responsible for spreading
disease, and in the rituals of the *ritsuryō* state there were specific rites,
such as the Chinkasai, prescribed for pacifying this particular deity.[4]
However, with this exception, prior to the seventh century in Japan
there were no *tatarigami*—deities whose sole function was to bring
down curses upon or to spread disease among human beings.

In contrast, in the Nara period, the dead souls of the politically
defeated were believed to be operating with malicious intent from the
beginning, as self-appointed bringers of disease and calamity. Moreover,
their actions transcended revenge against specific individuals to exert an
influence on society at large similar to that of the gods.

Differentiation between good and evil deities

Behind the emergence of spirits of the dead possessing such enormous power to influence politics and society was a shift in the nature
of the Japanese gods that took place in the late seventh century. With

the advent of the *ritsuryō* state, the most important of the *kami* were assigned specific abodes and charged with protecting the emperor and nation. This same period also saw the appearance of "imperial spirits" residing permanently in the *sanryō* as guardians of the reigning emperor. Having signed their contract, so to speak, with the state, this group of *kami* donned the uniform of guardian deities of the nation over the different robes they had worn as *tatarigami* whose actions transcended good and evil. Here I would ask the reader to recall the section in Chapter 1 entitled "Imperial spirits as guardians." In the imperial edicts of the Nara period, a truly diverse assortment of deities are invoked as guardians and protectors of the emperor—not only the traditional Japanese gods, but also the "imperial spirits," Vairocana Buddha, the Sutra of Golden Light, the Four Wisdom Kings, and more. This marks the first appearance in the Japanese islands of "good deities" with a clearly defined purpose.

The arrival of malevolent spirits of the dead, and the "vengeful gods" (*goryōjin*) deriving from them, was closely linked to these developments in the realm of the gods. The advent of official deities who inherited only the "good" side of the traditional *kami* entailed shearing off the "evil" side and being differentiated from it. In other words, the birth of "good deities" called forth "bad deities" and evil spirits. The ambidextrous function of the old gods to bless and to curse now bifurcated into light and darkness, good and evil; and two different types of gods with two different natures came into being. It was these newborn gods, representing the dark side, who would become *hitogami*, "deified humans."

The increase in the number of gods believed to reside in a specific place and the bifurcation into good and evil gods resulted in a greater sense of individuality and personification of deities who had previously been perceived only vaguely and homogeneously. In the Heian period, which began in 794, we see an increasing number of cases in which gods are represented in sculpture or paintings with a more specific individuality. This might be interpreted as conveying the message that these deities were always present in a specific place, with their watchful eyes perpetually surveying their surroundings. The gods, which had withdrawn from visibility since the Yayoi period, now made a comeback in the form of religious images, produced in great numbers beginning in the ninth century.

Some gods fused with spirits of the dead and became "plague gods" (*ekijin*), evil gods that delighted in spreading illness and human suffering. The images of *ekijin* presented by artists showed them in misshapen, demonic form. In contrast, other gods who had abandoned the evil aspects of their persona were presented in respectable and even imposing guise, depicted as powerful officials or clergy. These two different types

Figure 4-1 Image of a god (Matsuo Grand Shrine, Kyoto).

of gods of contrasting outward appearance had their origin in the bifurcation of the function and nature of the gods that took place in the early Heian period.

Of course not all of the myriad gods were clearly differentiated as benevolent or evil deities. The irrational nature of the *tatarigami* did not completely disappear. As folklore researchers have shown, the coexistence of good and evil traits within a single deity has remained a characteristic of the Japanese *kami* down to the present. And as we have seen in the case of the spirits of defeated political figures, it was also relatively easy for a malevolent deity to shift into being a benevolent one. In any case, the bifurcation into good and evil gods inspired movement along a variety of different vectors that brought about a rapid individuation and differentiation of function of the various deities from the Heian period onward.

2. Beginnings of the *Goryō* Cult

From spirits of the dead to *goryō*

In the Heian period, evil spirits were more active than ever before. Whenever there was an outbreak of disease or some other inauspicious event, the names of specific individuals who had paid for defeat with their lives were soon on everyone's lips. It is particularly noteworthy that veneration of the spirits of individuals believed to be responsible for creating these calamities arose spontaneously from among the populace.

The *goryō* spirits of the early Heian period appeared as an extension of the activities of these evil spirits. There is an entry in the chronicle *Nihon sandai jitsuroku* (Veritable Record of Three Generations [of Emperors] of Japan; 901) for Jōkan 5.5.20 (863) that is well known for recording the origins of the *goryō-e*, Buddhist religious services held to appease vengeful spirits. It relates that this practice spread from the Kinai region—centering on Kyoto—to surrounding areas in the summer and autumn of that year after many deaths in previous years from contagious diseases thought by the public to be the work of vengeful spirits (*goryō*).

Hence the imperial court attributed the epidemic of influenza that spring to *goryō*, and dispatched imperial emissaries to the Shinsen'en (a temple of Shingon esoteric Buddhism) to appease the spirits with sutra chanting, music, and dance. According to the *Nihon sandai jitsuroku*, six *goryō* were venerated at this ceremony: Emperor Sudō (Prince Sawara), Prince Iyo, Lady Fujiwara (consort of Emperor Kanmu), Fujiwara no Nakanari, Tachibana no Hayanari, and Fun'ya no Miyatamaro. All of these individuals, from Emperor Sudō on down, had been put to death due to the vicissitudes of court politics. They were seen as *enki*, "spirits of the falsely accused" that had taken demonic form and were working to spread disease. To counter this, the people now called these spirits *goryō* (which originally and literally means "honorable spirit"), and created shrines (*goza*) where they might be worshipped in order to appease them and avoid further calamity. The imperial court could not afford to ignore the popular enthusiasm for the *goryō* cult, and the *goryō-e* conducted at Shinsen'en and subsequently at other places and times were an effort not only to venerate these spirits as *kami* but also to place them under the control and supervision of the state.

In this era, what people sought from the gods was miraculous divine assistance. The *Nihon ryōiki*, an early ninth-century collection of Buddhist moral tales, depicts numerous examples of people offering prayers to the gods and buddhas for aid in achieving specific ends. It also happened to be a period of major instability in the system of complete state ownership of the land and people (*kōchi kōmin seido*) undergirding the *ritsuryō* state. The gulf between the haves and the have-nots was widening. Powerful individuals used their wealth to amass land and goods, while the poorer peasants were losing their land and being transformed into indentured servants. Meanwhile the upper strata of the peasantry, who had risen to be the leaders of their villages, drew closer to Buddhism as a spiritual support for their aspirations for an even better life.

While the Buddhist monasteries and temples were quick to open their doors to welcome people of a diversity of geographic and family background, the Japanese *kami* retained strong ties to a specific clan or local community, and thus did not possess such a free and open nature. But the *goryō* cult, as may be surmised from the way in which it drew adherents from the amorphous urban masses, was characterized by a ready abandonment of the exclusionary character of the established gods.[5]

The newly arisen wealthy classes and townspeople seeking miraculous assistance from the buddhas flocked to the *goryō* cult for exactly the same reason. The more powerful the *kami*, the more powerful its curse. In the terrible calamities produced by the *goryō*, the people saw the implicit power they sought from their gods. By worshipping the *goryō* they hoped, at a stroke, to transform this malevolent power into benevolent assistance.

Mass religious frenzy

The period from the late ninth to early tenth century when the *goryō* cult reached its peak was one in which a variety of popular cults suddenly burst forth from among the populace. The chronicle *Fusō ryakki* contains an entry for the ninth month of Tengyō 2 (939) which relates that in the streets of the capital people were setting up shrines with wooden images of deities such as Funado no Kami (a god of roads and borders) and the *goryō* and making various offerings to them, including incense and flowers. These were new types of *kami*, unbound by tradition, as may be gathered from the unconventional iconography of the images: they might wear caps or headdresses similar to those of the court nobility, their bodies painted with cinnabar, and a yin-yang symbol denoting sexuality inscribed on their lower abdomen.

Six years after this, in the seventh month of Tengyō 8 (945), a *kami* called Shidaragami appeared in the province of Settsu, and was carried in a portable shrine by a large mob into the precincts of the Iwashimizu Hachimangū shrine. Here as well, the assembled multitude—described in volume 7 of the twelfth-century chronicle *Honchō seiki* with some poetic license as "several tens of thousands of people"—made various offerings, including performances of song and dance. Toda Yoshimi has pointed out that the songs were "paeans to peasant prosperity and wealth," and sees this as a popular religious movement based in agricultural villages undergoing a period of economic and social transition.[6]

The deities Funado no Kami and Shidaragami had this in common with the *goryō* cult: they came from among the people and were supported by the anonymous masses. All of these cults were new religious movements rooted among the peasants and townspeople of the day and their aspirations for prosperity and riches.

Also worthy of note is that three of the six individuals whose spirits were venerated at the first *goryō-e* ceremony, such as Fujiwara no Nakanari, were not related to the imperial house. The first individuals in the history of the Japanese islands to be venerated as gods had been the spirits of emperors. Even in the Nara period, the main lineage of the *hitogami* was still members of the imperial family, such as Prince Nagaya and Emperor Junnin. In contrast, half of the *goryō* deities had no connection with the imperial house, which indicates that the range of people eligible for elevation to the status of *hitogami* was gradually expanding. In the period after the establishment of the *ritsuryō* state, the lineage of *hitogami* had broadened from the emperors themselves to other members of the imperial house, and now to members of the ruling elite in general.

Even as the *goryō* cult reached the peak of its popularity in the early Heian period, there is little to suggest that the earlier concept of imperial spirits had gained much acceptance among the masses of the people. During the Kofun and Nara periods, the mainstream of the *hitogami* had been of a familiar type: extraordinarily powerful individuals whose living glory carried over after death into their elevation as deities. The imperial spirits may be regarded as the climax of this phenomenon. This was a highly refined and systematized ideology, but it could not quite rid itself of its character as a deliberate creation of the ruling elite, and did not find much acceptance among the masses.

In contrast, the newly arisen *goryō*, while originating among the powerful nobility, possessed a quite different character, as they were personages who had experienced irrevocable failure and defeat in their lives. Spirits of the dead harboring such intense and volatile resentments were believed to possess a power like that of a plant which can either be a deadly poison or an extremely potent medicine — making them attractive to the masses of people seeking efficacious magic. Moreover, the individuality of the *goryō*, reflecting the different images and personalities of the figures from which they originated, resonated well with the tenor of the times, as the content of people's prayers diversified and the nature of the deities themselves diversified in response.

The difference in character between the imperial spirits, imposed from above, and the *goryō* cult, bubbling up from below, precisely reflected the differing social base each drew upon.

Sugawara no Michizane and the Fujiwara family

As the potential pool for *goryō* expanded beyond the imperial house, the greatest of all the vengeful spirits of the Heian period makes his appearance: Sugawara no Michizane.

Sugawara no Michizane (845–903) — venerated today as the patron deity of scholarship and letters — was originally from a cultured family of the mid-ranking nobility. But his extraordinary talent for scholarship was recognized and he rose in the world with unprecedented swiftness, eventually being appointed Minister of the Right. The emergence of Michizane occasioned considerable alarm on the part of the Fujiwara family, which dominated court politics at the time. Fujiwara no Tokihira, then Minister of the Left and viewed as a rival of Michizane, plotted Michizane's downfall and succeeded in drawing Emperor Daigo into his scheme. The result was that Michizane was exiled to Dazaifu in Kyushu in Enki 1 (901), where he died of disease two years later.

Immediately thereafter, a series of calamities began to befall the Fujiwara family that had plotted Michizane's expulsion from the capital. It was already an era in which *goryō* were believed to be active. People whispered that a variety of unusual natural phenomena—and the deaths of Tokihira, Emperor Daigo and others related to the plot— were *tatari* worked by Michizane's vengeful spirit. The imperial court and the Fujiwara family believed this to be the case as well, and set about restoring Michizane's good name and honor and having Buddhist services conducted to soften the wrath of his spirit.

This period also witnessed the establishment of *goryō*-related shrines. The enshrinement as deities of the *goryō*—spirits of individuals who had a strong impact on state and society—was an effort to integrate these spirits of the dead into some system capable of controlling them. However, once they had been ranked in this way as equals with the traditional gods, such shrines began to be built in different locales all over Japan, some of them collectively enshrining as many as six or eight of these *goryō* deities (*rokusho goryō* or *hassho goryō*). From the middle of the tenth century a festival venerating Sugawara no Michizane began to be held in the Kitano district of Kyoto after his spirit spoke through an oracle; this was the origin of the Kitano Tenmangū shrine which has endured to the present day.

Michizane's spirit had rained down merciless vengeance upon his enemies, but now, ensconced in a grand shrine, it underwent a remarkable transformation into a god receiving the prayers and supplications of the people. The eerie shadow of the vengeful ghost had all but disappeared. The irrationality of the *tatarigami*, with its unpredictable and

Figure 4-2 The Kitano Tenmangū Shrine and Sugawara no Michizane (Kitano Tenmangū, Kyoto)

peremptory demands, had been attenuated. Tenman Tenjin—Michizane's name as a deity—took up permanent residence in Kitano as a god who conferred his blessings upon all supplicants, from the emperors to the lowliest of the common people. If the mainstream of deification of human beings in the Nara period had been the imperial spirits, in the Heian period it became the *goryō* cult, reaching its apogee in the cult of Tenjin.

Exorcising evil spirits

The spirits of a few personages such as the *goryō* deities and Tenman Tenjin became the focus of cults that elevated them into gods shared by society at large. But these were not the only dead souls working their dark mischief in that era. Evil spirits of the dead known variously as *jaki*, *reiki*, and *mononoke* appeared with increasing frequency from the Heian period onward. The shades of the dead haunt the pages of the diaries of the Heian court nobility and the literature of the era, much of it written by women of the imperial court. Whenever anyone fell ill, the first thing that was suspected was the activity of a vengeful spirit harboring a grudge against that individual.

In the "Wakana" (New Herbs) chapters of *Genji monogatari* (The Tale of Genji), Lady Murasaki, the wife of the protagonist, Prince Genji, falls gravely ill. Determining this to be the work of a *mononoke*, Genji summons a group of Buddhist priests known for their spiritual power to perform an exorcism (*kaji*). As the prayers and chanting begin, the *mononoke* departs the body of Lady Murasaki and enters that of the *yorimashi* seated beside her to effect such a transfer. Through the mouth of the *yorimashi*, the *mononoke* reveals itself to be the spirit of Lady Rokujō, one of Genji's former lovers.

As suggested by this example, *mononoke* were spirits who had left their bodies with strong feelings of resentment or hatred. Usually these were spirits of the dead, but in some cases they were *ikisudama*, spirits who had temporarily left the body of a living person. They could enter the bodies of the people who were the objects of their resentment—or others related to them—to cause great physical and mental suffering.

When it was determined that a *mononoke* was the cause of a person's illness, the chosen remedy was exorcism (*kaji*). Buddhist clergy, enlisting the power of the buddhas, would attempt to subdue and expel the *mononoke* possessing the victim. This was usually accomplished by seating a person beside the victim who would serve as the *yorimashi* into whom the evil spirit/*mononoke* would move when pressed to leave the body of the victim.

The modus operandi of the *goryō*, even when exacting personal revenge, as in the curses laid by Sugawara no Michizane upon the Fujiwara family, tended to be stirring up social unrest through the agency of natural disaster, plagues, and the like. Because these were calamities affecting society at large, when these spirits were transformed in character into deities, they became the object of an openly shared faith. On the other hand, minor vengeful spirits who did not succeed in becoming *goryō* were conceived of at a more personal and individual level, both in terms of their nature and that of their victims. During the era in which the Fujiwara family dominated the politics of the imperial court (from the late tenth to mid-eleventh century), *jaki* and *mononoke* were seen as individual spirits, and their *tatari* was directed not at the general populace but at specific individuals or families against whom they held ill feeling. This is why exorcism was thought to be an effective treatment.

Hayami Tasuku has observed that religious incantation in the Heian period, as typified by esoteric Buddhist practices, developed in the context of the establishment of individual worship among the court nobility, and thus can be seen as having similar roots to the development of Pure Land Buddhism during the same period. Moreover, he argues that the heightening of individual consciousness during this era encouraged the individuation and personalization of vengeful spirits, thus creating a demand for private esoteric practices for exorcising spirits afflicting specific individuals with their *tatari*.[7]

The deified *goryō* were unquestionably beings to be venerated and placated. The plague gods (*eyaminokami* or *ekijin*) who were the cause of epidemic diseases were similar in nature, and attempting to use exorcism to deal with them was futile.[8] On the other hand, the ghosts and vengeful spirits that preyed upon individuals were sharply distinguished from the *kami*, and became the object of forceful suppression through the power of Buddhist practices or those of Onmyōdō (arts of magic and divination grounded in yin-yang cosmology).

3. Characteristics of the Gods of Antiquity

Gods and humans sharing the same realm

In the Nara period, as the deities increasingly took up permanent and stable residences, the *kami* (in the narrow sense of traditional Japanese gods) were joined by buddhas, Buddhist sutras, and the various Buddhist guardian deities as beings transcending humankind (*kami* in the broader sense). The "imperial spirits," which derive from the *hitogami* tradition, were also *kami* in this latter sense. Then, in the Heian period, the *goryō* emerged as newly venerated *hitogami* that eventually manifested a power surpassing that of the spirits of the emperors. And with this addition of the various *hitogami*, we arrive at what was essentially the full lineup of the major forms of ancient *kami* (as transcendent beings or deities).

Yet in ancient times there were types of *kami* other than those we have considered so far. In some imperial edicts (*mikotonori*) of the Nara period, the emperor issuing them is described as a "living god" (*akitsukami*). In other words, the reigning emperor was considered to be a deity. There are also examples of figures such as Prince Shōtoku and the holy man Gyōgi (venerated as a bodhisattva)—and even saintly relics such as a lock of Prince Shōtoku's hair—that were regarded as *kami*. In ancient times the land was overflowing with a diverse and abundant variety of deities.

These *kami* not only differed in origin and nature, but in their geographic locale. The rites and rituals for worshipping them also varied. Yet they did have certain characteristics in common.

The first characteristic of the ancient gods that we should mention is that they were not beings who inhabited a world separate from this one—they shared common ground with humanity. The *kami* were nearby, in places close enough for human beings to always be aware of their watchful gaze. The mountains were their representative abode. In the Yayoi and Kofun periods the gods had not yet taken up fixed residences, and it was rare to see them. Because of this, worship took the form of summoning them to occupy a place where they could hear and be heard by their human supplicants.

With the implementation of the *ritsuryō* system at the end of the seventh century, certain specific *kami* were invested with the responsibility of serving as guardian deities of the reigning emperor, which also required that they be induced to settle in a fixed location. Moreover, as the functions of the deities became more specialized, they took on a more individual character. This was the reason why, from the ninth century onward, we see the mass production of images of *kami* (*shinzō*) with identifiable individual features. The creation of such images is an overt expression of the notion that these deities would always be resident in a fixed location, available for worship and supplication by the people. In order to seek an audience with a deity, people no longer had to use a specially gifted spiritual practitioner as an intermediary. All they had to do was visit the place—a shrine—that the god occupied.

The *kami* who protected the emperors or responded to the supplications of the people could not perform their functions from some remote other world or distant heaven. They had to adopt an attitude of continual readiness to respond to human requests and actively intervene in the affairs of human society. In this land, the ancient *kami* were this-worldly presences cohabiting the same space as human beings.

Because of this people strongly desired the *kami* to make their presence and their gaze immediately felt. Even the buddhas who were one contingent of the *kami* were not worshipped as abstract beings from another world but as concrete images permanently enshrined in a specific place. The gods of antiquity were grasped as fundamentally real, concrete, visible presences.

Having said this, I anticipate that some will object, saying that the traditional *kami* of Japan were invisible beings. It is certainly true that in the Yayoi and Kofun periods the deities of heaven and earth ceased to have shape and form. Yet when the *kami* wanted to make their will known to humankind, they almost never appeared as a bolt out of the blue. Their *yorishiro*—great trees or rocky outcroppings—served as symbols of their presence. In the *Nihon shoki* and the provincial gazetteers, there are episodes in which gods appear in dreams to impart direct instruction, but in most cases it is a person possessed by the god as a *yorimashi* who speaks on behalf of the deity. And in cases in which a god assumes human or animal form, this is no mere apparition—it is a manifestation of an actual, corporeal being—for example, a child born of the deity of Miwayama and a human woman.

In the ninth century, production of representational images of the gods goes into high gear. In picture scrolls (*emaki*), specific shrine buildings with their characteristic architecture sometimes stand as symbols of the enshrined deities. The traditional Japanese *kami* might appear not to have shape or form, but when they needed to make their presence known, they could manifest themselves in concrete physical forms—a statue, a *yorishiro*, a shrine building. Similarly, the spirits of the emperors might not possess physical form, and yet manifested themselves in their *yorishiro*—the imperial tombs known as *sanryō*.

So in fact one salient characteristic of the gods of ancient Japan was the raw and visible reality of their presence.

Mobility in the hierarchy of the gods

The second major characteristic of Japan's ancient gods is the absence of any absolute, transcendent deity dominating all others.

The chapter of the *Hitachi no kuni fudoki* (Gazetteer of the Province of Hitachi) devoted to Namekata district contains an episode in which Yatsu no Kami (local deities in the form of snakes) were interfering with the cultivation of the valley in which they made their nests, but were forcibly evicted from the valley by Mibu no Muraji Maro, who chastised them, saying, "What heavenly or earthly deities are you to disobey imperial authority?" [9] From the eighth century onward, as the deification of the emperors as "living gods" (*akitsukami*) progressed, we frequently encounter stories of this type, in which local gods are challenged with the superior authority of the emperor. Sakurai Yoshirō has characterized as "ancient" this way of narrating the origins of shrines in which the enshrined deities are posited as recognizing and obeying the rule of the emperor in his manifestation as a living god.[10]

Yet there are also episodes throughout the Heian period in which emperors are stricken with illness as the result of the *tatari* of some deity. One ritual clearly acknowledged the possibility of the emperor himself falling victim to *tatari*: the Ōmima no Miura, conducted twice annually in the sixth and twelfth months. The ritual involved an examination of the emperor's divine person to determine if in fact he was afflicted with a *tatari*. It took the form of a *miyaji* (an official of the Shingikan, or Office of Shintō Worship) reading a predetermined list of various deities and determining whether or not they were working a *tatari* upon the emperor. This presupposes the existence of *kami* more powerful than the emperor, beings who could extend their influence over him. Nor should we overlook the episode in the *Shoku Nihongi* in which Emperor Shōmu, proclaimed a living god (*akitsukami*) when he ascended the throne, also described himself as "a servant of the Great Buddha" when he went to worship at Tōdaiji.

In Book 14 of the *Nihon shoki*, Emperor Yūryaku desires to see the form of the deity of Mount Mimoro (Miwayama), and summons a man renowned for his physical strength, Chiisakobe no Muraji Sugaru, ordering him to go seize the deity and bring it to him. Sugaru succeeds in capturing a great serpent and brings it to the emperor. But because the emperor has not observed the proper religious abstinences, the serpent's eyes flash at him like lightning and he is seized with such fear that he flees into the interior of the palace.[11] A variation on this story is contained in the *Nihon ryōiki*, which relates that on the order of the emperor Sugaru caught the thunder god and brought it to the palace, where it gave off a blast of light that frightened the emperor, who treated it with great respect and sent it on its way again.[12] Emperors might be able to order the expulsion or capture of *kami*, but in some cases they might also bow down before the power of the gods.

There was a certain hierarchy of power and status among the ancient *kami*, but it was an unstable one. A particular *kami* might, at a certain stage, establish itself at the apex of this system, but there was no guarantee it would remain there forever. A certain mobility or fluidity reminiscent of human society may also be seen in the status hierarchy in the world of the gods.

Watsuji Tetsurō has analyzed the myths and legends in the *Kojiki* and *Nihon shoki* and classified the deities appearing in them into three types: (1) *matsuru kami* (gods that worship), (2) *matsurareru kami* (gods that are worshipped), and (3) *matsuri-matsurareru kami* (gods that both worship and are worshipped).[13] The majority of personified deities active during the Age of the Gods described in the ancient chronicles were gods who worshipped as well as being worshipped; the *yamatsumi* (mountain gods) and *kunitama* (gods of place) that were only worshipped tended to exist only as names, without special functions or activities that defined them. The worshipped *kami* are mentioned with far less reverence in the chronicles than the *kami* who worshipped.

In ancient Japanese society, there was no absolute, other-worldly deity who existed in a different dimension from the *kami* who filled every corner of the land. Because there was no incontestable alpha god, and because of the fluidity of the world of the gods, the imperial

Japanese state could not completely depend upon the mythic order it initially constructed. From the ninth century onward, it would engage in a concerted effort to construct a state bureaucracy and national rituals to support and maintain the emperor.[14]

The gods as *tatarigami*

The third characteristic of the ancient *kami* we may cite is their essential nature as *tatarigami*.

In the most remote antiquity, the *kami* were an existence inseparable from nature. Any disturbance in the natural order was perceived as the wrath of the gods—as *tatari*—and believed to cause illness. Therefore, it was thought that epidemics would naturally subside if the gods were pacified and appeased and the natural order restored.

Tatari always manifested as a unilateral action of the gods. It was impossible for humans to predict. What the gods desired was also completely irrational and unpredictable. Initially, even the name of the deity inflicting the *tatari* was usually unknown.

Yet even though a *tatari* might be an imperious and inscrutable instruction from the gods, perhaps accompanied by an equally inscrutable insistence on worship by a specific individual, eventually a rational explanation of the cause might be teased forth—trespass upon a sacred space, perhaps, or the felling of a sacred grove. And for the Ōmima no Miura ritual conducted twice a year, the gods capable of inflicting a *tatari* were limited to those of proper pedigree and inscribed on the list read on that occasion.

As the *kami* began to be visualized and classified into good and evil deities in the Heian period, their separation from nature and their personification proceeded apace. The representations of wrathful gods robed in the finery of the court nobility, or of plague gods taking individual form and freely stalking about the world, were a major shift from the traditional image of the *kami*. By this stage, the infliction of *tatari* had almost entirely become the work of evil *goryō*, *ekijin*, or *mononoke*.

On the other hand, it is noteworthy that in almost direct proportion to the decline in instances of *tatari* from about the middle of the Heian period, we see increasing use of the term *bachi* (punishment) for this

Figure 4-3 A mob of "plague gods" (*ekijin*) as depicted in the *Yuzu nenbutsu engi* (Legends of the Yuzu Nenbutsu Sect) (Cleveland Museum of Art)

activity of the gods. From the twelfth century onward, *bachi* almost completely replaces other terminology. In the *kishōmon*—written oaths, produced in great numbers, that are among the representative documents of the medieval period—the function of the gods invoked is inevitably to administer *bachi* if the oath were to be broken. The twelfth century also saw the establishment of the medieval social system, and the transition in the function of the *kami* from the *tatari* of antiquity to the *bachi* of the middle ages can be understood in this light.

In other words, in medieval times the *kami* were seen as meting out punishment (*bachi*) rather than inflicting *tatari*. Perhaps in response to this shift, the deities regarded as specializing in *tatari* began to be enshrined and venerated by local communities. They also started to be invoked in *kishōmon* as watchful dispensers of punishment.

When we look at the functions of the gods in medieval Japan, we see that reward and punishment (*shōbatsu*) frequently appear as a set. *Kami* did not only dispense punishment, they possessed the ability to render very finely grained judgments of human behavior and mete out reward or punishment according to certain standards—such as fidelity or loyalty to the god itself, as well as to the Buddhist dharma and to the state, which the god served as guardian. The gods demanded loyalty of human beings, and dispensed appropriate reward or punishment accordingly. This exercise of power might seem to have something in common with *tatari*, but in fact it is completely different in nature. The gods were now seen as beings who have expressed clear standards of behavior expected of humans, and who adhere closely to them in their response.

We have thus shifted from gods who inflict curses (*tatari*) to gods who dispense rewards and punishment (*shōbatsu*), from mysterious gods with inscrutable wills ("commanding gods") to gods whose responses have a certain predictable logic ("responsive gods"). In the transition from antiquity to the middle ages, the nature of the gods was altered in a major way.[15] This transformation of the gods naturally extended to the *hitogami* as well. What was the fate of the *hitogami* in the course of this transition? In the next chapter, I would like to pursue this question, while situating this metamorphosis of the gods in historical context.

CHAPTER 5

Escorts to the Other Shore

1. The Distant Pure Land

Transition to the medieval worldview

THE ANCIENT WORLDVIEW was one in which humans and the superhuman inhabited the same realm, and humankind could feel the presence of the deities and hear their voices in the midst of everyday life. But late in the Heian period (794–1185) this worldview would undergo a decisive shift, part of a larger transformation in the prevailing cosmology of the Japanese islands.

For the people of ancient Japan, "the world" was fundamentally *this* world—the world available to our senses. Gods and humans occupied the same space and breathed the same air. A concept did exist of spirits of the dead, such as those of the emperors, who might become completely purified and be elevated into *kami*, but even they did not depart this world for somewhere beyond the reach of humanity.

The transformation of this worldview—often described as "unitary"—began in the late tenth century, and in the twelfth century it was supplanted by something entirely different in nature. New forms of religious faith took shape, premised on the existence of an ideal world—a Pure Land (*jōdo*)—separate from this one, to which one might go after death if one led the right sort of life. In the Pure

Land cult, as it is called, the ideal world was the Western Paradise of the buddha Amida, believed to be located in the farthest reaches of the universe. People came to believe that their life in this world (*shaba no sekai*, Sanskrit *sahāloka*; the world that must be endured) was only temporary, and that rebirth in an otherworldly Pure Land was in fact the goal of human existence.

In other words, the image of another world imperceptible in this world suddenly took hold of people at the cognitive level. We have already discussed how at a certain point in the Jōmon period a world of gods and the dead separate from the sphere of everyday activities of the living came into being. But in antiquity, the abode of the gods was never more distant than mountains such as Mount Fuji. From the foothills people might even witness the gods dancing on high. Gods and humans shared the same living space. In contrast, in medieval society people came to believe that the realm of the gods existed in a place so remote that humans could not interact with them.

Undergirding the popularity of Pure Land beliefs in late Heian Japan was a perception that this world—so long after the passing away of the historical buddha, Shakyamuni—was one in which no buddhas existed. For a certain period of time after Shakyamuni's passing into nirvana, his teachings might have had the power to save people, but even the *buddha-dharma* (the Buddhist "law" or teachings) must someday lose its efficacy in leading

Figure 5-1 The Amida Buddha seen over distant mountains (Zenrinji, Kyoto)

people to enlightenment. This was the advent of the age of *mappō* ("the latter days of the law"), which was believed to have commenced in Eishō 7 (1052). From the latter part of the eleventh century onward, people believed themselves to be living in this period of the degeneration of the Buddhist teachings.

And since they lived in such degenerate times, it was difficult to attain enlightenment on the basis of the teachings bequeathed by Shakyamuni. It was in this context that the Pure Land cult was born. The belief was that only by leaving this buddha-less world, and being reborn in a Pure Land in which a buddha actually existed, could one encounter the genuine Buddhist teachings and attain eternal salvation.

Deities had become something more than mere wonder-workers— they had become saviors, guides leading human beings to the Other Shore, to the world of truth. For the first time, the spiritual world of the Japanese islands now encompassed a faith that openly proclaimed salvation as its goal.

Stratification among the gods

This shift in the late Heian period from the unitary worldview of antiquity to the dualistic medieval worldview brought with it a radical transformation in the traditional gods. Gods, humans, and the dead had once shared the same realm. Now they were not only separated into this-worldly versus other-worldly beings, but a new hierarchy was also born amidst the gods themselves.

In the late Heian period, as the image of Amida Buddha as a lord and savior took on greater and greater weight, people came to feel that no matter how much they might raise their voices in supplication, it was inconceivable that they could visit the Western Paradise and look upon Amida while still in this life. Amida and the other buddhas stood on the Other Shore (*higan*); they were deities who had transcended this world.

But this created a problem. If this were indeed the evil era of *mappō*, then it would be quite difficult for the benighted people of this degenerate age to have faith in the existence of the buddhas in their Pure Land, no matter how eloquently one might preach of their majesty—and thus many who might have been saved would not be. But the buddhas of the Other Shore, in their wisdom, devised a plan to save the sentient beings of this world. And that was to assume a temporary form in our world: to appear as an avatar.

The term *suijaku* has often been used to describe manifestations of the other-worldly buddhas. Generally speaking, *suijaku* has meant the manifestation of buddhas in the form of traditional Japanese gods of heaven and earth, and it is true that in medieval times many of the *kami* were reinterpreted as avatars of specific *honjibutsu*—buddhas who were regarded as their primal or original form. But it was not only traditional *kami* who might be seen as *suijaku*: Buddhist images, and great saints and teachers such as Kōbō Daishi and Prince Shotoku, were also *suijaku*. In medieval times the realm of the gods and buddhas came to be comprised of two major groups: (1) the newly arisen, transcendental *honjibutsu* (buddhas of the other world), and (2) the immanent traditional *kami* (gods and buddhas of this world) now posited as their avatars, or *suijaku*.[1]

Attendant upon this spatial separation, human beings were also divided into (1) the dead, reborn into the realm of the buddhas; and (2) the living, resident in this world. In the middle ages, the ideal for the dead was to leave this world to be reborn in the distant Pure Land. There were those who after death remained in this world, but these were unhappy souls who for one reason or another had been denied such a rebirth. Religious rituals for the dead in medieval Japan were primarily directed toward giving the spirits of such people a proper send-off on their voyage toward the Pure Land. Those who had already successfully arrived in the otherworldly buddha realm had been transformed into beings whom the voices of the people of this world could no longer reach.

Kami as saviors

In Chapter 4, I mentioned that one of the characteristics that distinguished the medieval deities from their ancient counterparts was their "rational" nature. Contributing to this development was, as already discussed, the spread of the Buddhist worldview and the incorporation of the traditional Japanese *kami* into it.

Accompanying the formation of the dualistic "this world/other world" cosmology of the middle ages, the traditional Japanese *kami* were posited as *suijaku* (manifestations or avatars) of the *honjibutsu* (original or primal buddhas) of a distant other world. The reason why the *kami* had appeared as *kami* in the Japanese islands was to acquaint all sentient beings with the Buddhist dharma (law or teachings) and to direct their gaze toward the Pure Land: "We of this latter-day world, as we consider the afterlife, should for our own sake always remember to offer our prayers to the *kami*." As this passage from Kamo no Chōmei's collection of didactic Buddhist tales *Hosshinshū* (ca 1214) eloquently expresses, the fundamental nature of the medieval gods had become one of saviors after death. The mission given to the Japanese gods as *suijaku* of distant buddhas was to use the power of either the carrot or the stick to awaken the benighted masses of humanity of a degenerate age to the eternal truth of the Buddhist law. As a result, in the middle ages many people visited Shintō shrines to pray for rebirth in the Pure Land.

There is a famous image—sculpted by Kaikei and preserved at Tōdaiji—of the Shintō deity Hachiman portrayed in the guise of a Buddhist monk. An inscription in ink found inside the hollow wooden sculpture contains the Sanskrit seed syllables for the Amida trinity (Amida Buddha and attendant bodhisattvas Kannon and Seishi), a long list of donors, artists, and others associated with the gift of the image to the temple, and a quotation from the monk Genshin's *Ōjōyōshū* (Essentials for Rebirth in the Pure Land, 985): "At the moment of death all obstacles shall be removed, you will come face to face with Amida Buddha, and be immediately reborn into the Pure Land."[2] This expresses quite clearly the role that the deity Hachiman was expected to play as an escort to the Pure Land. In the Kamakura period (1185–1333) a large number of mandalas were produced featuring the Kasuga Shrine in Nara; they took the form of a landscape painting of the shrine and its environs, above which were arrayed images of various *honji-butsu*—a composition which gives visual expression to the perception that the shrine served as a portal to the other world (fig. 5-2). The most important reason that the *kami* had appeared on this earth was to lead humanity across to the Other Shore.

In an earleir time, the *kami* had an inseparable relationship with the people who prayed to them. The ability to pray to a particular god was limited to the members of the clan or community who held that god in common as an ancestral or tutelary deity. The *goryō* cult of the early Heian period was the first to root itself among the broad mass of the people. Today anyone may visit and pray to Amaterasu Ōmikami at the Ise Grand Shrine, but in ancient times private offerings were strictly forbidden and only the emperor was allowed to pray there.

Figure 5-2 A Kasuga Shrine Mandala (Minami Shichō Jichikai, Nara)

In contrast, the medieval gods had taken on the character of saviors, transformed into beings who heard the supplications of the anonymous masses.[3] Anyone who wished could freely visit a shrine. In the *Shasekishū*, a collection of Buddhist parables written at the end of the thirteenth century, one story described people fleeing the fighting and turmoil of the Jokyū Rebellion of 1221 and taking refuge in the precincts of Atsuta Shrine, regardless of whether they were ritually pure or not. And it is recorded that the god of the shrine approved, declaring that "The reason I descended from heaven to this land was to nurture and aid the myriad people."

In the *kishōmon*, the written vows and supplications produced in great numbers in medieval times,"Amaterasu Ōmikami, Lord of the Country of Japan" is often invoked as the being monitoring the fulfillment of the vows, regardless of the geographic location or social status of the writer. Hachiman and the deity of the Kamo Shrine also appear with frequency in this role. An era of free competition among these "national gods" for the allegiance of the people was about to arrive.

The medieval gods, having deepened their character as saviors and opened themselves to the masses of the people, could no longer behave like the *kami* of antiquity, the irrational "commanding gods" who appeared and disappeared so whimsically and confronted people with unreasonable demands. The medieval gods were permanently enshrined in a specific place, and had already given mankind clear instructions on the path they were to follow through life; the extent to which people complied was what determined the quite rational system of rewards and punishments that would be meted out by these "responsive gods."

Downfall of the living gods

In antiquity the emperors had ruled over the people as living gods (*akitsukami*) directly descended from the highest of all the deities, Amaterasu Ōmikami. But in contrast to this imperial image built up by the ancient monarchy, from about the twelfth century onward a very different perspective on the emperors makes its appearance—conceiving them as objects of the curses (*tatari*) or punishments (*bachi*) of the gods and buddhas.

Of course even in ancient times there were cases in which an emperor might be stricken by the *tatari* of one of the *kami*. There were certain more primal deities that could command even the emperors. Yet at the same time, the emperors were also depicted as agents who could control many of the *kami* and bend them to their will. The new image of the emperors that began to appear in the late eleventh to twelfth century, when political power was exercised by retired emperors in a system known as *insei*, "cloistered government," was one in which the emperors could see their fate determined by the deities— who might send them to hell, to political failure, or to an early death.[4]

In the "Encounters in Hell" section of the *Kitano Tenjin engi*—an illustrated history of Kitano Tenjin Shrine produced in the Kamakura period—the soul of Emperor Daigo is portrayed as burning in hellfire.[5] And in the *Zenkōji engi* (History of Zenkōji temple) is a depiction of the sudden death of Empress Kōgyoku and her descent into hell.[6]

Behind this changing image of the emperors was a more fundamental transformation of worldview. With the formation of the dualistic worldview of the middle ages, many of the ancient *kami* were posited as intermediaries between the people of this world and the invisible and distant other world. But the emperors did not present themselves as avatars (*suijaku*) like these other gods, nor did the majority of their medieval contemporaries see them as such. Hence the emperors had become sharply distinguished from the otherworldly divinities possessing the highest religious authority, and were seen as beings strictly of this world. The emperors, who in ancient times had belonged to the category of superhuman beings or divinities, had at this stage been shut out of the top class of the deities (the buddhas of the other world).

Moreover, the emperors could not humble themselves to join what might be described as the second-tier deities—the deities of this world serving as avatars of the otherwordly buddhas. The dualistic medieval worldview was structured according to the Buddhist *honji-suijaku* schema, and it was problematic for the emperor to be seen as functioning in the role of a *suijaku*, given that there was a taboo on direct involvement in Buddhist worship and ritual on the part of the reigning emperor. At this point the religious authority undergirding the emperor was limited to the ancestral god of the imperial family, Amaterasu Ōmikami. In other words, imperial legitimacy was being provided by a second-tier, this-worldly deity—which meant that the authority of the emperors themselves had fallen to the third tier.

We must also note that in medieval times the Japanese *kami* did not even occupy the top ranks of the deities of this world. Amaterasu Ōmikami, in theory preeminent among the gods, was in fact perceived as a minor deity whose power did not rival that of Buddhist guardian deities such as Bonten (Brahma) or Taishaku (Indra), or even Daoist gods such as Taizan Fukun (Lord of Mount Tai) or Enma Hōō (King of Hell).[7] Dependent as it was on the sacred aura of such a divinity, the sacralization of the emperors ran up against certain decisive limitations. The suspension of the Daijōsai enthronement ritual during the medieval period was not for economic reasons—it was because its function in sacralizing the emperor had been rendered virtually meaningless.

Esoteric rites surrounding the emperor

My assertion here—that in the transition from antiquity to the middle ages, the desacralization of the emperor proceeded apace, until the emperors came to be perceived as occupying the same level as ordinary humans—does not necessarily conform to the findings of contemporary research on the imperial system. In fact, mainstream academic research argues, quite to the contrary, that the emperors cloaked themselves in a thick aura of religiosity through the development of esoteric rites and practices, such as the enthronement ceremony, and succeeded in elevating themselves once again into transcendent, sacralized beings.

It is possible, I suppose, to interpret such efforts to sacralize the status of the emperor as an attempt to revive the emperor's religious authority at a time when, overall, the emperor's authority was being relativized and desacralized. The most significant factor in the secularization of the emperor's status was that in the course of the transition from ancient to medieval times the emperors had been shut out of the realm of the supreme deities and had fallen back into the human world. In order to once again clothe themselves in the sacred, the emperors would have to become something close to the supreme deities. The simplest way to accomplish this would be to rebuild relations with the deities, and assume the mantle of their religious authority. But the Japanese gods who had previously supported the imperial house were seen as beings of this world, subordinate to the primal or original deities (honjibutsu) of the other world.

If the goal, then, was to bolster the status of the emperor, the deity with whom the emperors needed to form a bond was not the this-worldly Amaterasu Ōmikami, but one of the otherworldly *honjibutsu*, the Buddhist deities. Various rites that became prominent during the middle ages, such as the esoteric enthronement ritual (*sokui kanjō*), were attempts to create a hotline, as it were, between the emperor and buddhas such as Dainichi Nyorai, the cosmic buddha, and channel their power and authority to himself.

However, these efforts did not bear fruit. This direct connection the medieval emperors were attempting to establish with a transcendental power was not a circuit that they could succeed in monopolizing. The methods involved were unrelated to the unique bloodline and ancestral deities of the imperial family; by seeking the basis of their legitimacy in the external and universal authority of Buddhism, the imperial house had taken up what proved to be a double-edged sword. This method of attempting to legitimate the position of the sovereign through his relationship to a primal authority or supreme being was always accompanied by the danger of revolution or rebellion, because anyone might lay claim to the same authority. And there were major figures such as Nichiren (1222–1282, founder of the Nichiren sect of Buddhism), for example, who clearly approved of a transfer of sovereignty from the imperial house to the Hōjō family that in his time dominated the Kamakura shogunate as regents.[8]

The frequent appearance in medieval texts of episodes such as the falling into hell of Emperor Daigo and Empress Kōgyoku is one of the more blatant expressions of a situation in which the emperors found themselves unable to monopolize a relationship with the buddhas of the other world.

The Japanese emperors in world history

The emperors, despite their best and most desperate efforts, did not succeed in adequately adapting to the changing cosmology in the transition from antiquity to the middle ages. Falling from their status as living gods (*akitsukami*), but also failing to clothe themselves in a religious authority sufficient to replace that status, the emperors confronted a critical phase in their history. They would find that the key to their survival lay, not in the personal embodiment of some sacred power, but in their political position at the apex of the state structure that had developed since the ninth century.

The relativization of monarchical authority that occurred during the period of transition from antiquity to the middle ages was not a phenomenon limited to the Japanese islands. The establishment of the world religions—Buddhism, Christianity, Islam—led to religious authority being concentrated in the transcendent or supreme beings posited by these faiths, such that kings lost their inherent sacredness as gods in their own right. Instead, they owed their sovereignty to an authority conferred upon them by a higher power. Religious structures—temples, mosques, and cathedrals—replaced the palaces of the monarchs as the grandest and most extravagant works of architecture.

In the European world, from 800 CE, when the Frankish king Charlemagne was crowned Holy Roman Emperor by Pope Leo III, imperial authority was regarded as legitimate only if given divine approval through the consecration and anointment embodied in this type of coronation ceremony. Kings no longer ruled over their people by wielding personal sacred authority; they could maintain their status only with the backing of an omnipotent God.

In the Islamic world as well, the legitimacy of sovereigns such as the caliphs and shahs was predicated on just and fair rule in obedience to the will of Allah, the ultimate authority. In China, the doctrine of the mandate of heaven (*tianming*)—that the sovereign was mandated by heaven to rule in its stead—arose during the Western Zhou dynasty (1046–771 BCE). This eventually developed into the concept of "revolution" (*geming*, lit. "renewal of the mandate"), which recognized the possibility that a ruler might lose the affection of the people and the mandate of heaven, and by so doing, lose the throne, to be replaced by a new sovereign of greater virtue. In *Mencius*, the third-century BCE classic, we find a passage explicitly affirming the killing of an evil tyrant and his replacement with a new ruler, which became part of a Chinese philosophical tradition legitimating dynastic change.

The issue of the religious authority of the Japanese emperors should no doubt be considered within this kind of world-historical perspective.

2. The Cult of Holy Men and Sacred Places

Establishment of the *oku no in*

As mentioned previously, as the concept of a remote other world (*higan sekai*) spread in medieval times, the *kami*, holy men, and even Buddhist images of this world were posited as *suijaku*—avatars or manifestations of the primal or original buddhas (*honjibutsu*) of the Other Shore. This gave birth to a new type of "human god" (*hitogami*) that had not previously existed in ancient times—the *hitogami* as savior.

The conception of holy men (*seijin*) as beings who could serve as bridges between this world and the other world resulted in a sudden florescence of cults surrounding such figures. Medieval temples and shrines, responding to this increased demand resulting from the tremendous popularity of the Pure Land cult, and the faith in saints and *suijaku* attendant upon it, built new facilities within their precincts specifically devoted to the veneration of holy men. Such structures, which were frequently sited in the deepest recesses of a temple or monastery's grounds, often with a commanding view of their surroundings, later came to be called *oku no in*, or "inner sanctums." The Okunoin at Kōyasan (Mount Koya), where legend has it that the great teacher Kōbō Daishi lives on in a state of deep meditative concentration (*samadhi*), is the classic early example of such a sacred place.

Kongōbuji, the great temple and monastic complex at Kōyasan, was founded by the monk Kūkai (774–835; later venerated as Kōbō Daishi) at the beginning of the ninth century as the central practice and training center for the Shingon sect of Buddhism. From the beginning, Kūkai conceived the topography of the Kōyasan site in the image of an esoteric Buddhist mandala, at the heart of an eight-petaled lotus blossom. Eventually, when Kūkai met his death in Jowa 2 (835), his remains were cremated and buried in what is today the Okunoin, atop a hill somewhat removed from the central complex of monastic buildings.

However, beginning about a century after his death, a new legend concerning Kūkai was born—the belief that he had not died at all but had entered into an eternal *samadhi*. In *Eiga monogatari*, an eleventh-century historical tale, Fujiwara no Michinaga, an imperial court official who represents the high point of the Fujiwara family's political dominance, is depicted as making a pilgrimage to Kōyasan, where he comes face to face with Kōbō Daishi, who "appears as if asleep."

The Okunoin at Kōyasan as a cultic sacred space experienced another fundamental alteration in the late Heian period under the impact of Pure Land beliefs. The *Ippen hijiri e* (a set of illustrated handscrolls depicting the life of Priest Ippen [1239–1289], founder of the Ji sect of Pure Land Buddhism, produced not long after his death) tells us that Ippen visited Kōyasan, "where the Sanjisatta [Kūkai] manifested (*suijaku*) himself" (*sanjisatta* referring to a bodhisattva who has achieved a particular level of enlightenment), because he hoped to enlist this karma in his own effort to be reborn in Amida's Pure Land. In *Ichigon hōdan*, a collection of Pure Land texts from the late thirteenth and early fourteenth centuries, there is a story in which the monk Chōgen makes a pilgrimage to the Okunoin at Kōyasan, and in the middle of the night hears a voice chanting the *nenbutsu* (the mantra of Amida fundamental to the Pure Land teachings) emanating from Kōbō Daishi's mausoleum. And there were those who believed, in the words of the *Kōyasan-ki* (a sixteenth-century chronicle of Kōyasan), that "Kōbō Daishi is none other than the living body of Amida Buddha," in other words, that he was an avatar of the buddha venerated by the Pure Land sect as its principal deity.

In medieval times, Kōyasan was thronged with itinerant Pure Land priests drawn by this vision of Kōbō Daishi as an avatar. The poet-priest Saigyō joined them. In the nearby valleys of Odawara-dani and Renge-dani, Amida-dō halls were constructed, and the sound of pilgrims chanting the *nenbutsu* filled the air.[9] Hoping to avail themselves of Kōbō Daishi as a guide or escort to rebirth in the Pure Land, many made pilgrimages to Kōyasan or were interred there. At the time of its founding Kōyasan had been conceived as the ultimate "pure land" of esoteric Buddhist thought, but in the middle ages it was transformed into a stronghold of the Pure Land faith, whose followers were aiming at a successful voyage to the Other Shore.

Holy men as avatars

Prince Shōtoku (574–622; one of the architects of the early imperial state) rivaled Kūkai as a central object of the cult of holy men or saints that arose in medieval times. Even at venerable temples such as Hōryūji and Shitennōji, both founded by Prince Shōtoku in the Asuka period (538–710), portions of the monastic cloisters outside the central enclosures were rebuilt during the twelfth century as Shōryōin—chapels dedicated to the veneration of Prince Shōtoku's spirit. These were new sacred places for the Pure Land cult, attracting the passionate devotion of those eager to be reborn in the Pure Land, from members of the imperial house to the common people. In the *Shūi ōjōden* (ca. 1139), a collection of stories concerning rebirth in the Pure Land, a monk named Senmyō makes a pilgrimage to the Shōryōin at Shitennōji to pray for rebirth in the Pure Land, "who made a candle of one of his fingers in offering to the image of the prince." When the temple Kōryūji was rebuilt after a fire in Kyūan 6 (1150), a shrine called the Jōgūōin was built to venerate Prince Shōtoku, which eventually developed into the

Figure 5-3 The Shōryōin at Shitennōji in Osaka

118

Keikyūin temple. All of these facilities are believed to have had functions equivalent to those of *oku no in*.

The site of Prince Shōtoku's grave in Shinaga, Osaka, also became a sacred site for the Pure Land cult in the twelfth century, attracting many pilgrims seeking rebirth in the Pure Land. A stone inscription is preserved there of a poem said to have been written by Prince Shōtoku himself, the "Byōkutsu-ge" (Tomb Gatha), in which the prince says, "I am leaving the corporeal body born of my parents in this tomb for the sake of saving all sentient beings in the latter days [of the Dharma] (*masse*)." The famous Pure Land teacher Shinran visited this site as a young man and made a copy of the text of this poem. The great variety of images of Prince Shōtoku produced during the late Heian and Kamakura periods reflects the aspirations of the people of that era for rebirth in another world.

Nor were Kōbō Daishi and Prince Shōtoku the only holy men who became objects of cults. In the *Nihon ōjō gokuraku ki*, a tenth-century collection of biographies of those reborn in the Pure Land, the priest Gyōgi, who worked among the common people in the Nara period, is described as an avatar of the bodhisattva Manjushri. Emperor Shōmu was regarded as an avatar of the bodhisattva Kannon, and Fujiwara no Kamatari as an incarnation of Vimalakirti. Sugawara no Michizane, central focus of the *goryō* cult of the early Heian period, was also integrated into the *honji-suijaku* paradigm of medieval times. His *honji* was described in the *Kitano Tenjin engi* as "the manifestation of eleven-headed Kannon Bodhisattva," who, in order to guide the people of this world, "descended from Amida's Pure Land to appear as Tenman Tenjin."

In the Kamakura period the founders of new Buddhist sects rejected avatars and other intermediaries, replacing this with an ideal of a faith that would connect the sentient beings of this world directly and immediately with the *honjibutsu* of the other world. However, after the deaths of these founders, their followers and sectarians tended to profess that the true nature (*honji*) of their patriarch was that of a specific buddha or bodhisattva, as will be described in the next chapter.

In the *Gukanshō*, an early thirteenth-century history, the priest Jien writes, "In order to save all sentient beings the bodhisattva Kannon has manifested in our Japan in the form of a number of personages from Prince Shōtoku to Fujiwara no Kamatari, Sugawara no Michizane, and Jie Daishi (Ryōgen); yet there are few who fully perceive the significance of this." In the middle ages, individuals who possessed unusual powers differentiating them from the common crowd—whether they were religious or secular figures—were seen as manifestations of otherworldly buddhas and bodhisattvas who had taken new form in this world in order to lead its people to salvation.

Youths, women, and untouchables

The figures we have touched upon so far were all familiar names to the broad public, appearing after their death in tales and legends; but there were a host of others, less well known, who were seen as emissaries from the Other Shore. One such group was clerics of outstanding virtue and ascetics who had acquired mystical powers and were venerated as avatars or incarnations of deities even during their lifetimes. The Kamakura-period monk Eison, described in an imperial edict issued by Emperor Go-Fushimi (r. 1298–1301) honoring him as "a flesh-and-blood buddha of these corrupted latter days," was a representative example. In the *Gempei seisuiki* (Chronicle of the Rise and Fall of the Minamoto and Taira Clans, book 25; a 48-volume expanded version of the *Heike monogatari* [Tale of the Heike]), the clerics Chōgen and Jōkei are characterized as "Shakyamuni in flesh and blood" and "Kannon in flesh and blood," respectively. In *Gyokuzui*, the diary of early thirteenth-century court noble Kujō Michiie, the author describes Gyōshō Shōnin, the priest from Kōyasan who tutored him in the Buddhist precepts (*jukai*), as "perhaps a living incarnation of the Buddha."

In Book 17 of *Konjaku monogatari shū* (Anthology of Tales from the Past), there is a story about a monk named Zōnen from the province of Mutsu who is called "an embodiment of the boundless compassion of Jizō Bodhisattva." From a tender age Zōnen had assiduously devoted himself to practices venerating Jizō Bodhisattva and instructing the people through his example. Toward the end of his life, he disappeared without a trace into the mountains, after which the people lamented,

"[Zōnen] was truly the bodhisattva Jizō in flesh and blood. But our sins are too heavy, and he has suddenly abandoned us to make his return to the Pure Land." They believed that Zōnen had been sent as an emissary to lead people to the Pure Land.

Nor was it rare for completely anonymous laypeople to be regarded as avatars of buddhas and bodhisattvas, as suggested by the following summary of a story from *Uji shūi monogatari*, a collection of tales from around the beginning of the thirteenth century.

There once was an old nun who lived in the province of Tango. Hearing that the bodhisattva Jizō walked the earth at dawn, every morning she would get up and wander the countryside in hopes of meeting him. A gambler saw what she was up to, and offered for a fee to introduce her to Jizō. But the Jizō he introduced her to was a boy of about ten years whose nickname was Jizō. Not realizing she had been tricked, the nun was overcome with joy and began praying to the boy—whose forehead suddenly broke open to reveal the flawless and perfect face of Jizō Bodhisattva looking forth. The nun prostrated herself with tears of gratitude, and was immediately reborn into the Pure Land.

This tale is summed up with a brief moral: "And so we should believe that if only we hold them deeply enough in our hearts and minds, the buddhas and bodhisattvas will grace us with their appearance." Or, as in this case, borrow the form of a youth in order to lead people to the Pure Land.

Along with boys or youths, in the middle ages certain women were also regarded as avatars (*suijaku*). In the *Imakagami* (Mirror of the Present), a historical tale compiled in the twelfth century, it is argued that Murasaki Shikibu was a Buddhist avatar, and that she wrote *Genji monogatari* (Tale of Genji) in order to lead people to the Buddhist path. Kamakura-period story collections such as *Jikkunshō* and *Kojidan* contain stories which describe the leader of the prostitutes at Kanzaki, a major transport center on the banks of the Yodogawa, as "a flesh-and-blood Fugen." Often looked upon with prejudice, here the women of the pleasure quarters are seen as manifestations of the bodhisattva Fugen, appearing in this world to save suffering humanity.

This idea of individuals ordinarily looked upon with contempt as actually being incarnations of sacred beings was sometimes extended to the *hinin*, or untouchables. In medieval Japan the *hinin* were ostracized from the society of ordinary people, but formed their own groups and often provided services cleaning temples and shrines and serving at funerals. And in medieval times it was widely believed that the bodhisattva Monju (Manjushri) would appear in the form of *hinin*. The priest Eison, mentioned earlier, was famous for his relief work with the *hinin*, and would sometimes conduct Buddhist services in which one of the *hinin* would stand in as a living embodiment of Monju.[10]

Places of pilgrimage

As the religious fervor directed towards saints or holy men who might serve as guides to the Other Shore mounted, it became common for temples to possess an *oku no in*, or inner sanctum, where a holy man with a significant connection to the temple was venerated, as a second sacred space in addition to the *kondō*, or main hall, in which the principal Buddhist deity (*honzonbutsu*) of the temple was enshrined. The cosmology of ancient temples was based on concentric circles: the *kondō* was the most sacred space and occupied the center of the compound, which was surrounded by roofed corridors or galleries (*kairō*) extending from an inner gate (*chūmon*), thus defining stages in the transition from sacred space to the secular world outside. But throughout the Japanese islands in medieval times, there was a broad shift toward a cosmology based on an ellipse defined by two sacred centers or foci: the *kondō* and the *oku no in*.[11]

In fact, it was the *oku no in* that actually became the nucleus of the medieval temples, which were undergoing a renewal as sacred sites and places of pilgrimage (*reijō*). This deep mutual connection between the Pure Land faith and the construction of *oku no in* gave additional impetus to the cults of holy men and popular aspirations to rebirth in Amida's Pure Land. Sacred sites regarded as a portal between this world and the other world began to appear all over the country in the late Heian period, commencing an era of mass pilgrimage by clerics and laypeople alike.

As a result, temples were transformed from what had traditionally been insular places of scholarship and religious training to more open sites of pilgrimage. This new type of temple (or pilgrimage site) welcomed the general public regardless of regional or familial origin. The main actors in this process were the "human gods" (*hitogami*) inviting people to the Other Shore as avatars of buddhas and bodhisattvas.

It was not only the social class of the pilgrims that had changed. The primary purpose of pilgrimages and retreats to temples and shrines had originally been to seek divine assistance with this-worldly concerns: advancement and promotion, recovery from illness, escape from poverty and other difficulties. For example, the author of *Kagerō nikki*, the diary of a late tenth-century court lady known to us only as "the mother of Michitsuna," undertakes a religious retreat to Ishiyamadera to pray for a reconciliation with her estranged husband. Yet by the twelfth century the nature of what pilgrims were seeking would radically change. While prayers for this-worldly benefits certainly did not disappear, the issue of the afterlife rapidly rose to overshadow them. The concern of the populace shifted from miracles to salvation, and before long the next world took on overwhelming significance in the lives of the people of this world.

From the twelfth century onward, collections of legends surrounding particular temples such as the *Ishiyamadera engi* and the *Kokawadera engi*, took as one of their most important motifs the question of what one should do to be reborn in the Pure Land. This phenomenon was a response to the expansion in importance of the other world during the late Heian period and the development of pilgrimage sites as portals or conduits to it, as noted above. People made pilgrimages to sacred sites where avatars (*suijaku*) of the buddhas were enshrined in order to offer prayers for their own peace and happiness in the afterlife.

But this principle could be applied to the dead as well as the living. By bringing the soul of the deceased—or the cremated remains that served as its *yorishiro*—to a sacred site, it was believed that they might be given a send-off on their voyage to the distant Pure Land. It was this worldview that created the popular custom in the middle ages of seeking interment of the remains of the dead at such sacred sites.

3. Searching for the Primal Deity

Images of the other world

The period of the establishment of medieval society, from the late tenth through the twelfth centuries, was also the period in which the Buddhist worldview broadly permeated and shaped the mentality of society. With the formation of a this-world/other-world cosmology, living human beings became separated from the gods and the dead with whom they had previously shared a unitary world. The invisible buddhas of the other world took on a vastly heightened reality and large numbers of people longed to take flight to join them in their other-worldly Pure Land.

However, I would like to point out that the expansion of the other-world paradigm in the late Heian period was not an effect of the spread of Buddhism and the Pure Land sect, but its cause. The sudden proliferation of images of the other world is something we may observe across the globe in different historical periods—in the Japanese islands it happened to occur during the late Heian period. Having reached this stage, Japanese society found the Pure Land faith an amenable mode of thought, adopting it along with the paradigm of the other world.

Such heightened concern with the other world is inextricably intertwined with the impulse to seek a primal being that both transcends and lies behind the things of this world. Buddhist theology offers detailed depictions of another world in which saviors reside. Convinced of the existence of this universal realm transcending earthly geography and ethnicity, Buddhists from many different lands and social positions sought to make their way there. This was expressed in the attempts by Buddhists connected with the Pure Land cult from the time of Genshin (942–1017; scholar-monk, author of the *Ōjōyōshū*

[Essentials of Rebirth in the Pure Land]) onward to depict in words and images Amida's Western Paradise. The teachings of representative figures of Kamakura Buddhism such as Hōnen and Shinran were also born out of this milieu.

The Pure Land cult was the dominant trend of the middle ages, but esoteric Buddhism (*mikkyō*) and the *hongaku* ("original enlightenment") teachings of the Tendai sect were also important strands. In contrast to the Pure Land faith with its ideal of rebirth in the other world, both *hongaku* thought and esoteric Buddhism sought to discover the ultimate Pure Land within the reality of the present world, and are often understood as having aspirations diametrically opposed to those of the Pure Land teachings. However, early medieval esoteric Buddhism certainly did not see the present, visible world as the Pure Land. Even if the ultimate truth or primal reality was ubiquitous throughout the universe, ordinary people were incapable of perceiving it. In this sense—a conviction that an absolute reality exists beyond the range of human perception, and that the central question is what one must do in order to access it—it seems to me that esoteric Buddhism and the Pure Land sects occupied similar positions.

The *Shasekishū*, a collection of Buddhist didactic tales from the end of the twelfth century, articulates a basic tenet of the *hongaku* worldview: "Though we all have the *dharmakaya* [the absolute nature of the Buddha-mind], delusion and enlightenment are created by the discriminating mind." But from there it unfolds the *honji suijaku* paradigm, "In other words, the manifestation of the *dharmakaya* in this world are what we call *kami*," stressing the role played by the Japanese *kami* in saving the sentient beings of our world. And even the great masters of both exoteric and esoteric Buddhism, who venerated *hongaku* and *mikkyō* as the ultimate teachings, longed to take flight into the other world when confronting death.

The Kamakura-period Shingon monk Dōhan, in his *Himitsu nenbutsu shō*, writes disapprovingly that many "of today's Shingon practitioners" are seeking rebirth in the Pure Land through recitation of the *nenbutsu*, yet at the same time he preached the use of Shingon *dharani* as a means to achieve "rebirth in the Pure Land and the rapid attainment of enlightenment."[12] Nor was Dōhan the only figure in the world of medieval esoteric Buddhism to stress the power of mantra (or *dharani*) as a means to achieving rebirth in the Pure Land.

This fascination with the idea of an ultimate existence beyond, or behind, the present world of reality was the keynote of medieval thought. An instinctive sense that all human beings were enfolded equally within the breast of an immense transcendental being was something held in common by the people of medieval Japan.

Coming to grips with primal being

Buddhist thinkers were the first to give theoretical expression to this burgeoning sense of a primal being or ultimate reality, employing concepts such as Amida Buddha or the *dharmakaya*. The various Japanese *kami* were posited as emanations (*suijaku*) of these more fundamental existences as defined by Buddhist theology, and thus were able to occupy a stable position within the cosmology of the era. But there was at least one group of people who resisted these intellectual and spiritual trends—those who believed in the traditional Japanese gods of heaven and earth and whose life and livelihood was devoted to serving them.

In the Japanese islands, by the Yayoi period (ca 300 BCE–300 CE) at the latest, worship of the gods had come to play an important part in the maintenance of the community. This function was inherited by the official system of worship and religious ritual developed under the *ritsuryō* state. With the importation of Buddhism and its ongoing fusion with the indigenous deities, the system of ritual and devotion surrounding the Japanese gods was gradually incorporated into the practices of the Buddhist sects. Despite this, there continued to be large numbers of priests and priestly families or clans professionally engaged in the worship of the indigenous deities—a group that wanted to avoid the fusion with Buddhism and defend the unique character of local beliefs and traditions.

More than anything else, in ancient Japanese society the Japanese *kami* were the source of the religious authority that made the emperor a living god (*akitsukami*). There was a taboo preventing the reigning emperor from having any direct association with Buddhism. The principal buildings of the palace complex (*dairi*) in which the emperor made his residence—the Shishinden and Seiryōden—were not built in a style recalling that of Buddhist temples, with their stone foundations and tiled roofs. In a period in which the fusion of Buddhist and Japanese deities proceeded apace, here a consistent stance was taken for "the separation of gods and buddhas" (*shinbutsu kakuri*) and the integrity of the worship of the Japanese *kami*.[13]

At the level of the state as well, the indigenous system of ritual and worship continued to possess great significance even as it underwent changes in character. The *ritsuryō*-system rituals aimed at bringing all the shrines in the nation under the central control of the state, but by about the middle of the Heian period this had broken down, and by the late Heian period imperial emissaries were still being sent only to the major shrines of the Kinai capital region and environs. This eventuated in a system of twenty-two shrines (*sha*) in the heartland surrounding the imperial capital in Kyoto, and one major shrine (*miya*) per province in more remote areas that received regular emissaries from the imperial government. This system became the framework for worship of the traditional gods during medieval times.[14] The role of the traditional deities and their worship was still quite significant in maintaining the unity of the imperial court and the outlying provinces even in this era.

Ise Jingū—the Grand Shrine at Ise—is the prime example of a shrine that found its raison d'être in defending a separate identity from Buddhism for the worship of the Japanese *kami* during the transition from antiquity to the middle ages, consistently prohibiting Buddhists from pilgrimages to the shrine. Even at Ise, it is clear that advancing Buddhist syncretism made its influence felt, but the shrine, through the use of *imikotoba* (substitute words used to avoid the use of Buddhist terminology) and other customs, was strongly oriented toward demarcating the worship of the indigenous gods from the Buddhist religion.

In the second half of the thirteenth century, as Buddhism made ever more serious inroads into the realm of indigenous beliefs, a new wave of religious thought arose at Ise. This movement, promoted by Watarai Yukitada and other priests of the Outer Shrine (Gekū) at Ise, is known as Ise Shintō. The *Shintō gobusho* (Five Books of Shintō), the sacred scripture of Ise Shintō, developed a monotheistic conception of supreme being who at the beginning of time created this world and rules over it. The intellectual raw materials for this were provided by the Buddhist and Daoist thought that had become so pervasive in medieval times.[15]

The transcendent deities Kuni-no-toko-tachi-no-kami and Amaterasu Ōmikami were referred to as "the Kami of the Great Origin" or "the Kami of the Void" (as Kuni-no-toko-tachi-no-kami was called in *Gochinza hongi*), or "the Peerless and Supreme Original Kami" (as Amaterasu Ōmikami was described in *Hōki hongi*). In *Gochinza hongi*, Amaterasu Ōmikami was described as "the primal form of all the myriad things" (*banbutsu no hontai*), while Toyouke Ōkami was described as "the totality of all the myriad things" (*banbutsu no sōtai*). As may be seen from these examples, Ise Shintō was attempting to wrest the primal being that the Buddhists had first articulated with the concept of *honji* away from the world of Buddhism and return it to the realm of the worship of Japan's indigenous gods of heaven and earth.

Honji suijaku and its opponents

One historical figure who was influenced by Ise Shintō, and attempted to develop an even clearer theoretical model for a primal deity from the perspective of faith in the traditional Japanese deities, was Jihen, who was active during the Nambokuchō period (1334–1392). In his treatise *Toyoashihara jinpū waki*, he wrote that the reason Kuni-no-toko-tachi-no-kami was also called "Kami of the Void" is because "[It] has only a name and is without form. Thus, even if heaven and earth come to an end, this deity will not. The forms of things may change, but [its] path never alters. Because it is ceaselessly arising and ceaselessly forming the land, it is called Kuni-no-toko-tachi-no-kami [lit., 'land-ceaselessly-arising-kami']."

The deity that appears here may be described with the word *kami* but is an entirely different being from those described in the myths and legends described in the ancient chronicles such as the *Kojiki* and *Nihon shoki*. Here a particular individual *kami*, Kuni-no-toko-tachi-no-kami, is elevated to the status of an absolute, immortal, indestructible being responsible for creating the cosmos. In this same work, Jihen divided the Japanese *kami* into three separate categories: (1) "deities of *dharma*-nature" (*hosshōshin*), (2) "enlightened deities" (*ukaku no kami*), and (3) "unenlightened deities" (*jitsumei no kami*), such as ghosts or spirits of animals. The *hosshōshin* transcended the *honji-suijaku* paradigm, for they were conceived as beings identical with the *dharmakaya*. This liberated the *kami* from the status of avatars or manifestations and awarded them the position of primordial being or *honjibutsu* previously monopolized by a Buddhist deity.

It is in this context that we encounter Yoshida Kanetomo, a Shintō scholar of the Muromachi period (1338–1568). Kanetomo promoted a complete reorganization of the shrine system and the independence of Shintō from Buddhism, creating a Daigengū Saijōsho (Ceremonial Site and Shrine of the Great Origin) that was intended to serve as a center for the worship of the Kami of the Great Origin (Kuni-no-toko-tachi-no-kami), and of the entire pantheon of *kami* from more than three thousand official shrines throughout the country. He also systematized what has been described as an "inverted" *honji-suijaku* theory, employing the metaphor of biological growth: "Japan gave birth to the seed; in China the branches and leaves appeared; in India the flowers and fruit. Because of this Buddhism is the fruition of the Law; Confucianism forms its branches and leaves; and Shintō is the root of all. The other two teachings are both manifestations of our Shintō."[16] Here, Shintō is awarded the status of being the "root" (*konpon*) of the world's other philosophies and teachings, with both Chinese Confucianism and Indian Buddhism regarded as emanations of it.

There are various interpretations of the relationship between *honji-suijaku* theory and its inversion, but I think it is virtually impossible to find a fundamental difference between the two as modes of thought. Both can be seen within the framework of the medieval imagination and its pursuit of primal being. The only difference lay in whether this primordial being was theorized with the teachings of Buddhism or posited as an indigenous *kami*.

Thus, in medieval Japanese theology, a metaphysical investigation of the divine was in progress that attempted to transcend sectarian frameworks such as Buddhism and Shintō and resulted in the development of a concept of an ultimate deity at the center of the universe who created this world and presides over it. Or, as Yamamoto Hiroko has put it, "The medieval theologians universally sought an ultimate deity and aimed to deal with the *kami* on a more metaphysical level."[17] This was nothing less than the creation of a unique philosophical realm in the form of a medieval rereading and reinterpretation of the myths of the ancient Japanese chronicles.[18]

Discovery of the god within

The casting of the divine in salvific and transcendental terms gave birth to a new and unprecedented type of god. In ancient times, the presence of the *kami* always confronted human beings. They were external to humanity, sources of miraculous power and energy. In contrast to this, in medieval times we see the appearance of modes of thought that began to seek the presence of the divine within the human heart and mind.[19]

In the *Nakatomi no harae kunge*, a text from the end of the Heian period, the *kami* are divided into three classes: (1) *kami* of original enlightenment (*hongaku*), (2) *kami* of acquired enlightenment (*shikaku*), and (3) *kami* of no-enlightenment (*fukaku*). The *kami* of the great shrines of Ise were categorized as *hongaku*: "They are the wondrous embodiment of the essence of the principle and nature (*rishō*) of the original purity... that is eternal and unchanging." Because of this, the text explains, they are called the Honored Kami of the Great Origin. The wind from the world of things does not stir them, the sea of the mind is deep and overflowing without waves. There is no *dharma* outside the treasure-body and the single mind. Thus, this is called "original enlightenment."[20]

This idea that neither the *kami* nor the realm of enlightenment was separate from mind would become a standard trope of medieval interpretations of the ancient myths and chronicles. We see similar ideas expressed throughout the medieval literature: "Mind is the source of the gods" (in the *Hōki hongi*); "When purified both within and without, there is no separation between my mind and the mind of the gods" (in *Daijingū sankei ki*).

A logic associating the experience of ultimate enlightenment with a Buddha-nature (*busshō*) inherent in human beings was always present in Mahayana Buddhism, but underwent an escalation in the context of the ascendancy of *hongaku* thought beginning in the late Heian period. In one of the earliest texts in the tradition of Tendai-sect *hongaku* thought, the *Tendai Hokkeshū gozu hōmon yōsan* (Essentials of the Oxhead Doctrine of the Tendai-Lotus School), we find a passage which reads: "The original nature of mind makes no discrimination between sacred and profane. This is called the innate buddha-nature." This mode of thought—seeing the nature of mind as originally enlightened—asserted that the fundamental essence of the ordinary human mind was identical with that of the eternal and indestructible buddhas. Humankind thus holds within it an inseparable connection with the ultimate truth of the cosmos, the *dharmakaya*. In medieval times, this perception was widely preached in simple and easily understood language, as in the thirteenth-century travel narrative *Kaidōki*: "The as yet unblossomed lotus of our hearts / awaits only spring to bloom"; or again, as in the testament of Hōjō Shigetoki (*Gokurakuji-dono goshōsoku*), "In the heart of each of us is a lotus, upon which resides a buddha in its glory."

As the names used in medieval texts clearly demonstrate—from the "*kami* of original enlightenment" of the *Nakatomi no harae kunge* to the "*kami* of *dharma*-nature" or "*dharmakaya* buddha" (*hosshin nyorai*) of Jihen's *Toyoashihara jinpū waki*—the conception of a primordial *kami* in medieval times was profoundly influenced by the developments of Buddhist thought in that era. The Buddhist attempt to explore the nature of the absolute was imported into the world of the Japanese gods and employed as an argument for their absolute nature. The gods, which had once worked their influence upon humans only from without, were not only recast as beings pervading the cosmos and wielding salvific power—they were also seen as the "original nature" of fundamental enlightenment that every human being inherently possesses.

As I will argue in the following chapter, this idea would later become the key which permitted ordinary people to become venerated as deities. The logic that would open the door of deification to the common people thus was born out of the Shintō thought of medieval times, developed in response to and resistance against the teachings of Buddhism. From late medieval times onward, examples of the deification of human beings grew rapidly in number, and underlying this phenomenon was not only the pervasive influence of *hongaku* thought but also the deepening view of humanity within medieval Shintō itself.

According to Mark Teeuwen, the term "*shintō*" ("way of the gods") was originally pronounced "*jindō*" in Japan when it was imported from China, and the change in pronunciation from *jindō* to *shintō* occurred in the fourteenth century. Behind this change lay a transition in the meaning of the word *shin* (*kami*, god, deity) itself from a collective to an abstract noun.[21] This development was intimately connected to the medieval reinterpretations of the ancient myths and chronicles discussed above.

But even these radically innovative movements in the realm of traditional beliefs could not win back the leading position in the world of medieval religion from Buddhism. The salient weakness of beliefs in the traditional gods was that they lacked the function most eagerly sought in religious faith by the people of the age—a theory and practice that would convey the dead to rebirth in the other world. Shintō had no established funerary practices. Even in Ise, the epicenter of intellectual activity in medieval Shintō, the shrine priests had no choice but to leave their own funerals in the hands of Buddhist clergy.

CHAPTER 6

The Undeparted Dead

1. Divinity in Grasses, Trees, and the Earth Itself

The *nenbutsu* of the grasses and trees

ELABORATE REPRESENTATIONS of the Other Shore and the world after death seemed to reach a peak from the twelfth into the thirteenth century and then began a rapid decline in the late thirteenth century. Once again, the spiritual world of the Japanese archipelago was undergoing a tectonic shift.

In late medieval times—from the fourteenth to the sixteenth centuries—this transition was accompanied by an attenuation of the fervor with which society aspired to rebirth in the Pure Land. Supplications for such rebirth continued to be reproduced in large numbers on votive stelae (*itabi*) and in written vows (*ganmon*). But the principal concern of the people seems to have been shifting from matters of the afterlife to leading a fulfilling life in this world.

We may interpret this phenomenon as one in which the Other Shore gradually receded from view as the things of this world took on relatively greater weight. The secularization of society that would continue from the early modern period into modern times was seeing its first genuine stirrings. As people lost their sense of the reality of the other world as a place to be reborn after death, they began to choose

paths to a fulfilling life and happiness in this world over the idea
of salvation in the world to come. In *Ippen shōnin goroku*, a record of
the words of the Pure Land priest Ippen (1239–1289), we come across
the following passage:

> *Nenbutsu* practitioners discard both wisdom and foolishness.
> They discard the realms of good and evil. They discard the rea-
> soning maintained by noble and humble, high and low. They
> discard fear of hell, aspiration for the Pure Land, and further dis-
> card enlightenment in all the schools: thus discarding all things,
> they say the *nenbutsu*. It is this *nenbutsu* that perfectly accords
> with Amida's all-surpassing Primal Vow.
>
> When in this way you raise your voice more and more in
> utterance, here is neither Buddha nor self, much less any reason-
> ing of this or that. The realms of good and evil are all the Pure
> Land. Outside of this, do not aspire, do not renounce. Among
> all living things—mountains and rivers, grasses and trees, even
> the sounds of blowing winds and rising waves—there is nothing
> that is not the *nenbutsu*.[1]

Here, the perspective we see in earlier Pure Land teachers such as
Hōnen—rejecting this world as polluted and debased—is completely
absent. Shinran had asserted that rebirth in the Pure Land could be
assured in this world, making the true believer an equal of the buddhas
(*nyorai tōdō*); but in his case this was accompanied by an even harsher
perception of himself as an "evil person" than that of Hōnen, and
a deep repentance for his attachment to the things of this world. Such a
denial of this world is nowhere to be found in the words of Ippen, who
was able to see the society of his day as equivalent to the Pure Land, and
to hear the voice of the Buddha in the sound of the wind and the roar of
the waves. Here we find no longing for an ideal society in the afterlife,
transcending the things of this world.

Ippen shōnin goroku, with its willingness to envision present reality
as the Pure Land and to perceive the image of a buddha in ordinary
people chanting the *nenbutsu*, seems to bring us closer to the Tendai

hongaku thought popular during the late Heian period than it does to the lineage of the Pure Land tradition from Genshin to Hōnen. Yet while these two modes of thought both perceived a universal world of truth underlying the reality of this world, their actual functioning within society was diametrically opposed.

Hongaku thought and Esoteric Buddhism took the position that the Buddha and the Pure Land did not exist separately from this present world and the people living in it. However, in the early medieval period it was inconceivable that the ultimate truth residing at the heart of the cosmos (the *hosshinbutsu*, or *dharmakaya*) would reveal its true form to or speak directly to the mass of humanity. Ordinary human beings were incapable of perceiving the existence of the *dharmakaya* or of hearing its teachings directly. Intermediaries—*suijaku*—were indispensable.

As a result, in the early middle ages, when elaborate representations of the other world pervaded society with a deep yearning for the next world, *hongaku* thought and Esoteric Buddhism, with their perception of the traces of the buddhas behind all the phenomena of this world, would play the role of making the entire world into a mystical experience, rather than serving as affirmation of secular reality.

Mountains as the body of the divine

This mode of thought would act to affirm everyday life in secular society only in the late medieval period, after conceptions of the Other Shore receded in importance and the tension between this world and the other world dissipated. The early medieval quest to discover a transcendental presence (the divine) in the hearts of human beings deepened in the late medieval period into one shared by the society in general, regardless of sectarian differences between Shintō and Buddhism. People came to see the operation of the divine not just in human beings but in nature. It is this transition in the spiritual realm that gave rise to the perspective quoted above from *Ippen shōnin goroku*. Here are two *waka* by the leading Zen monk of the Muromachi period, Shōtetsu (1381–1459), from his collection of poetry *Sōkonshū*:

Arimayama / hotoke no mi yori / idasu yu ni /
kiyoki satori mo / nadoka nakaran
Arimayama / bathing in the hot spring / that flows from the body
of the Buddha / who would not be purified and enlightened?

Yama mo mina / moto no hotoke no / sugata nite /
taezu minori o / toku arashi kana
These mountains, too, / are the form of the primordial Buddha /
The storms unceasingly preach the sacred teachings

For Shōtetsu the mountains themselves were the ceaselessly changing form of the Buddha, and the winds that stirred the trees on their
slopes were none other than the voice of the Buddha preaching the
dharma. Shōtetsu's disciple Shinkei inherited this perspective from his
teacher, and wrote:

Neither the true Buddha nor the true poem can have fixed form.
They simply manifest their feelings and virtues in response to
time and circumstance. Our hearts are like the dharma-body
of the Buddha, altering its immeasurable and boundless form
to bring forth all the phenomena of heaven and earth. This is
what is called *tōrushin*, the dharma-body in emanation. Neither
the dharma-body of the Buddha nor the dharma-body in emanation can possess a true form. And only the poet who does not
get stuck in any one place can achieve a true perspective. Thus,
when asked "What is the Buddha," one of the ancient masters
answered, "The oak tree in the garden." But when someone
later related this to one of the master's disciples, he was told,
"My master never said such words. Do not slander him!"

The myriad phenomena are all the dharma-body of the Buddha
Because of this I pay homage even to a grain of dust [2]

Here all the phenomena of heaven and earth are presented as manifestations of the *dharmakaya*, or ultimate reality, which resides in even
every grain of dust in the universe. The Buddha possesses no fixed or

definite form, transforming ceaselessly over time; all the infinite forms it assumes are embodiments of truth. And it is important for poems as well not to be bound by particular formal properties, but to express living, vibrant emotion in response to the ceaselessly changing environment.

Not only human beings, but plants and animals, and even rocks and gravel—all the existences of this world are seen as possessing the buddha-nature (busshō), and the reality right before one's eyes is seen, exactly as it is, as a manifestation of the ultimate truth. This perspective is summed up in the phrase "[even] the grasses, trees, and earth will all attain buddhahood" (sōmoku kokudo shikkai jōbutsu), which became a widely-known expression in the late medieval period. The logic of this was that if all the phenomena and things of this world partook of the fundamental buddha-nature, then they should actually be capable of attaining buddhahood. The ideal world does not exist in some separate space or dimension imperceptible to us, hidden from the world of our reality. The scenery immediately before our eyes is itself the Pure Land. Those mountains towering in the distance are the Buddha. Or, conversely, there are no buddhas or Pure Land to be sought outside the nature and phenomena we see every day.

In Chapter 3, we saw that in antiquity, while the idea of kami making their abode in the mountains became common, the concept of the mountains themselves as deities still did not exist. The spread of forms of religious belief and practice that conceived of a mountain as the body of the deity and worshipped it as such was a development that only became possible with the diffusion, in late medieval times, of a mode of thought that discovered divinity in the midst of nature and asserted that "[even] the grasses, trees, and earth will all attain buddhahood." Envisioning the mountains as gods—frequently seen as the prototype of Japanese views of nature—was certainly not an animistic tradition stretching back into the depths of antiquity. It was in fact a mode of thought deriving from highly abstract ideas that appeared in the process of the internalization of the divine in medieval Japan.

The conception of the divine embodied in "[even] the grasses, trees, and earth will all attain buddhahood" permeated the world of the arts in the Muromachi period (1338–1568). In the Noh drama, the spirits of plants such as cherry, willow, or plantain trees appear in human form to converse with human beings. In the play *Bashō* (The Plantain Tree), we find the following lines: "The green of the willow, the crimson of the cherry—all plants just as they are in their color and scent will become Buddha."

The changing appearance of plants throughout the four seasons is here described as the visage of buddha-nature. In Muromachi writings on aesthetics, this *hongaku* ("original enlightenment") concept of the incipient buddhahood of grasses and trees is almost always deployed as a means of emphasizing the importance of responding artistically to the four seasons of the natural world.

The emergence of ghosts

Another noteworthy aspect of the Noh drama is the frequent appearance of ghosts (*yūrei*). *Sumidagawa* (The River Sumida), by Kanze Motomasa, relates the story of a woman who has come all the way from Kyoto to what were then the remote provinces of eastern Japan in search of a son who was abducted by slave traders. At the crossing on the river Sumida, she learns from the ferryman of a child who died and was buried on the opposite shore exactly a year before. Urged by the ferryman to recite the *nenbutsu*—chanting the phrase *namu Amida butsu* (homage to Amida Buddha)—as an offering at the grave, her voice is joined in chorus by a voice from the grave mound, and the wraithlike form of her child appears. But when dawn breaks, all that can be seen are the long grasses thickly covering the mound.

In the early middle ages, the proper place for the dead was in the other world of the Pure Land, and those who remained in this world were regarded as fundamentally unfortunate, unhappy beings. In the Noh, there are even plays, such as *Motomezuka* (The Burial Mound), in which a ghost appears and relates the agonies it is suffering in hell. But the majority of the dead in Noh remain in their graves, where they may respond to a summons from someone, or perhaps emerge of their own volition to engage in dialogue with the living. Becoming a ghost was not something restricted to special individuals; like the child in *Sumidagawa*, ghosts might have been perfectly ordinary human beings. Overall, the concept of them either as fearsome, vengeful creatures, or

Figure 6-1 The true age of ghosts began from the late middle ages, as people ceased to set off for the Other Shore after death. *Yūreizu* (Portrait of a Ghost; Zenshōan, Tokyo).

as miserable beings excluded from salvation, was rather shallow.

In *Uneme* (The Lady-in-Waiting), the ghost of a lady-in-waiting who drowned herself in Sarusawa Pond in Nara appears to a traveling priest and asks him to perform rites for her so that she may attain nirvana. The priest complies, and tells the ghost of the Buddhist teaching that all living things, even the grasses and trees and earth, are all, without exception, destined to become buddhas. The ghost then declares that like the dragon girl, she has "transformed into a man," achieved buddhahood, and been reborn into "the Spotless World of the South." She then performs a final dance in celebration of the longevity of the emperor and his reign, and disappears into the depths of the waters.

The "dragon girl" is a reference to a passage in the Lotus Sutra concerning the eight-year-old daughter of the dragon-king Sagara. Having been born female, it was thought that attaining buddhahood would be impossible for her, but through the teaching of the Lotus Sutra she is transformed into a man, becomes a buddha, and is transported to the Spotless World of the South, to preach the dharma for the benefit of all sentient beings.[3]

In *Uneme*, the Spotless Land to the South where the dragon girl is reborn is recast as Sarusawa Pond, and the lingering there of the ghost of the drowned lady-in-waiting becomes her opportunity to achieve salvation and rebirth. The boundaries between this world and the next, between reality and the Pure Land, have become amorphous and porous. Here we can see that the concept of "rebirth" has been transformed into something completely different in nature from that of the Pure Land faith of the early medieval period. And it is the fading reality of the other-worldly Pure Land that has brought about this fundamental change.

The buddhas are no longer located in some distant realm beyond human perception—they are somewhere within this world. The Pure Land for which the dead are bound is also somewhere in this world. The dead shall find their peace not by journeying to a remote Pure Land, but by finding some appropriate place for themselves in this one, living harmoniously there in dialogue with the living—this is what people gradually came to believe.

2. Shape-Shifters

Holy men as avatars

In the middle ages, particularly in early medieval times, a variety of individuals—holy men, saints, eminent Buddhist clergy—were believed to be avatars or emanations of the primordial beings of the Other Shore. Medieval belief in deified humans (*hitogami*) was structured in accordance with Buddhist cosmology, positing a select group of people integrated into the *honji-suijaku* paradigm as saviors (deities) linking this world with the other. If one were to distill the function of deities in ancient times (*hitogami* included) into a single word, it would be "miracles"; in medieval times it would be "salvation."

However, this does not exhaust the various other types of *hitogami* that came into existence in the middle ages. For example, there were individuals who charged themselves with a mission whose fulfillment required that they remain in this world even after death. For example, Kujō Michiie, a member of the court nobility who served as imperial regent in the Kamakura period (1185–1333), left a will in which he wrote that if he were successfully reborn into the Pure Land he would use his "heavenly eyes," and if he was not, and must continue his journey among the Three Realms, then he would use his "fleshly eyes" to continue to watch over his estate, and mete out punishment (*bachi*) to any of his descendants who violated the terms of the will.[4] On his deathbed, Ashikaga Yoshikane, rebuilder of the temple Bannaji, left a written vow to become a *kami* after death to serve as the protector of this temple.[5] In both cases, the individuals involved vowed to become *kami* after their deaths in order to fulfill a self-selected mission as protector deities.

The logic permitting individuals to proclaim their own elevation into gods is difficult to situate within the context of medieval thought as we have seen it thus far. In the *honji-suijaku* paradigm, the *suijaku* not only functioned as escorts or guides to the Other Shore but they were also thought to dispense a variety of this-worldly benefits in order to lead people to

Figure 6-2 A protective amulet featuring an image of Ryōgen (Kiyomizudera, Yasugi City)

embrace the Buddhist teachings. And they were also capable of meting out fierce punishment to those hostile to the teachings, as their mission was to orient all people toward the true path.

In the *Goshūi ōjōden*, an eleventh-century collection of stories of rebirth, Ryōgen, the former chief abbot of the great monastic complex at Mount Hiei (Hieisan), is said to have initially postponed being reborn into the Pure Land after his death in order to protect the integrity of the Buddhist teachings at Hieisan, but that now he had left a "dharma-protector" (*gohō*) on the mountain in his stead, and had achieved rebirth. It was believed that *suijaku* could move freely back and forth between the Pure Land and this world while in pursuit of their mission.

However, it seems a bit of a stretch to try and force the cases of Kujō Michiie and Ashikaga Yoshikane into this pattern. Though their vows may seem at first glance to be based on Buddhist paradigms, there would seem to be something entirely different at work here.

Patriarchs as deities

What might that be? One thing that comes to mind is that, beginning late in the Heian period (794–1185), we see among the local landholders and village headmen comprising the upper strata of the peasantry a custom of interring the dead within the family compound. In the middle ages, however, not everyone connected with the family was accorded this privilege, which came to be restricted to special individuals such as the founder of the family or the builder of the house. Katsuda Itaru has observed that because such courtyard graves frequently became identified with the trees planted near them, the spirits of the dead were thought to reside in the trees and their spiritual power to protect the house, its land and fields, and the later generations of the family.[6]

Minamoto no Yoritomo, founder of the Kamakura shogunate, was buried on the slopes of Kitayama, overlooking both the headquarters of the shogunate at Ōkura and the town of Kamakura. At Chūsonji temple in Hiraizumi, the remains of three generations of the Ōshū Fujiwara family in northern Japan are enshrined in the Konjikidō, sited atop a hill with a splendid vista. The historian Irimada Nobuo says that these two sites were selected because they were places from which the townspeople could not help but feel they were being observed by the gaze of the patriarchs of these houses in their role as protector deities.[7] These deified patriarchs thus had the power even to determine subsequent urban planning.

We can understand founding fathers becoming deities to protect their descendants in the context of a lineage of deified dead since ancient times, from "imperial spirits" to figures such as Fujiwara no Kamatari. Buddhism incorporated these *hitogami* into its soteriology, positioning them as avatars (*suijaku*) of the primordial buddhas. Even so, the idea of an individual with special status within a clan or family remaining in this world after death, to protect his descendants and mete out punishment to their foes, was widely shared within medieval society at a level distinct from such theological explanations.

And while the mummified bodies of three generations of the Ōshū Fujiwara family interred within the Konjikidō (Golden Hall) were perceived as being the guardian deities of Hiraizumi, they also became the object of a widespread cult that viewed them as saviors who could act as intermediaries between this world and the Other Shore. It is possible to see in this one of the defining characteristics of the *hitogami* in medieval times: that they never lost their nature as emissaries of the afterlife. After the fall of the Fujiwara house, the Konjikidō was opened as a site of pilgrimage and prayer for people seeking rebirth in the Pure Land, as well as a place of interment.[8]

When viewed as examples of medieval *hitogami*, Kujō Michiie and Ashikaga Yoshikane exhibited another unusual characteristic: not only did they aspire to become *kami* after their deaths, they were convinced that this desire would in fact be fulfilled. They represent the appearance of a new type of *hitogami*—secular individuals of unusual power who became elevated to godhood not by the veneration of others after their deaths, but by the force of their own will and aspirations.

The *hitogami* of Suwa

Another unique aspect of the medieval *hitogami* was the appearance of *ikigami*, or individuals who were perceived as deities while still living. One of the best known examples is from the Suwa cult.[9]

In the archives of the Ōhori family in the collection of the Suwa Municipal Historical Museum in Nagano Prefecture is a document entitled "Ōhori Suwa Nobushige gejō utsushi," a petition for a prohibition on new and unorthodox rituals at the Shimosha, the Lower Shrine at Suwa. The document uses some quite interesting language in identifying the Ōhori, chief priests of the Upper Shrine, with the enshrined god.

The petition states that from the time Suwa Daimyōjin first manifested (*suijaku*) in Suwa he performed his function as a pacifier and protector deity of the realm in a guise that was directly available for worship to the people as an *arahitogami* (manifest god), but that later, in view of the state of the people, he decided to hide his form from them. At that time, the god declared that the chief priest of the shrine would perform the functions of the god and should be worshipped in his stead: "The chief priest should be treated as the enshrined deity (*gotai*), being a separate embodiment of myself" (*Ware bettai nashi, hōri o motte gotai to nasu beshi*).

Another reference to the priests at Suwa is found in the *Azuma kagami*, a historical chronicle of the Kamakura shogunate completed around the end of the thirteenth century: "The Daimyōjin proclaims his will through the pronouncements of the shrine priest Ōhōri."[10] In other words, the chief priest had taken on the role of speaking for the god as his representative.

In the above petition the origins of Suwa Daimyōjin are explained in the language of the *honji-suijaku* paradigm, demonstrating the pervasive influence of Buddhist thought. But *ikigami* ("living god") beliefs are also clearly in evidence in the way in which the chief priest is conceived as the living representative of the god and identified with him.

Another example of medieval *ikigami* beliefs is found in the *Shinjin ekeizu* from the province of Wakasa,[11] an illustrated hand-scroll that begins with pictures related to the founding of the Ichinomiya (First Shrine) and Ninomiya (Second Shrine) in Wakasa, followed by portraits of each generation of shrine priests from the earliest, Takafumi, onward. The portraits are presented as two-generation pairs, seated facing one another. The individual on the right, representing odd-numbered generations, is seated on a raised dais in front of a three-fold screen, while the one on the left, representing even-numbered generations, has no such background and is seated on an ordinary tatami mat.

It has been pointed out that this unique mode of representation is based on the thinking described in this passage from the *Shinjin ekeizu*:

The two deities [of the Ichinomiya and Ninomiya shrines] made an agreement, saying that the descendants of Takafumi would forever serve as the administrating priests (*shamu kannushi*) of the shrines. One generation would be regarded as *kami*, the next as ordinary human beings. Their family surname should be written Ryū (笠). Later generations must not alter these instructions.

Thus, the special accoutrements used in representing the odd-numbered generations were intended to express the status of these individuals as *kami*.[12]

We have thus reached an era in which, while it was still restricted to powerful rulers, important priests, and other special individuals, people might will themselves into becoming gods—in some cases elevated to that position even while still living—without having to go through the elaborate rites and rituals that had achieved such a status for the imperial spirits of antiquity.

Suffering transformed

In connection with the medieval *hitogami* that we have discussed thus far, it should be noted that medieval tales also include numerous instances in which people are reborn as *kami* after enduring great suffering.[13] A representative example is the legend of Kōga Saburō. During lengthy wanderings beneath the earth he is transformed into a snake, but eventually sheds that form to manifest as the deity Suwa Myōjin. According to "Suwa engi no koto" (Story of the Origin of the Suwa Deity) in the *Shintōshū*, a mid-fourteenth-century collection of tales about shrines, Kōga Saburō was born the third son of Yoritane, a fifth-generation descendant of Emperor Annei and vice-governor of Kōga, who was a *jitō* (estate steward) in the district of Kōga in the province of Ōmi. Upon his father's death, Saburō's two elder brothers were passed over and he officially inherited the headship of the family. Saburō took as his wife Lady Kasuga, whom he met on a pilgrimage to worship the deity of Mount Mikasa, but while they were on a hunting expedition at Ibukiyama, she was abducted by *tengu*, mountain spirits. Saburō searched for his wife throughout the mountains of Japan, and finally discovered her from deep in a cave on the slopes of Mount Tateshina in the province of Shinshū. Lady Kasuga was rescued, but Saburō was left behind in the cave as a result of a trick by his elder brother Jirō.

Saburō followed the cave into the depths of the earth, visiting seventy-two countries. Eventually the king of a country called Iman and his daughter took pity upon him and helped him reach the surface again at Mount Asama—but he had been transformed into a serpent. Through the intervention of mountain deities such as Hakusan Gongen and Fuji Sengen Daibosatsu, Saburō was able to shed this form, be reunited with Lady Kasuga, and then be transported to the Asian mainland, where he acquired supernatural powers. Returning to Japan, he then manifested as the god Suwa Daimyōjin in the Upper Shrine, while Lady Kasuga manifested as the goddess of the Lower Shrine.

In medieval society numerous stories of this type—simple folk tales concerning a person who overcomes trials and suffering to be reborn as a god—circulated in large numbers and won the sympathies of the people. Kōga Saburō only temporarily assumed the form of a serpent, but it was not at all unusual in medieval tales for people to transform into evil beings. The early Kamakura collection of *setsuwa* tales by the priest Keisei, *Kankyo no tomo*, contains a story entitled "The Spiteful Woman Who Became a Living Demon," which I will summarize here:

> There was a girl in the province of Mino who was being visited regularly by a certain man. But eventually he stopped coming to see her, and she became depressed and reclusive. Then she startled everyone by braiding her hair into five knots atop her head that she hardened into horns by dipping them in sugar syrup, donning a pair of red culottes, and disappearing into the night.
>
> After about thirty years had passed, a rumor spread that in the same province a demon had taken up residence in an abandoned temple in the fields, and that it was trying to capture and eat young boys who were tending the oxen. In order to expel this creature the local people armed themselves, surrounded the old temple, and set fire to it. What should then appear from within the burning temple but a five-horned demon dressed in red culottes! The demon confessed that it was what had become of the girl who had disappeared so many years ago. After killing the man who had spurned her, she was no longer

able to return to human form, and had hidden away in the old temple. After relating this tale, the demon leapt into the fire and ended its life.

Perhaps the most famous story of a living person transformed into an *oni* (demon) is that of the *onibaba* of Adachigahara. In the Noh play *Kurozuka* (*Adachigahara* in the Kanze school) two mountain ascetics (*yamabushi*) take lodging for the night at the home of an old woman in Adachigahara in the northern province of Mutsu. When they accidentally discover evidence that makes them suspect her, she becomes enraged and assumes her true form as a demon. She, too, had been a woman with a tragic past.

But it was not only demons into which people transformed. In Book 7 of the *Gukanshō* there is a story in which Imperial Princess Ikami, wife of Emperor Kōnin, becomes so filled with anger and hatred that she transforms into a dragon and kicks Fujiwara no Momokawa to death. This is the same Princess Ikami we have encountered before as one of the *goryō* deities after her death, but in this tale she has transformed into a dragon while still alive.

Similarly, the *Hokke genki* (Book 2) and *Konjaku monogatari shū* (Book 14) relate a story in which a woman from the province of Kii transforms into a serpent in order to murder a monk for whom she has nurtured an unrequited love. The monk, who realizes she is pursuing him in altered form, takes refuge in the temple Dōjōji, where the monks of the temple hide him inside a large bell. But the serpent twines itself around the bell and melts it with the poisonous fires of its vengeful hatred, killing the monk. In the illustrated scroll *Dōjōji engi*, the woman is graphically depicted running as the upper half of her body is being transformed into the fire-breathing serpent (fig. 6-3).

Thus in medieval times living human beings might be transformed into gods and buddhas—or into demons from hell. To put it another way, in the middle ages the distance between humans and deities had shrunk considerably. While the image of the distant and ideal Pure Lands with their transcendent deities continued to flourish, this earthly realm remained populated by a restless mob of people and *kami* who had missed out on salvation.

147

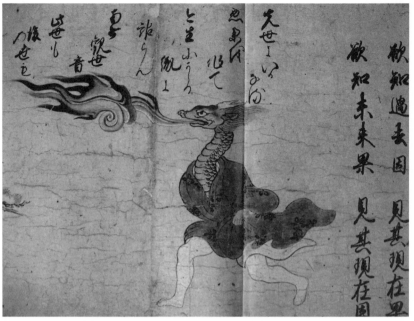

Figure 6-3 Detail from the *Dōjōji engi* (Dōjōji, Hidakagawa)

Closing the gap between gods and humans

Why did the middle ages see the gap between gods and humans close so rapidly, with such a wealth and variety of stories woven around the *hitogami*? It seems plausible that the process of internalization of the divine that we discussed in the previous chapter played a major role in this. The expansion of the other world in medieval times and the accompanying deepening of thought and discourse concerning a transcendent or supreme being eventuated in the discovery of the god within. This provided *hitogami* beliefs with a doctrinal grounding, probably contributing to their spread in medieval times.

As long as deities were located externally to human beings, as they were in ancient times, it was no easy matter for an ordinary human to become a god. For a human to be elevated to the status of a deity required the possession, while still living, of immense power and authority—such as that of the emperors—and, after death, careful and scrupulous ritual observances. In contrast, medieval Shintō doctrine grasped the *kami* as something inherent or internal; the oneness of human nature with the transcendent or supreme being was emphasized.

The idea of the sacred as something inherent in human beings was present in Mahayana Buddhism from the beginning, and this was incorporated into native thinking about the gods both through the development of Shintō thought sympathetic to Buddhism as well as by systematization of a theology by shrine priests attempting to resist Buddhist influence. The concept began to permeate society that every human being possesses a sacred essential nature which when manifested makes it possible to become a god or buddha.

However, in the early middle ages the mainstream logic behind humans becoming deities was to be seen as a savior figure integrated into the *honji-suijaku* paradigm—the *hitogami* as bright moons illuminated by the otherworldly light of the primordial buddhas. For the god within to shine with its own light and come fully to the forefront as the principle underlying the creation of the *hitogami* would require a long period of gestation from late medieval into early modern times.

3. *Gonsha* and *Jissha*

The venerated dead

In the period of transition from antiquity to the middle ages, the Buddhists had managed to secure a near monopoly on the right to interpret cosmology. Japan's traditional gods of heaven and earth were posited as avatars (*suijaku*) of otherworldly buddhas and bodhisattvas (*honjibutsu*), and seen as intermediaries on the path to ultimate salvation. *Honjibutsu* were designated for all of the best-known *kami*, without exception, and shrines were thronged with people seeking rebirth in the Pure Land over which these deities presided.

The resistance to these developments came from a certain group of shrine officials at Ise and elsewhere. They challenged the Buddhists' exclusive right to cosmological interpretation head-on, attempting to reestablish the Japanese gods as the primordial beings. *Hongaku no kami*—"originally enlightened gods"—was the concept born of this struggle over cosmology.

But the dispute between Buddhist and Shintō worldviews did not end with their conflict over the right to interpret the supreme being (or beings). In addition to the deities that made their homes at the famous and powerful shrines such as Ise and Kamo, there were a myriad of *kami* inhabiting humbler locales throughout the land. There were also many types of deities whose identity as *kami* or buddhas was unclear. There were the founders of clans or families revered by descendants as *hitogami*. There were shrines which venerated animals such as foxes or wolves. And there were many ghosts and vengeful spirits with malicious intent which, unlike Tenman Tenjin and the *goryō* deities, had failed to be elevated into *kami* and worshipped accordingly.

How to deal with this truly vast assemblage of local beliefs and deities and position them within a sensible theological and dogmatic framework was one of the weightiest and most inescapable questions confronting medieval Buddhists. The method conceived for dealing with this problem was to classify the *kami* into two groups: *gonsha* (or *gonge*) and *jissha* (or *jitsurui*). This divided all the gods inhabiting the Japanese islands into those which were avatars or manifestations of buddhas (the former) and those—in all their many forms or formlessness—who were not (the latter).

"Kōfukuji sōjō," a petition to the imperial court by the priest Jōkei (1155–1213) requesting a ban on the "*nenbutsu*-only" practice advocated by Hōnen, listed the "error of betraying wonder-working *kami* (*reishin*)" as the fifth error of the *nenbutsu* practitioners, criticizing their rejection of *kami*-worship—"If you pray to the *kami*, you will certainly fall into hell"—in the following terms:

> I will not touch here upon the gods and spirits of the *jitsurui* type. But when it comes to the manifestations (*suijaku*) of the *gonge*, these are unquestionably sacred. The great monks of ages past all deeply respected them.... Even the monks of these Latter Days (*matsuyo*) respect the emperor and his officials, and still more the wonder-working *kami*. This sort of loose talk must be stopped.

Jōkei here divides the *kami* into two classes—*jitsurui* and *gonge*—and while he won't speak to the first, he sees refusing to worship the latter as being unacceptable.

Rejection of the *jissha*

This division of the *kami* into the two categories of *jitsurui* and *gonge* was not peculiar to Jōkei; it was common to many medieval Buddhists. *Shoshin honkai shū*, a work believed to have been written by Zonkaku (1290–1373), argues that the *gonsha no reishin*—*kami* that are manifestations of the buddhas—are worthy of veneration, but that the *jissha no jashin*—evil *kami*, spirits of the dead, and so on—should be shunned. The *jissha* are "the type who, humans or animals, cause *tatari* and suffering and are worshipped as *kami* in an effort to placate them." Although venerating such evil *kami* is counter to what is "right and proper," in fact many of the *kami* worshipped by people are of this type, according to this text.

Categorization of the *kami* is something we come across frequently in a wide range of other medieval texts:

Generally the gods are of two types, *gon* and *jitsu*. The *kami* known as *gonsha* come forth from the capital of the dharma-nature and mingle with the dust of this impure world, coming to the aid of its ignorant and deluded beings. The *kami* called *jissha* arise from evil spirits, dead souls, and the like, and work *tatari* upon people.[14]

Concerning *gonsha* and *jisshin*
Amaterasu Ōmikami, Hachiman Daibosatsu, and similar *kami* who work as buddhas to the benefit of people are called *gongen* or *gonsha*. The *kami* known as *jisshin* are those spirits of horses, cattle, and so on that cause *tatari* after they die.[15]

Some sources did not stop with two categories of gods. One medieval Shintō text (*Nihongi Miwa-ryū*) developed a tripartite division by adding the *hongakushin* (*kami* of original enlightenment) discussed in the preceding chapter, renaming the *gonsha* as *shikakushin* (*kami* of acquired enlightenment) and the *jissha* as *jitsumei jaōshin* ("unenlightened serpent-king *kami*"). Jihen's classification of the gods into "*kami* of dharma-nature" (*hosshōshin*), "enlightened deities" (*yūkaku no kami*), and "unenlightened deities" (*jitsumei no kami*) followed a similar logic. In all of these classifications, the spirits of dead humans or animals were defined as evil or malicious spirits unworthy of worship, and sharply separated from the *gonsha* who were avatars or manifestations of the buddhas.

In medieval times, not only Buddhist clergy associated with the orthodoxy of the major temples and shrines, but even sects of believers in the traditional Japanese gods labeled many obscure and mysterious local deities as *jissha*, and worked resolutely to expunge them from their systems of worship.

The revenge of the *jissha*

The deities suffering rejection as *jissha* did not bow meekly in the face of such treatment. Jien's *Gukanshō* (ca 1220) is a work which attempts to interpret historical developments in the context of a complex interaction of principles characteristic of two different realms: *myō* (the world of gods and buddhas) and *ken* (the human world). Jien describes one of the principles of *myō* as the existence since ancient times of vengeful spirits (*onryō*) that could "cause the loss of dynasties and the downfall of men," and gives as examples Princess Ikami, Fujiwara no Asahira, Fujiwara no Motokata, and Fujiwara no Akimitsu. In more recent times, he argues, the spirits of the abdicated emperor Sutoku and of Fujiwara no Tadazane had caused disturbances and unrest in the world and harm to the populace.

In late medieval times the activities of *onryō* and other spirits that might be classed as *jissha* grew even more pronounced. The *Taiheiki*, a military epic written in the late fourteenth century, gives vivid descriptions of the activities of vengeful spirits. In the section of Book 27 entitled "Unkei's Prophecies," numerous *onryō* assemble at the *oku no in* of Atago Shrine to plot ways of disturbing the world. Among those present are Tarōbō, the great *tengu* of Mount Atago; former emperors who after death have become leaders among the demons, such as the abdicated Emperor Sutoku, Emperor Junnin, Empress Ikami, and the retired emperors Go-Toba and Go-Daigo; and prominent monastics who had been transformed into great demon kings, such as Genbō, Shinzei, Kanchō, Jie, Raigō, Ningai, and Son'un.

In Book 25 as well, Ōtō no Miya and other *onryō* of the imperial court assemble at the Six Cedars of the temple Ninnaji to discuss how to wreak havoc in the world. The plan they come up with is to possess various members of the Northern Court, destroy the relationship between Ashikaga Takauji and his younger brother Tadayoshi, and alienate their ally Kō no Moronao.

These *onryō* and demon kings, unlike the *mononoke* who might bring curses upon individuals, were believed to possess immense power to influence society, and were frequently worshipped locally as *kami* in the manner of the *goryō* deities mentioned previously. Buddhists and Shintōists with secure positions in the orthodox religious world labeled such deities as *jissha* and attempted to have them ejected from their belief system and cosmology. But these efforts did not succeed, as we see from the examples of the activities of vengeful spirits in the *Taiheiki*. The *onryō* of former emperors Sutoku and Go-Daigo were widely accepted throughout the Japanese islands, and demonstrated enormous influence.[16] It was an era in which vengeful spirits were still seen as capable of affecting the course of history.

The otherworldly Pure Land recedes into the distance

Even in the middle ages, with its ideal of rebirth in the Pure Land, many of the dead were thought to remain in this world—not merely to make travel arrangements for the Other Shore—and to interact with the living in a variety of ways. There were those lost souls who had committed grave sins while alive and fell into the realm of hungry ghosts after death, or wandered about graveyards. There were demon kings who found the meaning of their existence in wreaking vengeance upon a society they believed had wronged them. Conversely, there were spirits of those individuals who had willed themselves to become *kami* and remain in this world to protect their descendants.

In medieval times, the world was comprised of many varieties of the dead, in company with the living.

In the later middle ages, when the magnetic force of the other-worldly Pure Land became attenuated, it began to be believed that more ordinary individuals—in addition to the more special cases just mentioned—might also remain eternally in this world. *Hitogami* that did not fit cleanly into the vocabulary of *honji-suijaku* commenced playing prominent roles on the center stage of history.

For it happened to be an era in which the ideal world of the Other Shore was gradually losing its reality. The main concern of people with regard to the gods and buddhas was shifting from salvation after death to peace and security in this world. The emergence of the *hitogami* in this world had taken place against such a backdrop, but now their activities began to pull the focus back from an invisible realm after death and into this one. The profusion of *hitogami* began to erode, from within, the *honji-suijaku* paradigm and the dualistic worldview upon which it was premised, bringing about a fundamental transformation in that mode of thought. And so it was, in late medieval times, that large numbers of a new type of *hitogami* pushed through the rents in the fabric of *honji-suijaku* theory and sprang into vigorous activity on the stage provided by this world.

CHAPTER 7

The Ideology of Tōshō Daigongen

1. *Kami* in Competition

Religious uprisings

I N THE JAPANESE ISLANDS the Other Shore began to perceptibly recede from view during the late middle ages, from about the fourteenth century onward, as people began to seek a more fulfilling life in this world rather than salvation in the afterlife.

In the Nanbokuchō period (1334–1392), local communities called *sō* began to form throughout western Japan. During the earlier Heian and Kamakura periods, villages had been run by an oligarchy of the upper peasantry. In contrast, the *sō* created a system in which policy was determined through discussion by assemblies of almost all the constituent members of the community.

The establishment of these voluntary organizations of peasants fostered spiritual autonomy among the people. United in the *sō*, the peasants sought to enrich and secure their livelihoods by presenting estate proprietors with a variety of demands, including reductions in the annual taxes on production. The *sō* thus provided the infrastructure for the struggle mounted by peasants on the landed estates (*shōen*) to secure better rights and conditions. These so-called "estate revolts" (*shōke no ikki*), which started as economic struggles at the level of single villages or estates, began in the course of the fifteenth century to change in nature, involving tightly organized cooperation among a number of estates and villages for more explicitly political ends—marking the beginning of the era of full-scale peasant uprisings known as *tsuchi ikki*.

Meanwhile, in urban areas such as Kyoto the merchant class showed marked growth from the Nanbokuchō period onward. As a result, this imperial capital of antiquity was rapidly transformed into a new city of commerce. In the wake of the Ōnin War (1467–77), the powerful merchants known as *machishū* played a vital role in leading the restoration of the devastated city. Their solidarity, backed by the organized military force they developed, placed de facto rule over the city of Kyoto in their hands in the sixteenth century. In villages and cities, the people were developing broad-based organizations for self-rule and challenging the daimyo and shogunate with demands for reductions in taxes and other burdens.

Looking at society as a whole, the late medieval period was one in which images of the other world were gradually drained of their power. Yet at the same time, throughout the middle ages we continue to see forceful assertions of the objective reality of the other world, and the positing of specific buddhas as supreme or absolute beings. Hence the vein of religious thought we see in figures such as Shinran and Nichiren, who emphasized the *honjibutsu* as lords and saviors. This idea was widely accepted by the common people of the late medieval period, as their own power dramatically increased—and less as a basis for salvation after death than as a spiritual support for confronting secular authority. People used their belief in a direct connection with a vastly powerful personalized deity transcending this world as a source of strength and succor in their resistance to the ruling powers.[1]

We can see such beliefs strongly at work in the popular unrest of the fifteenth and sixteenth centuries—on the part of sectarian Buddhist groups such as the Hokke *ikki* and Ikkō *ikki*, or that of Japanese Christians. Uniting under a transcendental personified deity—Shakyamuni Buddha, Amida Buddha, or Deus (as the Christian God was known in Japan)—people sought equality, not in the next world or in the world of ideas, but in the real world, by ridding it of the rulers who oppressed them. This led to the creation of "domains of the *buddhadharma*" (*buppōryō*) by adherents of the Jōdo Shinshū (True Pure Land) sect in various areas in western Japan, and of the self-ruling zone known as the "domain of Lord Shakyamuni" (*Shakason goryō*) established by the *machishū* of Kyoto, many of them adherents of the Nichiren sect.[2]

Religious policies of the military unifiers

However, these leagues of religious adherents were confronted by the power of the great warlords such as Oda Nobunaga and Toyotomi Hideyoshi. The resulting conflict was horrific, frequently resulting in complete massacres. After fierce fighting, the Ikkō *ikki* were completely suppressed, the Christians extirpated. Even powerful temples such as Enryakuji and Kōfukuji had their domains confiscated and their legal exemptions stripped from them. Early in the Edo period (1600–1868), all religious forces were compelled to bend the knee to the newly unified secular authority. Religion capable of relativizing secular authority had been extinguished as a social force. The unified regime did not merely strip religious organizations of their secular power: it aimed at forcing them to submit in the realm of ideology. The classic example is the suppression of the Fuju Fuse branch of the Nichiren sect.

In Bunroku 4 (1595), Toyotomi Hideyoshi planned a vast religious ceremony at Hōkōji in the Higashiyama district of Kyoto, inviting a thousand monks from all the major sects to participate. The adherents of the Nichiren sect in Kyoto were deeply divided over how to respond. One of the leaders, Nichiō, advocated refusal. He argued that Nichiren had taken the Lotus Sutra as the one true faith and had rejected compromise with other sects; on these grounds, the proper stance for Nichiren believers was neither to receive (*fuju*) nor to give (*fuse*) offerings to adherents of other sects. Since Hideyoshi was not a follower of their sect, Nichiō argued, receiving offerings from him was wrong. Against this, Nichijū argued for compromise, saying that an exception should be made in the case of offerings from Hideyoshi, since he was the sovereign of the country (a position that came to be known as *ju fuse*, or "receiving but not giving").

We should not overlook that fact that the *fuju fuse* controversy within the Nichiren sect had to do with more than the overt issue of whether to accept offerings from the ruler of the country—there was a difference in worldviews underlying it. Nichijū and the others advocating the *ju fuse* position premised their argument on the idea that the sovereign was the highest authority in the land, so the very fact of living in this land was an acceptance of the sovereign's grace and offerings and thus the sovereign's will should be obeyed. Against this, Nichiō said, "This world of ours is, in its entirety, the domain of our lord Shakyamuni Buddha…. What ruler of a minor country can usurp the domain of Lord Shakyamuni?"[3] His position was that the ultimate possessor of sovereignty was none other than Shakyamuni Buddha as a supreme or absolute being, and that simply living in this land did not mean that one had accepted the offerings of its sovereign.

As a result of this debate, the various branches of the Nicheren sect divided into two factions. Those who accepted secular power, even as that power changed over the years, survived throughout the early modern period as the officially recognized Nichiren sect. On the other hand, the Fuju Fuse group, who insisted on the existence of a religious authority transcending all forms of secular power, was subjected to repeated persecutions and in Kanbun 5 (1665) was finally completely outlawed and forced underground.

The deification of Nobunaga and Hideyoshi

The unifiers were not satisfied simply to have the religious forces bow to their authority. The great warlords had seen firsthand the terrifying power of the Ikkō *ikki,* and in order to prevent the populace or enemy forces from using faith as an excuse to foment further rebellion and disorder, they took on the task of integrating religious authority into the structure of their rule, using it to legitimate their own rule. To achieve this, they sought to become gods in their own right.[4]

One can see the warlords' aspirations toward godhood in the case of Oda Nobunaga. A report sent by the Jesuit missionary Luis Fróis to the head of the Jesuit order on 5 November 1582 provides a detailed account of Nobunaga's efforts to sanctify himself.[5] According to this report, Nobunaga, who had already brought most of the country under his rule, "wished to be venerated, not as an ordinary mortal man, but as immortal, like a god." To this end, he had built a temple called Sōkenji atop a hill behind his castle at Azuchi, where he desired to have people worship him as "the divine presence" (*shintai*) and as a "living god or buddha."

People who worshipped there were guaranteed long life and riches, a peaceful and secure life, and heirs if they had none. Conversely, it was asserted that "evil non-believers will face ruin in both this world and the world to come." Other sources backing up this account of Nobunaga's efforts at self-deification are hard to come by. Reliable sources detailing a similar process of self-deification do, however, exist for Toyotomi Hideyoshi, who seized power in the struggle to succeed Nobunaga. Such deification was clearly an aspiration of his while still living, and the foundations for it were laid immediately after his death in Keichō 3 (1598). A central figure in the execution of this plan was Bonshun (1553–1632), a scion of the Yoshida family of Shintō priests.

Only a month after Hideyoshi's funeral, construction began on a mausoleum. The buildings were completed in a little more than half a year, and his spirit formally enshrined there. His name as a deity was originally supposed to have been "Shin ("New") Hachiman," but in the end he was called Toyokuni Daimyōjin.

The role of Yoshida Shinto

Behind the selection of the posthumous name Toyokuni Daimyōjin— contravening Hideyoshi's own expressed desires—was the influence of the Shintō thought developed by the Yoshida family from which Bonshun had emerged. We have already seen how Yoshida Kanetomo had attempted to position Shintō as the root of all other religions with a paradigm based on plant morphology (Chapter 5, section 3). Yoshida Shintō was in essence an effort to wrest the control of cosmological interpretation back from the monopoly of the Buddhists and restore it to practitioners of the native beliefs.

Figure 7-1 Hōkokusha (Toyokuni Shrine) in Kyoto, dedicated to Toyotomi Hideyoshi

But the Yoshida family also initiated another radical reform that would alter the function of Shintō in society, creating unique funeral rites in order to break the monopoly Buddhism also held over offerings to the dead.

Developments from the Ise Shintō of the Kamakura period (1185–1333) to Yoshida Shintō had stressed the uniqueness of faith in the native gods in contrast to Buddhism, but even the Shintō priests had been compelled to hand over services for the dead to the Buddhist clergy. For generations, even the heads of the Yoshida family had died chanting the *nenbutsu* and praying for rebirth in the Pure Land, and no one thought this unusual. Their corpses were then cremated and the ashes interred in a graveyard, or else transported to the necropolis of the great monastic complex at Kōyasan and buried there.

This all changed in the fifteenth century with Yoshida Kanetomo. The new custom was to bury the intact body in the earth, build a small shrine (*reisha*) over the grave site, and venerate the deceased as a *kami*. From Kanetomo onward, the head of each generation of the Yoshida family was enshrined in this way.[6] Concurrently, Buddhist clergy ceased to be invited to participate in the funerals of these Shintō priests, and the creation of Shintō funerary rites from which all Buddhist elements had been eliminated proceeded apace. By about fifty years after Kanetomo, during the late sixteenth-century headships of Kanemigi and Kanemi, a unique set of Shintō funerary rituals and customs had been perfected.

In this veneration of the dead with a *reisha* we can glimpse the tradition of thought discussed in the previous chapter of the divine being immanent in humans. This tradition lived on in the words of Yoshida Kaneo in the Edo period:

> What we call the divine is the indivisible primal energy of heaven and earth. In heaven it is the heavenly gods, on earth the earthly gods, in man the spirit, our hearts and minds.... The source of our birth is the source of heaven and earth; the source of our end is the source of heaven and earth. The duality of life and death is simply that when energy gathers together we have life; when it disperses there is death. If we but realize this, then there is no Pure Land, and there is no hell. There is only that which comes from the divine (*kami*) and returns to the divine (*kami*).

In this passage we see a borrowing of Neo-Confucian theory that interprets the cycle of human life and death in terms of the concentration and dispersal of divine energy. Death is not a point of departure for a journey to a Pure Land or to hell, but a return to the divine source. The cycle of life and death is grasped as something fully completed within this world of ordinary reality.

Bonshun was a son of Yoshida Kanemigi, and his motto was to escape from Buddhist influences. So it is only natural that he put up fierce resistance to the selection of a posthumous name for Hideyoshi—Hachiman Daibosatsu—that would have had such a strongly Buddhist flavor in the minds of the populace.

2. The Deified Ieyasu

Myōjin or Gongen?

Tokugawa Ieyasu, who successfully weathered the civil strife that followed the death of Hideyoshi and unified Japan under his own rule, ended his seventy-five years of life in the fourth month of Genna 2 (1616) at the castle in Sunpu (present-day Shizuoka) to which he had retired. Before he passed away, Ieyasu is said to have left a will with instructions to inter his remains at Kunōsan, a mountain on the outskirts of Sunpu, and then, after the first anniversary of his death had passed, to build "a small hall" at Nikkō to enshrine his spirit. In this same document Ieyasu expressed his intent to become "a guardian of the eight provinces" (*hasshū no chinju*) of the Kantō region.[7]

The precedent had already been set by Hideyoshi, and since Ieyasu had left such explicit instructions for his veneration as a deified spirit, the process began immediately after his death. Once again, the figure playing a central role in making the arrangements for this was Bonshun. As per his will, Ieyasu's remains were buried at Kunōsan, and preparations made for the ritual of his deification as a *daimyōjin* according to the practices of Yoshida Shintō, in what appeared to have been a prearranged plan.

But problems arose. Another close advisor of Ieyasu, the Tendai priest Tenkai, expressed opposition, and wanted Ieyasu deified as a *gongen* in the traditions of Sannō Ichijitsu, a branch of Shintō that developed within and was closely associated with the Tendai sect of Buddhism. A debate ensued, argued before Ieyasu's successor as shogun, Hidetada, which pitted Tenkai against Bonshun and Sūden (another longtime advisor of Ieyasu).

In the end, it was Tenkai's plan that was adopted. The intention to deify Ieyasu as a *gongen* was officially presented to the imperial court, and the court responded with the emperor's approval of the action and a suggestion of four different possibilities for Ieyasu's posthumous name: Tōshō (Illuminating the East), Hinomoto (The Origin of the Sun), Iryō (Powerful Spirit), and Tōkō (Light of the East). Hidetada selected Tōshō Daigongen (Great Avatar Illuminating the East). In the fourth month of the following year, after the first anniversary of his passing, Ieyasu's spirit (and his physical remains) were officially transferred to the newly constructed Tōshōgū at Nikkō and enshrined there—creating a new sacred site for the Tokugawa shogunate.

Figure 7-2 The Mausoleum of Tokugawa Ieyasu at the Tōshōgū in Nikkō

The new nature of Ieyasu as avatar

But why was Ieyasu deified as a *gongen*, or avatar? What was the rationale behind choosing such an explicitly Buddhist designation? *Gongen* meant the "temporary manifestation" of a primal, original, or source buddha (*honjibutsu*), an idea grounded in the *honji-suijaku* paradigm. And in fact the source buddha for Tōshō Daigongen was posited to be Yakushi Nyorai, the buddha of medicine or healing, and an image of Yakushi was enshrined in the Honjidō hall at Nikkō. This was in marked contrast to the case of Hideyoshi, in which a concerted effort had been made to expunge Buddhist influences. But was it really a reversion to the *honji-suijaku* paradigm of the middle ages?

An excellent source for understanding how Tōshō Daigongen was conceived at the time is the *Tōshōsha engi* (Origins of the Tōshō Shrine), compiled during the time of the third shogun, Iemitsu. Two different versions of this text exist: the so-called *mana* version, written in a form of classical Chinese, and the *kana* version, written in a more vernacular Japanese style.

One of the first things that strikes one on reading these texts is that discussion of the deities focuses almost exclusively upon Sannōshin, protector deity of the Tendai sect, and upon Tōshō Daigongen, with virtually no explanation of Yakushi Nyorai as the *honjibutsu* of both of these deities. In medieval *honji-suijaku* theory the role of ultimate savior was performed by the *honjibutsu*. The *suijaku* performed an important role as the point of direct contact with the sentient beings of this world, leading them toward the *honji*, but the central existence in the realm of all the gods and buddhas was the otherworldly *honjibutsu*. However, while these texts describe at length the great powers of the *suijaku*, Tōshō Daigongen, they do not touch on the meaning or significance of his *honjibutsu*.

Scroll 1 of the *mana* version, believed to have been written first, contains a scene in which Ieyasu asks a Tendai priest, "In the Shintō of Sannō Daigongen, how is *honji-suijaku* understood?" He receives a rather uninformative reply, in which the nature of *honji-suijaku* is left completely unexplicated: "Sannō Shintō does not posit *sōgen* [identity], nor *honjaku engi* [relationship of origin and manifestation], nor yet *ryōbu shūgō* [a merging of Shintō and Buddhism]; even as a priest this is something I cannot simply and easily explain."

In contrast, what is discussed in considerable detail is a method of "ruling the country and benefiting the people" (*chikoku rimin*) supposedly transmitted in the lineage of Sannō Shintō. Grounded in the perspective of the Tendai sect of Buddhism—*zokutai jōjū*, that this world itself is the eternal Pure Land—the principal elements of this teaching were to support the law of the sovereign (*ōhō*) in order to achieve a peacefully governed realm and "prosperity and longevity of family and lineage." This, the *mana* version of the *Tōshōsha engi* asserted, was the desire of Tōshō Daigongen.

Here, Sannō Gongen and Tōshō Daigongen are completely liberated from the role assigned the medieval *suijaku*, that of intermediaries between this world and the other world. Their principal duties have become preserving the peace of this world and the stability of the state—not providing salvation after death.[8]

The changing *honji-suijaku* paradigm

We noted that while the *Tōshōsha engi* posits Tōshō Daigongen as a *suijaku* according to *honji-suijaku* theory, scarcely any interest is shown in the *honji* of which he is a manifestation, nor in the reasons or process behind that manifestation. This silence regarding the *honjibutsu* stands in marked contrast to the vivid and concrete terms in which the role of this *suijaku* is depicted. The *honjibutsu* seems to fill no defined function or have any raison d'être other than to stand behind the *suijaku* as a kind of higher-order aura of sacredness.

Another aspect of the *honji-suijaku* paradigm as presented in the *Tōshōsha engi* is that, in contrast to the invisible and otherworldly *honjibutsu* of medieval times, here the *honjibutsu* is presented in strictly this-worldly terms. In the *mana* version, the most detailed reference to the *honjibutsu* is contained in a passage describing the Honjidō hall: "The *honjibutsu* Yakushi Nyorai, in the form of its marvelous and brilliant enlightenment, here newly displays the glorious features of the buddha." This is followed by a passage describing the specific iconographic details of the enshrined image of Yakushi. In the *kana* version of the text, Yakushi Nyorai appears in a passage in which the parents of Ieyasu make a pilgrimage to an image of Yakushi at Hōraiji temple to pray to be blessed with an heir—a supplication that is fulfilled by the birth of Ieyasu. There is more than a hint here of Ieyasu being a rebirth of Yakushi Nyorai.

In both cases, the *honjibutsu* is an image enshrined in a temple. This is not the medieval concept of the image as a *suijaku*, behind which lay the original, primal world of enlightenment. Here *honji-suijaku* does not function as a paradigm vertically uniting worlds existing in two completely different dimensions; it has become a connection completed entirely within this world. This use of the *honji-suijaku* paradigm to horizontally connect two items or points within this world—Buddhist images and Japanese gods, or India and Japan—is typical of its functionality in early modern Japan.

So the *honji-suijaku* paradigm itself might persist, but in the *Tōshōsha engi* it should be understood as having a completely different import. One reason might be the cosmological shift that took place in late medieval times—the fading reality of the other world versus the rising significance of this-worldly concerns. This alteration in worldview—the basic operating system software governing people's cognitive circuitry—converted the function of the *honji-suijaku* application software running on it into something completely different.

Kami as defenders of morality

The historical documents related to Tokugawa Ieyasu offer another example of how the medieval *honji-suijaku* paradigm had been transformed. Ieyasu issued the following pronouncement regarding the prohibition of Christianity:

> Our country has always been the Divine Land (*shinkoku*). From the beginning it has revered the gods (*kami*) and venerated the buddhas. The buddhas and gods, united through manifestation (*suijaku*), do not differ. In affirming the way of loyalty and propriety between lord and subject, and in sealing enduring pledges of vassalage or alliance, everyone swears oaths to the gods as evidence of their good faith and trust.[9]

In its equivalence of gods and buddhas this text employs a logic reminiscent of the *honji-suijaku* paradigm. Hence, at first glance it would seem virtually indistinguishable from medieval ideas of Japan as the divine land or land of the gods. However, the *suijaku* that unite the gods and buddhas are not perceived here in terms of their role in linking the other world of the Pure Land with this world. Rather, the *kami* are seen as providing a foundation for what is essentially a Confucian ethic of loyalty and proper relations between sovereign and subject.

The concept of the remote other world that consistently underlay medieval ideas of *honji-suijaku* and the divine land has completely disappeared. Replacing it are the present world of everyday life and the Confucian ethics that attempt to order it. In this text as well, *honji-suijaku* does not denote a vertical relationship linking this world with the other world, but instead a shift toward a horizontal relationship between gods and buddhas unfolding on the stage provided by this world.

Although the deifications of Hideyoshi as Toyokuni Daimyōjin and of Ieyasu as Tōshō Daigongen initially appear to have followed diametrically opposed paths, they actually have certain aspects in common — and not merely that they were efforts to sanctify a powerful ruler. In both cases, we see similar deviations from the medieval *honji-suijaku* paradigm—a logic that has slipped the bonds of the spiritual universe of the late middle ages and permitted these *hitogami* a freedom and vitality of action unconstrained by the earlier *honji-suijaku* framework.

Such an emphasis on the gods and buddhas as upholders of the secular order is widely observable in the early modern period. Sūden's *Hai Kirishitan bun* (A Rejection of Christianity), written in Keichō 18 (1613), states that Japan is "the land of gods and manifestations of buddhas (*shinmei ōjaku no kuni*), the homeland of Dainichi Buddha," once again employing *honji-suijaku* reasoning to affirm the unity of the Japanese gods with the buddhas. Then the text continues with a passage that assigns these gods and buddhas the role of overseers of morality: "Japan is a land of gods, a land of buddhas; it reveres the gods and venerates the buddhas; it is committed to the path of benevolence and righteousness and judges good from evil."

Similarly, the eighteenth-century Jōdo sect priest Daiga writes in his treatise *San'ikun* (Three Immortal Teachings):

The buddhas, gods, and sages in their profound and sacred wisdom took pity on the turmoil [of this world] and appeared in the Three Countries [India, China, and Japan] to spread their teachings for myriad generations so that people might by that means free themselves from delusion. Because of this, the Three Teachings [Buddhism, Confucianism, and Shintō] may differ in the paths they take, but they all arrive in the same place, which is to encourage good, chastise evil, and rectify the hearts and minds of the people.

In medieval theory, Shakyamuni in India, Confucius in China, and the *kami* of Japan were all saviors dispatched to this world by the primal or cosmic Buddha, and thus the fundamental mission of Buddhism, Confucianism, and Shintō was in fact to escort humanity to the Other Shore and connect them with this *honjibutsu* that was the ultimate reality. Here, however, this soteriological mission has been lost, replaced by the extremely secular goal of "rectifying the hearts and minds of the people."

3. Secular Rulers Aspire to Godhead

The ideology of the mausoleum

As aspirations for rebirth into the ideal world of the Other Shore receded in popular consciousness, the *hitogami* were released from their obligation to escort sentient beings to it and liberated from the yoke of serving as avatars and saviors. The result was a dramatic expansion in their existential ground and range of activity. Moreover, the late middle ages was an era in which the divinity inherent within all human beings was widely preached. The *hitogami* were no longer beings fundamentally different in nature from the common run of humanity.

The deification of Hideyoshi and Ieyasu also heralded a new era for the *hitogami*. From this time onward, there was a rapid increase in the number of figures who held important positions of secular power during their lifetimes and who were venerated as *kami* after their deaths. Central to this process were a number of the daimyo of the more important domains under the hegemony of the Tokugawa shogunate.

The earthly remains of Uesugi Kenshin, for instance, who passed away at Kasugayama castle in Echigo in Tenshō 6 (1578), were initially interred at a gravesite within the castle walls. Later, as the Uesugi family was transferred from one domain to another, Kenshin's remains accompanied them until arriving at a final resting place in Yonezawa castle. In Keichō 17 (1612), a mausoleum was constructed, with Kenshin's remains flanked by images of Bishamonten and Zenkōji temple's Amida Triad. In the Meiji era (1868–1912) the mausoleum was withdrawn from the management of the family's ancestral temple and became the Uesugi Shrine.

Another of the great daimyo, Date Masamune, rode out the vicissitudes of the Sengoku period, dying in Kan'ei 13 (1636). Before his death, Masamune instructed that his remains be interred atop Kyōgamine, a hill in Sendai regarded as a sacred place since medieval times. The following year his successor Date Tadamune built a mausoleum for him at that site called the Zuihōden, and at the foot of Kyōgamine a temple named Zuihōji was built to serve as the Date family temple. Kyōgamine became the site of mausolea built for successive generations of the heads of the Date family. From earlier times Kyōgamine, as the name implies, was the site of a sutra mound (*kyōzuka*), and also a place where memorial tablets for the dead (*itabi*) were erected. In the middle ages it had been regarded as a kind of portal between this world and the other world. So it was that Date Masamune chose the highest point of this sacred site as the place for his own remains to be interred and venerated.

In the early Edo period, when the daimyo of powerful domains passed away, mausolea were constructed for them similar to the Zui-hōden (and all ultimately modeled on Ieyasu's Tōshōgū at Nikko). These were something considerably more than simple gravesites— in each domain they were accorded special religious significance as sacred places. The main hall of the Zuihōden, built over the grave in which Masamune's remains were interred, enshrined a portrait image of him, before which were constructed a worship hall (*haiden*) and a Nehanmon ("Nirvana Gate"). All of this clearly indicates that the Zui-hōden was built from the beginning with the intention of worshipping Masamune's spirit. During the Edo period, the central pilgrimage path

Figure 7-3 The Zuihōden in Sendai. The Nirvana Gate stands at left.

to the Okunoin at Kōyasan became lined with mausolea of daimyo from domains all over the country. Among them were examples, such as that of Yūki Hideyasu, built in the style of a Shintō shrine, complete with *torii* (fig. 9-1), in which we may detect the intention to worship the spirit of the deceased as a *kami*.[10]

Much earlier, the three generations of Ōshū Fujiwara at Hiraizumi and Minamoto no Yoritomo in Kamakura had been buried in sites in the hills overlooking the cities they had built, watching over them as guardian deities. In the Edo period, the daimyo of each domain took on this role. But in contrast to their medieval predecessors, the spirits of the daimyo of early modern times were absolved of the additional mission of escorting people to the distant Pure Land. Like Tōshō Dai-gongen, they were indisputably deities of this world.

The *ikigami* cults and Suika Shintō

Along with a significant increase in the number of personages who through force of will arranged to be worshipped as gods, the Edo period also witnessed the proliferation of *ikigami*, or "living gods." The efforts we have described to deify powerful lords from Hideyoshi onward were all undertaken after the deaths of the individuals involved. In contrast, as the name implies, the *ikigami* were specific individuals venerated as gods while still alive.

The prototype for this type of *hitogami* was the reverencing of the emperors in ancient times as *akitsukami* (manifest or living gods). But it is questionable whether such beliefs ever were widely shared by the general society beyond the confines of the imperial court. There were also isolated examples in medieval times of important Buddhist cler-ics venerated as "living buddhas" and Shintō priests revered as *kami* while still living, but in fact the worship of a living person as a deity was still quite rare. An episode in the *Tengu zōshi*—a latethirteenth-century picture scroll caricaturing conceited and corrupt monks at large temples of various sects—does depict followers of the Pure Land teacher Ippen Shōnin drinking their leader's urine as "a medicine to cure all ills," but this is clearly a satirical mockery of their fanaticism. It was not until early modern times that the worship of living individuals—and laymen rather than religious figures—became a socially acceptable practice.

As far as the early modern period is concerned, the first example we should give of deification is that of Yamazaki Ansai (1619–82), a Neo-Confucian scholar who was also the founder of Suika Shintō. Ansai is said to have, while still living, imbued a sacred mirror with his own living spirit, and then had it enshrined and worshipped under an inscription that read "Suika Jinja" (Suika Shrine). This was approved and the name of the shrine was officially bestowed by Yoshikawa Koretari, head of the Yoshida sect of Shintō. Yoshida Shintō had played a significant background role in the early modern *hitogami* worship of Toyokuni Daimyōjin (Hideyoshi) and similar figures, and we see it here as well.

Koretari also bestowed a title of divinity, Hanitsu Reijin, upon the daimyo of Aizu domain, Hoshina Masayuki, who in Kanbun 12 (1672), the year of his death, had designated a gravesite for himself in the foothills of Mount Bandai. Scarcely a year passed before his mausoleum was elevated to the status of a shrine, Hanitsu Reisha, and Hoshina's spirit venerated there. From the middle of the early modern period onward, there were many cases in which daimyo houses applied to the Yoshida or Shirakawa families of Kyoto to have their founders and ancestors given such *shingō*, or titles of divinity.[11]

Matsudaira Sadanobu (1759–1829), who served as a senior councillor (*rōjū*) of the Tokugawa shogunate, believed that through practicing perfect fidelity (*shisei*) a person could become a god—and saw himself as no exception. Based on this notion, he had a wooden image of himself carved while he was still alive, and enshrined in a hall called the Kan'ōden in the secondary residence of his domain in the Tsukiji district of Edo. In addition, he applied to the Yoshida family for the *shingō* Shukoku Daimyōjin (Great Deity Protector of the Nation), and worshipped himself under this title. According to scholar of Shintō studies Katō Genchi (1873–1965), we may find numerous other examples of *seishi*—the veneration of living individuals as *kami*—during the early modern period. This practice also extended to a number of emperors of the era, such as Emperor Reigen and Emperor Sakuramachi.[12]

Hitogami beliefs and cult deities

In contrast to the cases discussed so far, in which deification was given the imprimatur of orthodoxy by the Shintō establishment, there were also examples in which a popular movement raised certain individuals to the status of gods. The classic example here is cult worship of the emperors.

In Tenmei 7 (1787), in the midst of a terrible famine, the imperial palace in Kyoto became the focus of a popular movement called *sendo mairi*. This consisted of multiple circumambulations of the earthen embankments enclosing the palace, accompanied by prayer and worship. The number of participants soon rose to at least ten thousand. Prayers were offered before the Nanmon and Karamon gates, where people tossed offerings of coins wrapped in paper upon which were written supplications for stabilization of the price of rice, for example. Considerable sums of money were thrown into the palace grounds in this manner.[13]

In the Edo period, the emperors had lost any real political authority or power, and their most important remaining public responsibility was religious—their principal role was to worship the gods. The *sendo mairi* were not purely religious in motivation, but it is indisputable that they were grounded in a common perception of the emperor as a sacred being. And contributing to this perception was the image of the emperors as being immersed in the ritual veneration of the *kami*.

Another *ikigami* example I would like to cite here is the cult of the "cat-picture daimyo" (*neko-e tonosama*). The heads of the Iwamatsu house, lords of a minor domain in the Nitta district of Kōzuke province, became renowned for the efficacy of their drawings of cats in driving away mice and rats, the mortal enemy of the silkworm-cultivating farmers of his region. As a result, the drawings were in much demand and produced in great number; they were venerated by the people as *kaiko no kamisama*, or protector gods of the silkworms. In the late Edo period this faith in the religious power of the lords of the Iwamatsu domain became even more fervent, and protective talismans from their hand—against smallpox and other epidemic diseases, as well as fox possession—were greatly sought after.[14]

It was not at all uncommon for the lord of a domain to be venerated as a god in early modern times. *Tōyūki*, a record of travels in eastern Japan by medical doctor Tachibana Nankei beginning in Tenmei 5 (1785), notes that almost every private home in the Echizen region had a protective amulet pasted on the facade reading "Hosokawa Etchū no Kami"—Hosokawa, Governor of Echizen. The personage being supplicated here was Hosokawa Shigekata, daimyo of the Kumamoto domain in Kyushu in the south of Japan, who had passed away that year. His name was being used as a protective device by the common people in this remote north of Japan. Shigekata was renowned as an enlightened ruler, and even before his death had been venerated with a festival by the people of his domain.

Neither the emperors, nor the heads of the Iwamatsu family, nor Hosokawa Shigekata had been particularly conscious of themselves as religious figures. Even the emperors, who were deeply involved in ritual observance, saw their role as that of worshipping the gods. Although a few emperors had themselves venerated as *seishi*, the majority did not engage in such self-aggrandizing behavior. However, despite this and regardless of their own intentions, they were looked to and venerated by those surrounding them as special beings who might act to resolve a variety of real-world problems.

In this sort of deification process, it is perhaps possible to see a spiritual formation unique to the people of the early modern period, who sought to create—using whatever materials came immediately to hand—divinities who could grant their wishes and desires.

Ruling power and the gods and buddhas

With the internalization of divinity that took place during the middle ages, the gap between ordinary people and deities shrank dramatically. However, especially during early medieval times, when the world of the Other Shore held such overwhelming reality, the *kami* of this world were unable to transcend their role as intermediaries. The *hitogami* did not shine with their own internal light; they merely reflected the radiance of the primordial deities of the other world. And since divinity in the form of *suijaku* was still fundamentally salvific in nature, the gap remained between the saviors and those in need of salvation—the people.

After the transition from the late middle ages, in the early modern period the world of the Other Shore began to recede from view, losing its potency and existential significance. Moreover, an age had arrived in which it was thought that all people carried the sacred within them. Having lost the backing of the other world, there was no longer any decisive line of demarcation between the *hitogami* and ordinary mortals. This intellectual landscape prepared the way for the full-scale adoption of Song Neo-Confucian thought, which taught that all human beings were endowed with a nature that was fundamentally good, and that any person could potentially become a sage, given sufficient study and application. This in turn further narrowed the gap between human and divine, and so it was that in the Edo period the world was overrun with gods on an essentially human scale.

In early modern times, the other world had shrunk, and the commonly accepted vision of all being embraced in the bosom of a primal, cosmic divinity evaporated. It was no longer possible for a specific religion with a unified epistemology to monopolize the spiritual world. Tōshō Daigongen (the deified Tokugawa Ieyasu), or the emperors as living gods, were also incapable of dominating the contemporary religious landscape in the way that the *honjibutsu* of the other world had in medieval times. In the end, they could not overcome being simply one among the plethora of gods and buddhas abiding in these islands.

In the end, this is what led to the sacralization of the ruling power during the Edo period: not so much ideology in the narrow sense—the concept of a divine ruler or the teachings of Confucianism, for example—as a vast array of ritual, ceremony, and symbol that gave visible manifestation to the power and glory of the shoguns.[15] At the apex of the hierarchy was neither a god nor a buddha, but the emperor as dispenser of official rank and title, including the title of *shōgun*. Thus, in the late Edo period, when a sense of crisis arose over the threat of foreign incursion and the country began to grope toward a unified nation-state transcending the divisions among the traditional domains, there was really no option other than the emperor as the keystone of a new national polity. As this new nation-state came into being from the late Edo into the Meiji period, it was inevitable that the emperor should once again come to the forefront as a uniquely Japanese existence with a tradition stretching back to the Age of the Gods.

CHAPTER 8

The Heyday of Living Gods

1. The Deification of Ordinary People

The transformation of human sacrifice

I N THE EARLY MODERN PERIOD, gods were not born solely out of the ruling class of emperors, shoguns, and daimyo—individuals who managed to become deities through the force of their own will began to emerge from diverse social strata.

The following is a paraphrase of an account in traveler and botanist Sugae Masumi's (1754–1829) *Tsugaro no ochi* of the origins of a deity local to the Tsugaru region of northern Japan:

Near Sakaimatsu on the outskirts of the town of Kuroishi is a village called Sekihachi because a system of dikes (*seki*) splits the river there into eight (*hachi*) streams. The dikes were not terribly effective because the swift currents of the river kept washing them away. But an individual named Sekihachi Tarōzaemon came forward to offer himself as a human sacrifice (*hitobashira*). In Keichō 14 (1609), after praying to the gods of heaven and earth for success in controlling the raging waters, he lay down where one of the stakes for rebuilding the dikes was to be driven, placed its point on his own abdomen, and demanded it be driven into the ground. It ran him through, and he was buried beneath the dike.

Construction was subsequently completed without a hitch, providing irrigation for about a thousand *chō* of paddy fields. From that time forward, Tarōzaemon's spirit was venerated as a god, known as Sekihachi Myōjin or Fukuda ("Field of Happiness") no Kami.

The practice of offering a human sacrifice as part of a major construction project is something seen in Japan since ancient times. The *Nihon shoki* records an incident from the seventh year (319) of the reign of Emperor Nintoku, relating that in conjunction with the construction of a dike at Manta, the river god appeared to the emperor in a dream and demanded the sacrifice of two specific individuals—a man named Kowakubi and another known as Manta no Muraji Koromonoko. Kowakubi wept and wailed but entered the water as a sacrifice, and so the dike was successfully completed; by a clever subterfuge Koromonoko was able to save himself.

And the medieval *Shintōshū*, a collection of legends and anecdotes about Shintō shrines, contains the story of the Lady of the Bridge (Hashihime) of Nagarabashi in Settsu province. The official in charge of its construction was at wit's end after several attempts to build it had ended in collapse. His solution was to seize a man, a woman who appeared to be his wife, and their small child, and make them into sacrifices for his bridge. The people had pity on the woman in particular, and constructed a shrine where they worshiped her spirit as Hashihime Myōjin.

In the *Nihon shoki* incident above it is the river god who demands the offering of specific individuals to be given in return for successful completion of the construction. The individuals involved were not volunteers, and neither the one who lost his life nor the one who survived were later venerated as deities. Also seen in the story of Yamata no Orochi (the Eight-Forked Serpent), this pattern of human sacrifices being offered at the demand of a *kami* is common in ancient lore. And while the Lady of the Bridge in the *Shintōshū* is later venerated as a deity, this was clearly not what she herself had in mind.

In contrast, Sekihachi Tarōzaemon gave his life of his own volition, moved by the suffering of the people he saw around him, not the
demand of some god. His motivation was not service to the gods but
devotion to his fellows, and it is this which led him to be deified by the
people of his region.

So while the content of these three stories all has to do with human
sacrifice, their structure is antithetical. Tarōzaemon gave his life to
resolve a worldly problem and was later celebrated as a deity—without
the agency or involvement of any transcendental otherworldly being—
by the people grateful for the benefits they enjoyed as a result of his
sacrifice. In this we can see a distinctive characteristic of the *hitogami*
beliefs of early modern times.

In the seventeenth century, Sakura Sōgorō was a village headman
who made a direct appeal to the shogun on behalf of his people and
paid for it with his life. His case is typical of the legends of *gimin*, or
"righteous men"—frequently leaders of peasant protests or uprisings
who were put to death for their actions—that sprang up in in every
region of the country during the early modern period. Such tales were
gradually embellished and their protagonists elevated into local deities
in a deification of ordinary individuals resembling that of the human
sacrifices mentioned above. These rebel leaders were reborn as gods
in this world as a result of the sacrifice of their own lives for the good
of others.

The cult of *sokushinbutsu*

A similar process of deification may be seen in the cult of *sokushinbutsu*
—ascetics who had themselves buried alive in order to enter nirvana as
"buddhas in this very body"—that gained popularity in the early modern period. Even today, the mummified remains of these *sokushinbutsu*
are to be found in various temples in the area surrounding the sacred
peak of Yudonosan in Yamagata Prefecture, where they continue to be
venerated by believers. The temples in which these *sokushinbutsu* are
enshrined preserve an oral tradition of their life and practices.

The first of the Yudonosan *sokushinbutsu* was Honmyōkai Shōnin,
enshrined at Honmyōji temple in Asahimura. Originally a lower

Figure 8-1 The site where Honmyōkai Shōnin is said to have entered nirvana

samurai named Togashi Kichibei, he became a fervent adherent of the
Yudono sect of Shugendō (a form of mountain asceticism featuring a
syncretic blend of esoteric Buddhism, Shintō, and Daoist practices). At
the age of forty he left lay life at Chūrenji monastery, after which he
engaged in ascetic practices at a place called Senninzawa ("Swamp of
the Immortals"). In Tenna 3 (1683), he left a will in which he vowed
to "become a buddha in this very body" to fulfill the prayers of the
people, and after giving instructions to exhume him three years later,
he entered nirvana in an underground chamber. Next was Chūkai
Shōnin, enshrined at Kaikōji in the city of Sakata. He was also a member of the Togashi family (Honmyōkai was his uncle). After two years
of ascetic practices at Senninzawa (including a rigorous fast known as
mokujiki involving abstention from all cereals), in Hōreki 5 (1755) he,
too, had himself buried alive and so entered nirvana.[1]

Another *sokushinbutsu*, Shinnyokai Shōnin, enshrined at Dainichibō temple, entered nirvana in Tenmei 3 (1783). In the eighth
month of that year, after a thousand-day *mokujiki* fast commenced in

Tenmei 1 (1780), he had himself buried alive on Dainichizan, a hill located about two kilometers from Dainichibō, where he awaited his entry into nirvana while ringing a bell and reciting sutras.

The years that Chūkai Shōnin and Shinnyokai Shōnin entered nirvana—1755 and 1783—were in the midst of the Hōreki and Tenmei famines, respectively. The Tenmei famine in particular is remembered as the very worst of the four great famines of the Edo period (1600–1868). Nor were these two the only *sokushinbutsu* who entered nirvana in famine years. Having noted this, folklorist Naitō Masatoshi writes, "The fundamental philosophy of the *mokujiki* fasts performed by the Yudonosan ascetics would appear to have been to starve their own bodies as a form of prayer and supplication on behalf of the many people starving in the famines."[2] Naitō sees the *sokushinbutsu* as a form of messianic thought passed down through Japanese folk beliefs.

The majority of the mummified buddhas of Yudonosan had come from the lower samurai or peasant classes. As a culmination of severe ascetic practices, they ended their lives by ceasing to take nourishment. Here, too, we see ordinary people giving their lives in supplication for the well-being of others, and their elevation into *kami* by people grateful for their sacrifice.

The rapid rise and fall of popular gods

The early modern period was characterized by people who became celebrated as deities in return for the sacrifice of their own lives out of compassion for the disasters and tragedies visited upon others. On the other hand, there were also large numbers of *hitogami* with much more limited functions and modest aspirations, working to resolve a host of less dramatic problems of everyday life.

The grave of Honda Tadatomo on the grounds of Isshinji temple in the Tennōji ward of Osaka (fig. 8-2), for instance, became a mecca for individuals vowing to quit drinking and families attempting to recover from the ravages of alcoholism. Tadatomo was the second son of Honda Tadakatsu, a trusted vassal of the Tokugawa family, and fought ably in the battle of Sekigahara in 1600, but during the 1614 winter campaign against Osaka Castle he disgraced himself with blunders

Figure 8-2 The grave of Honda Tadatomo (Isshinji, Osaka)

resulting from his excessive drinking. To restore his good name he fought fiercely in the summer campaign of 1615 and was killed in action. His dying words were a vow to come to the aid of anyone who was ruining their life because of drink, and he became known as "the god of temperance."

This is only one of an extremely large number of similar cases in which a person who suffered from a particular problem became celebrated after death as a deity who could help others in overcoming the same difficulty. All over the country, *hitogami* were believed efficacious against a variety of afflictions, from headaches and toothaches to hemorrhoids and eye diseases.

Beside the front gate of the Edo residence of the Tokugawa vassal Ogawa Shigesaburō in Ushigome Hayamizu Bansho was a small shrine believed especially efficacious against coughs and phlegm, and people whose symptoms were relieved by praying at the shrine had a custom of donating sacks of beans to it. According to *Mimibukuro*, a collection of essays by Edo city magistrate Negishi Shizumori (1737–1815), this custom dated to around the end of the Hōreki era (1751–64), when a retainer of the Ogawa family named Yamada Kōzaemon and his wife Oshimo both died after having suffered from phlegm for many years, vowing that "after our deaths, if anyone suffering from phlegm will simply remember us, we pledge to help them heal." The couple were then enshrined as Sōkō Daimyōjin (taking the initial Chinese character of each of their names), and attracted many local worshippers.[3]

In addition to cases such as these, based on vows made while the individuals were still living, we can see many other examples in early modern society of people celebrated as deities after their deaths in ways unforeseen during their lifetimes. For example, in Bunka 2 (1805) the infamous burglar Oniazami Seikichi was captured and executed in Edo. His remains were interred at Enjōji temple in Asakusa, and his grave soon became a popular pilgrimage site, to the point that by the end of the Edo period, a banner was placed there reading "Seikichi Daimyōjin." The remains of Seikichi Daimyōjin were eventually transferred to the cemetery in Zōshigaya, where to this day throngs of eager students pray at his grave for success in passing their entrance examinations. Nezumi Kozō ("Little Mouse") Jirokichi was another infamous thief who was worshipped as a god after his death. In other cases the spirits of drowned men cast up on shore were venerated as deities bringing good fortune.

The folklorist Miyata Noboru dubbed these new deities—arising one after another in response to the needs of the people and often just as quickly disappearing—hayarigami, or "faddish gods," and sees in them an ethos peculiar to the townspeople of Edo, who were able "to freely create gods and buddhas with a direct connection to the realities of their daily lives, and just as freely to believe in them, no matter what the shogunate might have to say in the matter."[4] Thus early modern society was one in which anyone might become a deity, given the right circumstances. And many people—regardless of their social status—both aspired to deification and achieved it. It was an age in which countless minor gods proliferated without the backing of any transcendent other world.

The mountains—abode of the ancestors

One of the first things that may come to mind when this proliferation of *hitogami* is mentioned is Yanagita Kunio's assertion that in Japan, after a certain period of time has passed, the spirits of all our ancestors become *kami*. The words of Yanagita quoted at the beginning of this book—that it "was an enduring custom of the Japanese people to take ones who once lived among us…. and enshrine them as deities to be celebrated, reverenced, and prayed to"—well express his thoughts on how the Japanese people perceive their ancestors.[5]

In his view, the Japanese people never really embraced the idea of the dead setting off on a journey to a remote and inaccessible world. Instead, the spirits of the dead lingered in the peaks of the mountains and hills overlooking our villages and, when invited for periodic festivals such as the midsummer festival of Obon and the spring and autumn equinoxes, would temporarily descend to commune with their surviving family members. The ordinary people of Japan thus shared a completely different concept of the other world from the Buddhist cosmology of myriads of Pure Lands located at an infinite distance from our own world.

Yet even in Japan, with the passage of a certain amount of time after death, the connection between the dead and the living underwent a significant change. In this same essay, Yanagita posits a temporal divide at the thirty-third year after death, when it is customary in many parts of Japan for the last Buddhist service for the deceased to be conducted, after which the deceased is thought to have become an "ancestor" or a "god." Moreover, "after a certain period of time has passed, the ancestral spirit is perceived as abandoning individuality to merge with a collective unity," he writes, at which point our ancestors "become an eternal ancestral god who protects the family and the land of our nation, or so it would seem the people of old once thought."

This assertion by Yanagita—that traditionally the Japanese have believed that the ancestors are eventually transformed into *kami*—has been enormously influential down to the present day, in both the field of folklore studies and beyond. However, as we have seen, the custom of venerating the ancestors as gods has not actually been "an enduring custom of the Japanese people." That would be impossible without (1) common acceptance of the dead residing eternally in this land, and (2) the establishment of an *ie*, or family system that would serve to remember and periodically offer memorial rites for the dead. Another important condition for the deification of the ancestors would be widespread acceptance of the notion of continuity between the human and the divine.

The concept of ancestors becoming *kami* did not actually become widely established in Japanese society until these conditions were fully met during the Edo period—and the latter half of the Edo period at that. This also happens to be the period in which the dead came to be referred to in everyday speech as *hotoke*, or "buddhas."

2. Changing Aspects of Pilgrimage

From avatars to magical buddhas

Behind the alteration in the nature of the *hitogami* that accompanied the transition from medieval to early modern times lay a change in the role people expected gods to play, which was in turn expressed by a shift in their forms of religious belief and practice. The mainstream of *hitogami* beliefs in the early medieval period had conceived of specific individuals as avatars or manifestations (*suijaku*) of otherworldly buddhas, positing their role as that of intermediaries between the sentient beings of this world and the buddhas of the Pure Land. In contrast to this, the leaders of so-called Kamakura Buddhism such as Shinran and Nichiren rejected *suijaku* and other mediation, pursuing instead a soteriological program that would connect ordinary people directly with the buddhas of the other world. These founding figures of their respective sects did not function as salvific intermediaries of *honjibutsu*, nor did they style themselves as prophets.

Yet after their deaths, their disciples soon reversed this and set about the transformation of the founders into "embodied buddhas" (*shōjin*). They insisted the founders had in fact been avatars, and encouraged their veneration as deities. Throngs of believers visiting the mausolea of the founder and praying for salvation before their images became an everyday sight. At Ikegami Honmonji in Tokyo, Nichiren's ashes were placed in a seated image of him made for the seventh anniversary of his death, and the image itself became the object of worship as "the living body of our founder." Moreover, Nichiren sect doctrine teaches that Nichiren was an incarnation of Jōgyō Bosatsu (the bodhisattva Superior Practices), and venerates him as an avatar of this sacred being. We can see this as a process by which he was transformed into an "embodied buddha" and his life gradually mythologized—a process which eventuated in the attribution to him of mystical powers such as the ability to prophesy the future, and the creation of a view of Nichiren as a superhuman being who was even able to ward off the Mongol invasions of Japan.

This deification of Nichiren was not unique; we see a similar phenomenon among the other leaders of Kamakura Buddhism. Shinran famously claimed in his *Tannishō* that "I do not have a single disciple," but after his death an image was made of him and enshrined and worshipped at his mausoleum in Ōtani.[6] The *Ippen hiijiri-e*, a set of illustrated handscrolls in the collection of Kankikōji temple depicting the life of Ippen Shōnin, shows a sculpture of Ippen enshrined in the Founder's Hall of the temple and being worshipped by his followers. These founding figures may have denied that they themselves occupied any privileged position as intermediaries between the buddhas of the Other Shore and the sentient beings of this world, but they still became the principal focus of folk cultic belief within their sects and were worshipped in their temples as sacred beings with salvific powers.

But yet another major transformation awaited the progressively deified founders of Kamakura Buddhism. Like the other deities of the later medieval period, the founders gradually lost their function as intermediaries connecting this world with the other world. No longer serving as salvific representatives of otherworldly buddhas, they were now perceived as beings who possessed supernatural powers in their own right. The image of Nichiren enshrined at the temple Myōhōji in the Horinouchi district of Edo was widely venerated by the common people of the city as a protector deity. The image of Nichiren's disciple Nitchō at Ikegami Honmonji was also believed to work powerful magic, and attracted worshippers suffering from eye diseases as well as students praying for academic success. This transition meant that during the Edo period the founders and their disciples enshrined in the temples of the major sects of popular Buddhism came to be perceived as "magical buddhas" (*reigenbutsu*) who would respond directly to the diverse secular needs and problems of the masses, healing their ills and protecting them from disaster and misfortune.

Sacred sites and the standardization of pilgrimage

The decline in the late medieval period of the image of the Other Shore and the transformation of sectarian patriarchs into magical buddhas also had a major impact on the nature of sacred sites. Once rebirth in the Pure Land after death had ceased to be the primary concern, the sacred sites at which *hitogami* were enshrined also lost their significance as portals between this world and the next; in early modern society supplications aimed at this-worldly benefits and aspirations took on increasing weight.

A variety of shrines and worship halls celebrating a diversity of gods and buddhas sprang up in the precincts of established sites, promising to respond to prayers for the safety of one's family, healing of illness, success in business, or the prosperity of future generations. In much the same fashion that specialized clinics have been established to care for a wide range of diseases and ailments, a division of labor developed among the various gods and buddhas in responding to specific this-worldly supplications on the part of the faithful. Among them, the sectarian patriarchs celebrated as *hitogami* also began to be perceived as beings who could bring about certain specific benefits to those who worshipped them.

As a result, in the early modern era the cosmology of sacred spaces took the form of a cluster of overlapping circles whose center points were the shrines and halls of the variety of gods and buddhas venerated within the precincts of the site. In contrast to the single-centered circle of ancient temple cosmology and the double-centered ellipse of medieval temples, this polycentric cosmology of early modern times allowed for the incorporation within a single sacred site of numerous worship halls for a diversity of gods and buddhas possessing distinctive but essentially equivalent functions.

We may cite Nakayama Hokekyōji as a prototypical example of such a sacred site. The basic layout of the temple that we see today was established in early modern times. Entering the temple precincts, we find arrayed in a large circle a Founder's Hall dedicated to Nichiren, accompanied by other worship halls dedicated to the Lotus Sutra; to Seishōkō, a deification of the Sengoku-era warrior Katō Kiyomasa venerated as a protector of the Nichieren sect; to deities adopted from Hindu origins into the Buddhist pantheon such as Kishibojin, Ugajin, and the ten Rasetsunyo; to the bodhisattva Myōken, and others. People visiting the temple would enter through the main gate and then make their way around this circle, offering specific prayers and supplication at each hall in turn. In contrast to the medieval pattern of pilgrimage and worship, in which believers proceeded directly to a specific site to pray for the single goal of salvation after death, the characteristic form taken by early modern pilgrimage to sacred sites was this circuitous, sequential round of prayer for this-worldly concerns.

The peripatetic quality of worship within a particular early modern sacred site, as opposed to the medieval focus on a single goal, was also characteristic of the larger pilgrimage journey. In medieval times, as already noted, the basic form of the pilgrimage was a direct journey to a specific sacred site and the return. Pilgrimages to multiple sites were not unknown—examples may be seen in *Nanto shichidaiji junrei ki* (Record of a Pilgrimage to the Seven Great Temples of Nara), thought to have been written early in the Muromachi period (1338–1568), and the pilgrimage tours of the retired emperor Go-Shirakawa—but except for a minority of the clergy and nobility, the pilgrimage of ordinary people normally was a simple round-trip to a single site. There were a few sacred places such as Kumano in the southern Kii peninsula that encompassed a number of individual sites, but in these cases as well, the pilgrimage was a means to arrive at the ultimate goal of salvation. The act of visiting and praying at a prescribed itinerary of sacred sites had not become an end in itself.

In contrast, beginning in late medieval times we see the establishment of multi-site circuit pilgrimages such as the eighty-eight temple Shikoku route and the thirty-three temple Saigoku ("Western Provinces") Kannon route; and the custom of embarking on lengthy walking pilgrimages over considerable periods of time, stopping to pray at each site in succession, gradually permeated the population. The pilgrimage routes were fixed and clearly defined, and the completion of the circuit an end in itself. In the Sengoku period (1467–1568), itinerant ascetics known as *kaikoku hijiri* traveled throughout the sixty-six provinces of the land, depositing copies of the Lotus Sutra at sacred sites in each province. By early in the Edo period (1600–1868), the custom of circuit pilgrimages (*junrei*) was firmly established in society, replacing the medieval form of single-site pilgrimage (*sankei*).[7]

Pilgrimage sites popped up everywhere. Guidebooks such as *Saigoku sanjūsansho meisho zue* (An Illustrated Guide to the Thirty-three Sites of the Saigoku Pilgrimage) and *Kii no kuni meisho zue* (An Illustrated Guide to the Province of Kii) were published, along with a host of pilgrimage maps, pilgrims' hymns (*goeika*), and travel journals. Now broad masses of people participated in circuit pilgrimages, such as the *o-Ise mairi*, that doubled as a kind of pleasure excursion and sightseeing tour. Even the word now common for a pilgrimage site (*reijō*) is a product of the Edo period.

From sacred sites to cemeteries

As pilgrimage sites satisfying a variety of real-world demands prospered during the Edo period, a number of sacred sites known since the middle ages as "burial grounds" began to develop into full-scale cemeteries. A site we have already touched upon several time, the Okunoin at Kōyasan, was known from the twelfth century onward as a sacred space in which to inter the remains of the dead. It became an article of widespread cultic belief that Kōbō Daishi had not actually died, but remained in a deep state of meditation within his mausoleum, and an increasing number of people wished to be buried in the vicinity of his divine presence.

According to a chapter in the epic *Heike monogatari* (Tale of the Heike), after his master, the bishop Shunkan, had died on the island of Kikaigashima, young Ariō hung round his own neck a vessel containing Shunkan's remains and carried them to the Okunoin at Kōyasan for interment, after which Ariō himself entered the priesthood at nearby Rengedani and prayed for the repose of his master's soul. In this same text, the remains of Taira no Shigehira, responsible for the deliberate burning of some of the most important temples in Nara, are said to have found a resting place at Kōyasan. People bringing remains for burial beside the pilgrims' path leading through the Okunoin would mark the grave sites with wooden stupas. But those depositing remains there, including friends and family of the deceased, did not intend to return to the Okunoin to visit these graves. Once the bones were interred in an appropriate place, what happened afterward ceased to be a concern. It was believed that the spirits of the dead, who continued to use their remains as a *yorishiro*, or abiding place in this world, would be conducted by Kōbō Daishi himself to rebirth in the Pure Land—and thus would not remain for long at their grave sites.

But this situation began to change in late medieval times. Rather than departing on a journey to rebirth in some distant, unknown, and otherworldly Pure Land, the spirits of the dead in the Okunoin began to be seen as residing right there, in a peaceful repose guaranteed by the benevolent proximity of Kōbō Daishi.

In response to this changed conception of the afterlife, during the Edo period the pilgrimage route at Kōyasan from Ichinohashi to the Okunoin gradually became lined with the mausolea of daimyo families, and regular pilgrimages to Kōyasan became customary. A cemetery accompanied by a great five-story pagoda was constructed, and gravestones erected. Kōyasan was no longer a way station on the voyage to the Other Shore; it became instead a place where mausolea and imposing gravestones served as *yorishiro* for the souls of the dead to remain there forever. In some cases, such as the mausolea of the daimyo, an effort to venerate the deceased as *kami* was made, as noted in Chapter 7 (section 3). Kōyasan continues to this day to be a site for pilgrimage to the graves of the individuals and families interred in its precincts.

3. The Conception of the Divine in Popular Religion

Ordinary people become "living gods"

Tarōzaemon, who became Fukuda ("Field of Happiness") no Kami, the deified *gimin* (self-sacrificing peasant heroes), the self-mummified *sokushinbutsu* of Yamagata—none of these were members of the ruling class such as emperors or daimyo. In early modern society it became possible for many common people leading quite ordinary lives to elevate themselves to godhood through force of will or the gratitude of their fellows. And among them were a few who were acknowledged as divine while still alive—individuals who were known as *ikigami*, or living gods.

A forerunner of this phenomenon was "Otake Dainichi," who lived in the early Edo period. Otake was a poor serving girl of great Buddhist virtue, but a small hall venerating her as "Dainichi Buddha in flesh and blood," the Otake Dainichidō, stands to this day in the precincts of

Figure 8-3 The Otake Dainichidō (Hagoro-chō, Yamagata Prefecture)

the Shōzen'in Koganedō temple in the village of Tōge in the foothills of Hagurosan in Yamagata Prefecture, one of the three sacred mountains of Dewa. Otake died in Kan'ei 15 (1638), but the family of her master, the Sakumas, built the Otake Dainichidō and entrusted it to the care of a local mountain ascetic named Genryō.

But the real outpouring of *ikigami* from amidst the common people would take place in the latter days of the Tokugawa shogunate, which saw the birth of a number of popular religions—Tenrikyō, Konkōkyō, and Kurozumikyō, among others—that had such "living gods" as their founders. Tenrikyō founder Nakayama Miki, Konkōkyō founder Akazawa Bunji, Maruyamakyō founder Itō Rokurobei, and Ōmotokyō founder Deguchi Nao were all men and women of peasant or commoner origin who received divine revelations and began spreading the message of a new faith. These founding figures had different styles of preaching, but all of them claimed to be divine—or at least never denied it. Yet, at the same time, it is important that they did not monopolize this claim to divinity, but worked to discover the sacred within their followers and humanity in general.

Jikigyō Miroku of Fujikō, a religious society based around the veneration of Mount Fuji that may be seen as a predecessor of the popular religions just mentioned, entered nirvana in Kyōhō 18 (1733) at Eboshi-iwa, a site near the summit of Mount Fuji, at the end of a prolonged fast. In a text which recounts the teachings of his final days, *Sanjūichi-nichi no onmaki* (A Record of Thirty-one Days), he speaks of the oneness of Sengen Daibosatsu (the deified Mount Fuji) with human beings, and stresses the dignity of mankind in the following terms: "It is a noble thing to be born a human being, for if in this body we conduct ourselves with proper attention, we are close to being gods and buddhas." He also taught that all human beings were equal, regardless of social position or gender: "Equipped as we all are with the 'three bodies,' among human beings there is no separation between aristocratic and common birth; no one is more noble than oneself"; "Simply heed this teaching: if you but rid yourself of evil, and purify yourself within, what difference is there between men and women? We are all the same human beings."

In the eighteenth century, such ideas did not lead immediately to radical demands for the abandonment of the hierarchy of social class and status. The conviction that every individual was at one with the divine did not evoke a denial of the discrimination implicit in the four classes of samurai, peasants, artisans, and merchants; instead, it produced a logic that people of each station, "by diligently pursuing their calling," might "find themselves born into a position in which they did not lack for wealth or status." However, it is also worth recognizing that even in the midst of the class hierarchy of Edo society, the idea of human equality was beginning to be articulated, based on this rather original conception of humanity.

The *ikigami* community

The popular religions of the late Edo period saw the appearance of a more self-conscious form of the *ikigami* concept. For instance, Akazawa Bunji, founder of Konkōkyō, encountered the primal deity Tenchikane no Kami in the course of recovery from a grave illness, and founded a community of faith taking this god as its central deity. Bunji himself was regarded as an *ikigami* who served as an intermediary with this god. But the status of *ikigami* was not in this case limited to the founder alone. Disciples who had received the teachings of the religion by "direct transmission" from Bunji also operated as *ikigami* and were given titles of deification—producing a system in which "living gods" were created in significant numbers from among the faithful. "The community of the faithful in early Konkōkyō was made up of a group of 'living gods' who recognized one another's divinity with 'godly names' (*shingō*)."[8]

The concept in Konkōkyō of a community of living gods clearly aspired to transcend the status and class hierarchy of secular society.

When we worship Tenchikane no Kami, we must next revere, venerate, and worship this god as everyone's Golden Deity, without exception—everyone's. Izanagi and Izanami no Mikoto were human beings, and Amaterasu Ōmikami, too, was a human being. Are not the emperors descended from her human beings as well? [9]

This was a statement of Bunji's from the period after the Meiji Restoration in 1868, but it plainly relativizes the authority of the emperor with its conception of the continuity of human and divine.

Kozawa Hiroshi, scholar of religious history, has noted that the equation of human beings with children of god(s) may be found in the words of most of the founders of the popular religions. After pointing out that this idea played a central role in undergirding each of their teachings of salvation, he writes that "the major premise of the founder's soteriology was that the nature of the god each founder believes in was that of a powerful salvific deity whose personal vow was to save all people from the depths of their suffering and distress, and that the equation 'human being = child of god' was first and foremost an explicit expression of faith in this boundless divine love."[10]

It has also been frequently observed that in the popular religions arising in the late Edo period we frequently see the divine manifesting as a primordial existence transcending secular society—a phenomenon which has been described as the appearance of "a powerful, monotheistic supreme deity."[11] Moreover, this was a divinity that did not preside over the afterlife or the Other Shore, but over this world. And it was not a cold and distant god passing down commandments from a remote other world, but a deity who resided within human beings and spoke to them, playing the role of a fountainhead for the birth of countless *hitogami* in this world.

During this same period, Edo-period moralists such as Ninomiya Sontoku and Ōhara Yūgaku were attempting to revive village communities by encouraging a grassroots, self-help movement of rural people. Thinkers such as Ishida Baigan also emerged, preaching the importance of strict self-discipline and respect for morality among the common people. Historian Yasumaru Yoshio has addressed the thought of Baigan and Sontoku, observing that the practice of the "secular virtues" they preached, such as diligence, thrift, and harmony, eventually brought about an internalization of this value system, and that this might be interpreted as a process of individual empowerment and independence uniquely suited to the formative period of modern society.[12] The *Myōkōnin den*—biographies depicting the lives of ideal practitioners of the faith that enjoyed widespread distribution among the adherents of the Jōdo Shin sect in the late Edo period—were also models of ordinary people leading healthy and fulfilling daily lives as a result of internalizing such secular virtues.

Behind these movements as well, we can see the new mentality of the era, which acknowledged the infinite potential inherent in human-kind and sought to actualize it in society. For a person to become a deity was no longer an awakening to a mystical state as it had been in medieval times. Each person could shine forth, in their own terms, simply by fulfilling the responsibilities assigned to them by their lot in life and station in society.

The structure of emperor worship

Thus far, I have argued that the early modern era was one which began to see the image of the divine in ordinary human beings; one which produced a profusion of figures who elevated themselves into deities through their own inner light, and not the reflected glory of a supreme being or *honjibutsu*, as in the middle ages. By the late Edo period, a significant number of *ikigami* had emerged—people who claimed to be "living gods" and who were acknowledged as such by others. The popular religions of the final years of the Tokugawa shogunate stood as the peak of this phenomenon.

On the other hand, the late Edo period down to the fall of the sho-gunate also saw the rising influence of a completely different pathway elevating individuals to divinity. This was a line of thought propounded by Suika Shintō, beginning with Yamazaki Ansai and the Yoshida Shintō teachings that influenced him, which saw loyal service to the emperor as something that could lead a person to posthumous deifi-cation. As noted earlier, in Suika Shintō the souls of certain specific individuals might be given a title of enshrinement and worshipped as deities. It was this tradition that provided the theoretical and practical means for deifying certain individuals because of their connections to the imperial house.

Wakabayashi Kyōsai was a member of the Kimon school founded by Yamazaki Ansai. He discussed the secret teachings of Suika Shintō in a treatise, *Shintō taii*, writing that any person devoting themselves fully to the service of the emperor, who is an *arahitokami* or living god, "would take their place among the lower orders of the myriad gods as divine spirits (*reijin*) continuing to protect and serve their sovereign lord and pacify the nation." Similar expressions may be found throughout the related literature of Suika Shintō from the eighteenth century onward. The flesh may wither but the spirit is eternal and indestructible, and through meritorious action in life human beings can gain entry into the realm of the gods. In this realm of the spirit is a hierarchy like that of the present world, centered on the emperors, but through selfless loyalty and service it is possible to leap over the status hierarchy of this world to take a seat much closer to the emperor in the next world. By proposing a new vision of peace and security in the afterlife in connection with the deification of the emperors, Suika Shintō has earned a place in Japanese history.[13]

In Tenpō 14 (1843), Kamo no Norikiyo, founder of Uden Shintō, presented a memorial entitled "Ari no omoi" (Thoughts of an Ant) to the shogunal commissioner of shrines and temples. In it, Norikiyo proposed the construction of a man-made Chūkōzan ("Mountain of Loyalty and Filial Piety") as a strategy for dealing with the increasing number of *muenbutsu* (departed spirits without survivors to tend their graves) in Edo as well as serving to commemorate paragons of loyalty and filial piety who might otherwise be forgotten.[14]

This was an ambitious plan to use the earth and gravel dredged from the Sumida and other rivers of Edo to construct a nine-level artificial mountain nine *jō* (about 27 meters) in height at the mouth of the Fukagawa. At the summit a shrine would be constructed, and the uppermost of the nine levels would venerate Ninigi no Mikoto and the thirty-two deities who accompanied him when he descended from heaven, the emperors, and Tōshōgū (the deified Ieyasu) and the vassal daimyo who had supported him from his early years in Mikawa. The second level (in descending order) was for empresses, empress dowagers, grand empress dowagers and others honored with similar rank; the third level was for grand ministers of state and persons of higher order. In this way, those who had performed meritorious service for the nation were arranged according to their station. The ninth and lowest level would celebrate individuals from the peasant, artisan, and merchant classes. The site was envisioned as a place of refreshment and recreation for the populace as well as a place of pilgrimage.

Norikiyo's Chūkōzan proposal was intended to revere as *kami* individuals of all classes who had made significant contributions to the nation, while at the same time integrating them into a hierarchy of the spirit world that had at its apex a deified Tokugawa Ieyasu and the emperors. Four years later, Norikiyo would make a revised version of this proposal and submit it once more to the shogunate, this time calling it Kōzan ("Incense Mountain"), and arguing that by forever enshrining there as deities individuals who had distinguished themselves by their loyalty and filial piety it would encourage the masses of the people to embrace the aspiration to be enshrined there themselves after death.[15]

From caste society to nation-state

We can see the emergence of such concepts of *hitogami* or *ikigami* as Japan moved into the final years of the Tokugawa shogunate, along with the rise of the new popular religions, as expressing a new mentality affirming the autonomy and potential of the individual. While Suika Shintō looked to the emperors and the popular religions to less exalted local gods, both represented a rediscovery of indigenous sources of divinity as the generative source of *hitogami*, rather than the gods of universal religions such as Buddhism or Christianity.

By the nineteenth century, the affirmative self-perception and aspirations for advancement on the part of ordinary people had already reached a stage where they felt stiflingly constrained by the rigid hierarchy of class and status under the Tokugawa shogunate. While the popular religions groped toward a conception of a millenarian *yonaoshi no kami* ("world-renewing god"), Suika Shintō, with its renewed focus on the emperor, held out the possibility for ordinary individuals to become *kami* through a direct connection with the sovereign and to vault over the restrictions of the existing social order. These developments, like the protests, uprisings, and riots in both rural and urban areas that spread in the late Edo period, were reflections of a deep level of popular consciousness that sought to destroy the existing social system and replace it with an egalitarian utopian order. This consciousness may also be detected in the *namazu-e*, or "catfish prints," that enjoyed widespread popularity in the final years of the shogunate and depicted the earthquake-causing catfish as possessing a dual nature as both destroyer and savior.[16]

The turmoil surrounding the fall of the Tokugawa shogunate and the Meiji Restoration was not merely a political struggle; a wave of human sentiment that had taken a millennium to mature dashed against a sclerotic social hierarchy, threatening it from below with a massive tectonic shift. Thus, even after the regime changed and internal disorder was pacified, there would be lengthy and persistent repercussions from amid a populace that sought—and would not cease seeking—"liberty" and "equality."

Even after the collapse of the Tokugawa regime, the question of how to enlist the potential of these popular movements on the side of the government and link them to the creation of a homogenous "people" who would voluntarily and actively support the nation-state was the most important challenge confronting the nascent Japanese empire.

CHAPTER 9

The Road to Yasukuni Shrine

1. Toward Human Gods

The discovery of divinity

B EGINNING IN THE PREHISTORIC JŌMON ERA and continuing to the fall of the Tokugawa shogunate, this book has over the course of eight chapters traced the birth and evolution of "human gods" or "deified humans" (*hitogami*) in the Japanese islands. In closing, I would like to offer a perspective on developments in *hitogami* beliefs in the modern era, but before I do so, let's briefly review the main themes raised thus far.

In the Introduction, I remarked that there are probably no human cultures which do not possess gods. We may assume that when people in the Japanese archipelago first recognized the existence of sacred beings with powers transcending the human, it was, as in other parts of the world, in response to awe-inspiring natural phenomena and animals possessing capacities humans could not hope to emulate. Initially, divinity was grasped as inseparable from the individual phenomena that inspired its perception. Thunder and lighting, or a volcanic eruption, were themselves apprehended with fear and awe, as gods. Individual animals were also seen as gods. Awe-inspiring crags and great trees were also perceived as divine.

This primitive conception of divinity eventually shifted to the next level. From perceiving specific objects and individual phenomena as divinities in and of themselves, there was a transition to positing the divine as a more abstract and primordial presence, a spirit or *tama* that lay behind phenomena and could produce miracles.

In the Japanese islands this transition may be thought to have occurred as a gradual process during the latter part of the Jōmon period, about four thousand years ago. The *dogū* figurines typical of Jōmon pottery were clearly modeled on human beings, but in the late Jōmon period we begin to see examples of *dogū* with heart-shaped faces or unusual goggle eyes that seem to represent something entirely different. The sacred was separating itself from the concrete things of this world and becoming progressively abstract. As it happened, this was also the era in which gravesites were separated from village settlements, and the idea of a geographically and spatially autonomous realm of the dead arose. The *tama* or spirits, liberated from the material constraints of animals, plants, or human remains, were idealized and elevated into transcendence. The reality of another world comprised of these invisible presences began to be shared by the Jōmon people.

This tendency toward abstraction of the divine progressed even further during the Yayoi period, which was an era in which deities ceased to be expressed in concrete form, as they had in the *dogū* of the Jōmon period. Images might be made of sacred trees that served as *yorishiro*, or temporary abodes of the gods; of shrines venerating the gods; or of shamans who served as the celebrants of religious rituals—but the gods themselves were no longer depicted. In this period, though there were apparently various visible signs of the presence of gods in the environment, they did not seem to occupy specific and fixed abodes. Thus, from the Yayoi into the Kofun period, the typical mode of worship involved inviting the *kami* to temporarily occupy a particular site of worship from which they were believed to depart when the rituals were completed.

The gods, who abhorred the pollution of the secular world, loved the quiet and solitude of the mountains. Though the mountains might serve as the abode of the gods, they were not themselves deities. In this period, the practice of worshipping the mountain itself as the embodiment of the divine—frequently said to be an ancient Japanese tradition—had not yet taken root. In fact, the perception of divine spirits inhabiting mountains and rivers, grasses and trees, and all the myriad phenomena of nature did not become generalized until medieval times and after. And when the gods of the mountains were worshipped, it was not done from afar; deities were summoned to a ritual space prepared in or near the mountains, where their voices could be heard and where they could be addressed by their human worshippers.

Based upon such conceptions of divinity, the first clear implementation of a strategy aimed at the deification of human beings took the form of the *zenpō kōenfun*, or keyhole-shaped tomb mounds. These tumuli were premised on the common contemporary belief that the *kami* resided in the mountains, and in addition to venerating the spirit of a powerful chieftain as a protector deity for the newly established state (the Yamato court), they were constructed as artificial mountains which these kingly spirits might make their abode. It is thought that rituals were conducted, not as a worship of the "mountains" themselves from the base of the tumuli, but by inviting the ancestral spirits to temporarily inhabit a *yorishiro* of one kind or another at sites in the vicinity of the tomb.

The establishment of shrines and the incarnation of gods

The conception of the divine just described, which formed the mainstream during the Yayoi and Kofun periods, reached a turning point with the reforms of the reigns of Emperor Tenmu and Empress Jitō in the late seventh century. This was a period in which a powerful monarchy was attempting to establish itself as a counter to the continental forces of Tang China and the Korean kingdom of Silla, and the strategy was to elevate the sovereign into a sacred being who could serve as the unifying power at the center of the state. To achieve this goal, the title emperor (*tennō*, lit. "heavenly ruler") was adopted, and a genealogy created linking the current sovereign in an unbroken line back to the sun goddess, Amaterasu Ōmikami. A number of the more important tumuli dotting the landscape as a legacy of the Kofun period were identified as the tombs of the prior generations of the imperial line. After their deaths the emperors were supposed to reside in these tombs as "imperial spirits," eternally protecting the reigning emperor and the nation. The concept, fostered since the time of the keyhole tombs, of the chieftain or ruler posthumously becoming a *kami* who watched over his successors now became more systematized and visible as an element of state policy, and the visage of the "human god" came into sharper focus.

It was also from about the end of the seventh century that the location of shrines became fixed and the idea that the gods resided in them permanently began to take hold. From the time of Empress Jitō's construction of the capital at Fujiwarakyō, the custom was abandoned of relocating to a new palace at the time of an imperial succession, and the emperors would henceforth reside in a capital city built on the continental model. The new imperial state posited many of the traditional Japanese *kami* as protectors and defenders of the state, like the imperial spirits, but the *tatarigami*, whose whereabouts and motives were obscure and inscrutable, were not suited to such a role. Thus the state built specific shrines so that the major deities might always have a permanent abode, and prescribed regular rituals—such as daily morning and evening food offerings—that made it clear that a god was in residence. In addition, the desire to impart a sense of authentic presence to protector deities gave birth to a new form of representation of deities—realistic images. The gods, who had for a long period of time lost corporeal form, were once again given flesh.

This change in the conception of divinity also produced changes in the nature of faith and religious practice. Where formerly the gods were invited to manifest themselves for the duration of a ritual and then depart, there was now a shift to forms, such as pilgrimage to shrines, where people went instead to visit the gods in their abodes. Worship at the imperial tombs now took the form of priests and court officials making offerings at these sites. As the authority of the *kami* increased and they came to occupy established and impressive shrines, the physical distance widened between the gods being worshipped and the people doing the worshipping. The gods became one-way recipients of veneration and worship, and the dialog between gods and men disappeared from public loci of ritual. The gods of heaven and earth dwelling as permanent residents of the official shrines needed to possess an unwavering will to protect the state and nation and inspire trust that they would forever continue to fulfill their duties in this regard. Thus, for the first time in history, "benevolent gods" (*zenshin*) equipped with a clearly defined raison d'être appeared in the Japanese islands.

On the other hand, this meant that the aspect of the traditional gods as *tatarigami*, or bringers of misfortune and woe, was spun off separately in the form of "malevolent gods" (*akujin*) and vengeful ghosts. In the Nara period, such ghosts began to proliferate, and the more powerful among these spirits that could visit *tatari* (curses and misfortune) upon the living were celebrated as gods, in an effort to transform the tremendous negative energy they possessed into something positive. Unlike the cult of the imperial ancestors, which was part of the closed universe of court society, the cults of the *goryō* deities were open to the masses, and became the principal form of *hitogami* worship.

From the ninth century onward, as the gods became more functionally differentiated they also became much more clearly defined as individuals, and began to be given a variety of representations. Now gods of diverse gender, form, and function were born in response to the variety of human needs and desires.

Gods as saviors

Throughout prehistory and antiquity in the Japanese islands, the gods were totally external presences confronting mankind. It was during the middle ages that humanity began to discover the sacred within itself. Behind this lay a deepening and systematization of thinking about transcendent or supernatural beings—the articulation of a theology. In the Japanese islands it was Buddhism that provided the intellectual raw materials for such an enterprise. Employing the logic of Buddhism, from the second half of the tenth century onward certain types of deity were elevated into supreme beings and saviors, creating and expanding a division between the human world (this world) and a world of primordial or cosmic deities (the other world). The other world inhabited by such deities—the Pure Land of Infinite Bliss of Amida Buddha being the prime example—was no longer a place that the common run of humanity could expect to easily enter. A cosmology was constructed in which this world and the ideal of the Pure Land confronted one another, and it was the Other Shore where the primordial deity resided that was seen as the "real" world, the world of truth. A sense that this world was only a temporary way-station in transit to that ultimate reality became widespread among the general populace.

Thus, in contrast to the miracles and wonders (*reii*) worked by the ancient gods, "salvation" emerged as the greatest concern of medieval people—to enlist divine aid in surviving life in this world to pursue the true goal of life, which was arrival in the other world of the Pure Land. In the reorganization of the world of the gods that accompanied these changes, many of the existing gods were posited as this-worldly avatars (*suijaku*) serving as intermediaries between mankind and the supreme deities of the other world.

The *hitogami* were not exempt from these developments. Holy men such as Prince Shōtoku and Kōbō Daishi were interpreted as avatars or manifestations of otherworldly "original buddhas" (*honbutsu*), and myriads of people made pilgrimages to the places these figures were enshrined, seeking their aid in order to be reborn in the Pure Land. Nor was this restricted to a few major figures—in the middle ages local *hitogami* sprang up in almost every part of the country to serve as salvific avatars guiding people to the Pure Land.

The deepening of theological interest in deities as saviors led, on the other hand, to a correspondingly deeper inquiry into the nature of human beings as the objects of salvation. The result was a discovery of the sacredness inherent in all humankind. Initially, this was conceptualized in Buddhist terms as the "Buddha nature" possessed by all sentient beings. This elicited opposing theoretical constructs from adherents of the traditional Japanese gods, who elaborated concepts such as *hossōshin* ("*kami* of dharma-nature") and *hongakushin* ("*kami* of original enlightenment"). A primordial being was immanent in all earthly phenomena, including the plants and trees and the earth itself—and in human beings as well. Individuals might discover the sacred spark within, and by manifesting it, elevate themselves into sacred beings.

In the early medieval period, the concept of "the god within" remained an ideal—it did not actually function as the logical basis for suddenly elevating the mass of humanity into deities. The ascension of humans into deities was usually explained according to *honji-suijaku* theory in terms of their relationship to the primordial *honjibutsu* of the other world. People in general remained the objects of salvation by the deities. But in the late middle ages, the world of the Other Shore began to lose its reality and vividness, and examples increased of humans who managed to make the leap into godhood without the reflected glory of an absolute god. And before long, the great warlords and unifiers of the realm would be deified and worshipped.

The flowering of the age of *hitogami*

In the early modern era, the *hitogami* came to be exempted from the role of guiding sentient beings to the Other Shore and liberated from the bondage of a salvific mission—which gave space for a dramatic expansion of their range of action and function in society. The *hitogami* were no longer beings who differed fundamentally in nature from the common run of humanity. In the new age virtually anyone, given the right conditions, might become a god—not through the reflected light of a more primordial deity, but by manifesting the divinity immanent within themselves. This served as the backdrop for the gradual social acceptance of the Neo-Confucian theory that all human beings might become sages by rediscovering and restoring the fundamental goodness of their original nature.

At the beginning of the early modern period, the first humans to be deified were the great warlords and unifiers such as Toyotomi Hideyoshi and Tokugawa Ieyasu. They were joined by the emperors and powerful daimyo, and by the second half of the Edo period class barriers to deification had been dramatically lowered. It was an age and a society in which people, regardless of class or social status, could aspire to be gods—and realize that aspiration.

Another noteworthy development in the beliefs of the early modern era is the striking increase in examples of *ikigami*—people regarded as deities while still living. This reached its peak with the new popular

Figure 9-1 The mausoleum of the daimyō Yūki Hideyasu at Kōyasan was designed to venerate him as a god.

religions that arose during the waning years of the Tokugawa shogunate. Many of the founders of these sects did nothing to deny their own divinity. But they also did not attempt to monopolize it, and broadly sought to discover a shared divinity among not only their followers and disciples, but among ordinary working people. They did not directly criticize the status hierarchy supporting the Tokugawa regime, but they did preach the equality of all human beings, regardless of class or gender, grounded in respect for the divinity inherent in all.

This heralded an age in which an individual might become a god purely through their own will and effort. The awakening of the divine would come, not as in medieval times through enlightenment in the religious sense, but by making oneself shine forth in society by fulfilling one's duties proper to one's place in the social hierarchy. And so it was that just before the fall of the Tokugawa shogunate, a plethora of lesser gods proliferated through the Japanese islands, independent of any reflected glory from an ideal other world.

2. What Study of the Divine May Bring to Light

The fiction of uniqueness

The sense of the sacred in the Japanese islands has gone through a number of metamorphoses over the long history that stretches from the Jōmon period to modern times. From a stage in which gods were apprehended in specific objects and phenomena, a process of increasing abstraction arrived eventually at their transformation into invisible beings. There was also a shift from *tatarigami* whose inscrutable will transcended good and evil, to protector deities with more stable and clearly defined intentions. A further shift was from gods as presences external to human beings to the concept of the internal presence of the divine. In concert with these altered conceptions of divinity, the nature of the Japanese *kami* and of the *hitogami* also continually changed.

There is a current of thought which asserts that the *kami* venerated in today's shrines (*jinja*) are uniquely Japanese, praising them as embodiments of the essence of the Japanese people in a tradition reaching back to the most remote antiquity. But it should be clear by now how divorced this view is from reality. None of these deities existed in splendid isolation from the rest; each was one among many of the myriad gods venerated in these islands, and survived to the present day only after undergoing a series of dramatic transformations down through the various ages of Japan's history.

Of course it is possible, as an academic approach, to study the Japanese *kami* in the context of the history of Shintō, dissecting and analyzing their intrinsic nature. But if we are interested in exploring the historical and intellectual significance of these gods, then we must work to understand their place within the cosmology of a particular era and how it defined them; a chronological approach that takes into consideration transformations in the nature of the *kami* is thus an indispensable part of our investigation. Such a stance may leave me open to the accusation that I am denying the traditions of Shintō that are the quintessence of Japanese culture. But this would be a completely misdirected criticism.

As we have seen, the gods of the Japanese islands became inter-twined with various currents of thought, domestic and foreign, and with other divinities introduced from overseas, undergoing significant transformation as a result. This was a product of the rich imagination of the people living in these islands. To explicate this is none other than to elucidate how the people of these islands have embraced this land and its natural environment, and the profound thought and insight they have accumulated therein. To attempt to force this into the mold offered by much of the discourse on Japanese culture—with essentialist appeals to antiquity and indigenous identity—can only end in reducing all of the rich imagination and thought that the people of these islands built up in dialogue with their gods into a single stereotypical phrase.

A reexamination of analytical concepts

Analysis of the deities of the Japanese archipelago within a broader context and historical perspective has an additional scholarly signifi-cance: the potential for contribution to intellectual inquiry beyond the history of religion or the history of Shintō.

A variety of developments can be cited to explain the transforma-tion of the gods through the ages. Salient examples are the establish-ment of permanent shrines that came with the introduction of the *ritsuryō* system, the spread of the Pure Land cults, and the suppression of religious forces by the great warlords and unifiers. But I think that there was an even more fundamental factor engendering the changes we have seen in the conceptions of divinity in the Japanese islands, one surpassing individual incidents, changes in state policy, or the importa-tion of foreign culture—a transformation in cosmology taking place at the deepest level of consciousness.

In the Japanese islands, the cosmology of ancient times, in which humans shared the same realm with supernatural beings such as the gods and the spirits of the dead, took a drastic turn in the eleventh century. A deepening and systematization of thought with regard to these transcendent or supernatural beings—a theology—took shape, elevating some of these beings to absolute supremacy and giving them the power of salvation, while at the same time bringing about the independence of the world of the gods (the other world) from the world of humankind (this world) and expanding its influence and power. The unipolar cosmos of antiquity had evolved into the bipolar cosmos of the middle ages.

A clear line had thus been drawn between the humans and the gods who had once occupied the same space, and they now resided in separate realms—this world and the Other Shore. The theology of the otherworldly domain of salvific deities expanded to immense proportions and was described and catalogued in precise detail. The resulting cosmology was characterized by a tension between the present world and the ideal world of the Pure Land. The world of the Other Shore, in which the deities resided, was seen as the "real" or "true" world, and this world as little more than a temporary way-station on the journey to it. A universal realm embracing all the people of the world, regardless of the color of their skin or the languages they spoke, was widely believed to lie behind this world.

In the places touched by this cosmology, religious authority was concentrated in specific transcendental and absolute deities of the Other Shore; and the mystical authority of kings and chieftains, who were after all secular rulers, was greatly diminished. In this stage of history, kings, having lost any inherent sacrality, could only be recognized as sovereigns as a result of the authority invested in them by otherworldly transcendent beings. The interring of members of the imperial family in enormous tomb mounds lost its meaning, and in their stead magnificent works of religious architecture glorified the power and authority of otherworldly divinities.

But eventually the medieval cosmology—with its sharp distinction between this world and the other world and its ideal of an ultimate arrival in the otherworldly abode of the supreme being—also reached a turning point. People began to lose their sense of the reality of the Other Shore, and with it the keenness of their desire to be reborn into the Pure Land. They no longer held the ideal of arriving in a distant other world after death. Instead, they now hoped to enjoy the life of this world to the fullest, and after death to sleep peacefully in some corner of it where they could continue to commune in some way with their descendants.

This transformation was closely related to what could be termed the secularization of society. The attempts of medieval theology to reconstitute through abstract reasoning alone a transcendent other world beyond the reach of direct human experience gradually lost ground as people's understanding of the natural world expanded and a spirit of inquiry into its concrete workings grew. The sense of being embraced by a supreme or absolute being transcending geography and ethnicity was lost; the divine became an issue internal to each individual. Deities which had functioned to bind the community in solidarity were replaced by a nationalism serving a similar role in uniting the hearts of the population.

Such a transformation of cosmology was by no means peculiar to Japan; I believe it is one commonly seen, with many variations, in most regions of the world. Isolated, individual events and the influence of foreign cultures alone do not produce such transformations in the nature of divinity. It is deep and quietly advancing tectonic shifts in the spiritual realm that summon such developments.

The challenge that faces us now is to adopt a global perspective and liberate the *kami* from the stereotypes of the standard discourse on Japanese culture, in order to elucidate the diversity and richness of the world of thought in these islands. The hybridization of various strains of thought and the coexistence of a diversity of deities are phenomena common throughout East Asia. Hence, it is possible that the results of such inquiry will be applicable beyond the Japanese islands, contributing to research on the religious worlds of East Asia that have tended to be lumped together under such rubrics as "shamanism."

I have not delved into such matters in this book, but even looking solely at modern Japan, there have been complicated patterns to the process of human deification. Anne Bouchy has drawn attention to the fact that many of Japan's *fugeki*, or spirit mediums, take the form of *kamigakari*—a term which should be expressed as "possession," not "shamanism."[1] Taking this into consideration, and moving ahead with a more precise analysis and reexamination of analytical concepts will no doubt lead to rediscovery of a spiritual world in the Japanese islands that cannot be grasped with established ideas of "religion." This should also offer a perspective that can relativize the traditional framework of Western research in the history of thought, which has emphasized a logic generated out of the doctrines of monotheistic religion. In future research I hope to use such a perspective as the point of departure for a fresh cross-cultural examination of the deities of other regions of the world.

History with and without gods

Another subject I would like to address is the restructuring of the relationship between scholarship on divinity and historiography. Traditionally historiography has treated the subject of divinity quite coldly. Historians have, without the slightest doubt, seen society and the world as constituted by human beings. Gods and deities have been seen as simply a variety of "false consciousness" born out of the process by which some human beings dominate others. Yet wherever one may look—past or present, East or West— no case exists of a society which does not recognize some form of divinity (or transcendent being). The origins of the gods extend back several tens of thousands of years into Paleolithic times, long before the birth of states or nations. In the Japanese archipelago as well, clear physical evidence dating back to the Jōmon period indicates a consciousness of the divine.

The understanding of premodern peoples was that this world was not made up solely of human beings. Transcendent beings such as gods and buddhas and the dead had an overwhelming presence. Animals and plants were also full-fledged members of this world. People lived their daily lives with a sense of the existence of these various other beings, and listening to their voices. They believed that human beings and beings other than human together shaped the cosmos. Thus the gods were an indispensable presence for humankind. Without the gods, people could not exist—nor could they form communities or states.

The sense of the presence of the gods and buddhas and the position they occupied was especially strong in society in the middle ages and before. The leading role in this world was not taken by humans, but by the gods and buddhas. It was their will that was thought to propel society at its most fundamental levels. If we accept this, then when we study premodern states and societies, it is insufficient to look only at human beings as the constituent elements of society. We must explicate how, and in what sort of relationship, human beings and beings transcending the human created a shared world.

This perspective is also indispensable in thinking about the problem of kingship. The creation of the sovereign was not just a matter of the human world—it was an act that imparted order to the entire cosmos, including the natural world and the other world comprised of the gods and buddhas and spirits of the dead. Conversely, for the king to occupy a secure position in this world, it was insufficient merely to construct the organization and institutions of rule and expand a power base; it was also imperative to establish a proper relationship with the gods, the buddhas, and the dead. Kingdoms unable to construct an appropriate relationship with these transcendent beings contained inherent weaknesses, no matter how powerful they might have appeared to be.

Of course divinity and cosmology do not operate independently. The forms of their expression are no doubt determined by the unique climate, topography, and ecology of each region. Then there are the modes of production—the base or infrastructure of Marxist historical theory—by which people derive their livelihood from this natural environment, and which also play a crucial role. The totality of these relations among human beings and nature gives the gods and the cosmology of each region their unique character and affects how that character is transformed.

Humanity is impossible without divinity. Deities and cosmology are determining factors in the form and development of communities and states. How adequately has existing historiography grasped this reality of the divine?

3. *Hitogami* in Modern Times

Transcending the social hierarchy

In early modern society, since everyone carried an element of the divine within them, everyone possessed the potential to become a deity. But in fact deification required some heroic act, such as the giving of one's own life for the sake of others, something the average person was not about to undertake voluntarily or lightly. In other words, for an ordinary person to become a god, some form of catalyst was necessary. This role was played by two different sorts of beings: the strongly indigenous *kami* of the popular religions, and the emperors as conceived by Suika Shintō and by Kokugaku, or National Learning, the nativist tradition of inquiry into Japanese culture that established itself in the course of the Edo period under the influence of scholars such as Motoori Norinaga. Both provided a boost to the possibilities for elevation into a *hitogami* transcending the class and caste discrimination of the times. In this we can detect the confidence of people in their own abilities and an aspiration for advancement unbound by the strictures of a fixed social order.

In the late Edo period, scholarship in the form of Confucianism and National Learning became widely distributed among certain strata of the non-samurai population, notably the upper peasantry and affluent merchants. Intellectual networks based on common interest in arts such as *waka* and *kyōka* poetry sprang up throughout the Japanese islands.[2] Many were interested in improving their farming methods, and busied themselves with agricultural reform along the lines proposed by Ninomiya Sontoku and others. There were even figures who embraced a strong concern with social reform and attempted to make their voices heard regarding political issues at the national level. A movement from below aspiring to change the sclerotic system of social caste and status spread to even the lowest strata of the common people as the Tokugawa regime neared its end, and rural uprisings and urban riots reflecting this occurred with increasing frequency.

The spread of popular talk of people becoming gods went hand in hand with these developments among the subordinate classes. Speech directly critical of the ruling establishment was itself rare, but by the nineteenth century the people of the Japanese archipelago had—at a subconscious level—begun to chafe at the restrictions of caste and class.

Underlying the fall of the Tokugawa shogunate, the Meiji Restoration of 1868, and the lengthy process of social change that followed was a millennial transformation in cosmology taking place in the Japanese archipelago. The undercurrent of the changes wrought during the final days of the shogunate and the Restoration years—changes that dismantled the Tokugawa class system and aimed at replacing it with a modern nation made up of equal citizens—was a new vision of man, aspiring to the social leveling expressed in the permeation of the concept of *hitogami* throughout society.

This movement continued even after the Tokugawa shogunate was replaced by the imperial state and its institutions. The strong desire of the masses of the people for equality supported a variety of grassroots political movements early in the Meiji era (1868–1912), including the Freedom and Popular Rights Movement.

Monuments to loyal spirits

The Restoration government came into being with a powerful boost from popular desires and agitation for fundamental social change. Therefore, the forcible suppression of popular aspirations for advancement was simply not an option. Rather, the most urgent challenge facing the government leaders was how to take the popular voluntarism that had grown up during the latter part of the Edo period, convert it into loyalty to the nation, and use it to strengthen the foundations of the new regime. Having thrown off the old system of caste and class and embarked on the construction of a modern state, it was essential to create a self-motivated nation of people who would not hesitate to sacrifice themselves for the sake of their country.

The policiy adopted by the Restoration government was to take the aspirations for advancement that had erupted from amid the masses of the people in the form of a desire to be deified as *hitogami*, and bind them to a devout reverence for the emperor posited as the spiritual axis of the new nation. A new national army—a standing army, theoretically blind to previous class distinctions—was created. Any member of the armed forces who, in the fulfillment of his duties, laid down his life in service to the emperor was promised rebirth as a *kami*, to be forever remembered and revered by his compatriots. In effect, the logic of creation of *hitogami* using the emperor as intermediary that had been articulated and practiced within the lineages of Suika Shintō and Kokugaku was now officially recognized at the national level and implemented on a much grander scale.

The first efforts in this regard were the *chūkonsha* ("shrines to loyal spirits") created to celebrate the sacrifice of the soldiers who had died fighting for the imperial forces in the internal conflicts surrounding the Meiji Restoration. These war dead were reverenced as *kami* because they had given their lives for the emperor. Accordingly, the emperor himself had to be something more than an ordinary human being—and so was deemed an *arahitogami*, or living god. The war dead would be forever at the emperor's side as protector deities of the nation, and their heroic acts eternally remembered and celebrated. The *hitogami* beliefs that would lead to Yasukuni Shrine in Tokyo drew on a tradition inherited from early modern times, but in a form more suited to the imperial state and nation. The mentality arising in the early modern period affirming the agency and potential of human beings would thus be bound within the logic of the imperial state.

Concurrently, mechanisms that might create *hitogami* without the emperor as intermediary were eliminated. These other forms of *hitogami* belief had to be ruthlessly extirpated because they threatened

Figure 9-2 The Gokoku Shrine in Fukushima, one of the *gokoku jinja* founded to enshrine the spirits of the war dead

to relativize the authority of the emperor. The popular religions drew much of their material on cosmology and the origins of the universe from the world of ancient mythology, and in this sense shared many aspects with the newly evolving mythos of the modern state. However, precisely because of this, when their cosmologies did come into conflict with the mythos supporting the emperor system, they were subjected to unwavering repression. It was not a question of whether or not the popular religions were directly critical of the emperor system; the point was that if they possessed a unique cosmology that did not accord with that of the imperial state, they were fated to be branded as heretics.

In addition, after the success of the Meiji Restoration, popular religions frequently gave voice to people's resentment whenever they felt that the newly constructed order had betrayed their hopes or threatened their livelihoods. Popular religious thought sometimes took on an apparently antimodern guise, as in its resistance to the modernizing policies of the Meiji government, because it was deeply rooted in the life experiences of the common people. For this reason it was regarded as especially dangerous, and attacked as heretical.

Thus in modern times *hitogami* beliefs diverged into two conflicting streams: one leading to Yasukuni Shrine, utilized by the government to enlist and bind the energies of the people to the service of the state; the other represented by the popular religions, which sought to retain their autonomy and independence as a grassroots movement.

The emotion invested in *hitogami*

The history of the quest for the divine is a history of humanity's pursuit of its own potential. The discovery of the innate sacredness of all human beings is the dawning of an awareness of the dignity and self-hood of every individual. The *hitogami* of the early modern period, devoid of the backing of a clearly defined primordial deity, signify none other than the separation of humanity from nature and the birth of the human as a specially privileged state of being. If humanism is one of the hallmarks of modernity, then the gradual recession of the world of the Other Shore and the foregrounding of the human that took place from the late medieval period onward is a phenomenon symbolizing the advent of modernity in the Japanese archipelago. This became a fundamental factor in the dismantling of the caste and class system during the reforms of the late Tokugawa and early Meiji periods, and the motive force behind the push for Westernization.

Yet even with the progress of modernization, a mode of thought which still broadly acknowledged the sacrality of the plants and trees and the earth itself was not entirely lost, as may be seen in such practices as Buddhist offerings to the spirits of felled trees (*sōmoku kūyō*) or the worship of certain mountains as the embodiment of the divine (*shintaisan*). We should note that this is a quite unusual feature of Japanese culture, particularly in comparison with cultures of the West, but I cannot engage in further examination of this perspective here.

Having come to be like gods, the people of modern times gradually came to place an excessive faith in their own wisdom and omnipotence. But this omnipotence actually signified that they had acquired the power to bring about their own destruction. We now live in an age in which the very survival of humanity is in serious question. Modernity brought with it a developing awareness of the limitless potential of the human race—but we have reached a point where it seems necessary to stop, look back, and reflect upon what this means for us, personally.

It is very difficult, using the philosophies born of modern times, for us as people of those times to view ourselves objectively. To truly relativize modernity, what is needed is the wisdom engendered and accumulated by the human race over centuries and millennia of the currents of time. But this cannot be some facile projection of what contemporary people imagine "Jōmon thought" or "Yayoi thought" to be. What is required of us is to rethink—from as broad a perspective and as long a temporal reach as we can—the meaning of the age we call modern and the meaning of the lives we live within it.

Afterword

AFTER TURNING FIFTY, I set out two themes upon which I wanted to stake my remaining life as a scholar. One was death; the other, divinity.

Death is the fate which unavoidably awaits us all. On the other hand, gods have constantly accompanied humankind as intimate partners from the most remote antiquity. If the purpose of the human sciences is to elucidate the nature of this inscrutable creature known as the human being, then these two themes that have consistently engaged humanity at the deepest levels should serve as excellent points of entry. And I wanted to pursue these two themes, death and divinity, not at the level of abstract thought, but using concrete material drawn from these Japanese islands that have always been my field of study, investigating them from a historical perspective.

In 2008, Iwata Shoin published my book on death, *Shisha no yukue* (Whither the Dead?). From that time onward, I have concentrated on the divine, and in the process have discovered what an unimaginably difficult theme it is.

This book is the product of four years of intense struggle in pursuit of the gods—and after reading the final proofs, I cannot help but feel that I have left a mountain of unexplored issues. In writing my books and academic papers I try to emphasize clarity of argument above all; in this regard, the present work leaves some major topics still to be addressed. The road ahead is long; I offer this up as an initial milestone on that journey.

In writing it I have benefited from the guidance of much previous research. For me, scholarship is a process of learning from what one respects, and in my work on this book I have happily encountered a number of earlier works worthy of such respect.

I would also like to take this opportunity to thank everyone who provided me with occasions to speak on related themes. To the extent my schedule allows, I make a point of accepting invitations to speak or to give papers, even when I am busy with my own work or the topic is outside my field of specialization. While this has sometimes caused problems with overlapping commitments, I look back on all of these occasions with pleasure and a feeling that they were rewarding experiences. More than a few ideas that have come to me in the process of preparing a talk or in the discussions that have followed have found their way into this book. I feel keenly how much my work as a scholar has been supported and nurtured by the community surrounding me.

On March 11 of last year I experienced the Tōhoku earthquake in Sendai. I have experienced a number of major earthquakes in my lifetime, beginning with the 1978 Miyagi quake, but this was by far the most severe and violent of them all. And it was followed by a tsunami reported to be unprecedented in scale. I could have easily lost my life in this disaster. A trivial decision became the dividing line between life and death. Like many others experiencing such natural disasters, I came to sense that my life is not my own, but something permitted by a much vaster power. How am I to make use of this experience in my ongoing inquiry into divinity? This feels like a new and weighty theme I must embody in my work.

Following upon *Shisha no yukue*, Iwata Shoin has once again undertaken the publication of a book of mine. Iwata Hiroshi, president of the company, has always shown deep understanding and sympathy, not only for my own work, but for ambitious proposals by a number of younger scholars I have introduced to him. In the present deteriorating climate in publishing, the presence of solid, reliable, conscientious academic publishers such as Iwata Shoin is becoming increasingly important. In closing I would like to express my gratitude to Mr. Iwata and my best wishes for the continuing prosperity of Iwata Shoin as it rides out the storms of our times.

Satō Hiroo
9 August 2012

Notes

INTRODUCTION

When Humans Become Gods

1. Steven J. Mithen, *The Prehistory of the Mind*.
2. Matsumoto Naoko et al., *Ninchi kōkogaku to wa nani ka*.
3. From the official website of Yasukuni Shrine (yasukuni.or.jp). Accessed November 11, 2011.
4. Yanagita Kunio, "Senzo no hanashi."
5. Yanagita Kunio, "Hito o kami ni matsuru fūshū."
6. Hori Ichirō, *Minkan shinkōshi no sho mondai*.
7. Miyata Noboru, *Ikigami shinkō*.
8. Komatsu Kazuhiko, *Kami ni natta hitobito*.

CHAPTER 1

The Birth of the Imperial Spirits

1. Yanagita, "Hito o kami ni matsuru fūshū."
2. W. G. Aston, trans., *Nihongi*, 228. *Nihongi* is an alternative title for the *Nihon shoki*.
3. Orikuchi Shinobu, "Dajōsai no hongi."
4. Terasawa Kaoru, *Ōken tanjō*.

5. Kumagai Kimio, "Kodai ōken to tama."

6. Aston, *Nihongi*, 317–18.

7. Aston, *Nihongi*, 96–97.

8. Motoori Norinaga, *Kojikiden*, fascicle 3.

9. Kōnoshi Takamitsu, "Kami to hito."

10. Edwin A. Cranston, trans., *A Waka Anthology, volume. I: The Gem-Glistening Cup*, 196.

11. Aston, *Nihongi*, 64.

12. Translation from Torquil Duthie, *Man'yōshū and the Imperial Imagination in Early Japan* (Leiden: Brill, 2014).

13. Kita Yasuhiro, "Ritsuryō ryōbo saishi no kenkyū."

14. Imao Fumiaki, "Ritsuryō-ki ryōbo no jitsuzō."

15. An English version of this passage is given in R.A.B. Ponsonby-Fane, *Studies in Shinto and Shrines* (original ed. 1942, reprint Routledge, 2014), 462.

16. Hori Ichirō, "*Man'yōshū* ni arawareta sōsei to, takaikan, reikonkan ni tsuite."

17. Satō Hiroo, "Shisha wa yama ni sumu ka."

18. "Mogasaki yokoanabo-gun," 1989.

19. *Izumi Shikibu shū.*

20. Kuroda Satoshi, *Chūsei shōzō no bunkashi.*

21. Kaneko Shūichi, "Kan-Tō kan ni okeru kōtei saishi no suii."

CHAPTER 2
From Dead Souls to Deities

1. Mithen, *The Prehistory of the Mind.*

2. Aizawa Tadahiro, "*Iwajuku*" no hakken.

3. Matsuki Takehiko, *Rettō sōseiki.*

4. Sasaki Fujio, "Kanjō resseki to Jōmon-shiki kaisō shakai."

5. Okamura Michio, *Jōmon no seikatsushi.*

6. Tatsumi Kazuhiro, *Seiju to kodai Yamato no ōkyū.*

7. Terasawa Kaoru, *Ōken tanjō.*

8. Tatsumi Kazuhiro, *Seinaru mizu no matsuri to kodai ōken.*

9. Isomae Jun'ichi, *Dogū to kamen.*

10. Harada Masayuki, "Dogū saishi no kōzō."
11. Harada Masayuki, *Dogū to sono shūhen II*.
12. Nelly Naumann, *Yama no kami*.
13. Sasaki Kōmei, *Yama no kami to Nihonjin*.
14. Umehara Takeshi, *Nihon no shinsō*.
15. Tsunematsu Mikio, *Saiko no ōbo*.

CHAPTER 3
New Deities and the Tumuli

1. The Kofun period is variously dated as extending from circa 250 or 300 to 538, 552, 645, or 710.
2. Poem attributed to Prince Yamatotakeru in the *Kojiki*. Translation by Edwin A. Cranston, *A Waka Anthology, Volume I: The Gem-Glistening Cup* (Stanford: Stanford University Press, 1993), 23.
3. Mori Kōichi, *Nihon no kodai bunka*.
4. Egami Namio, *Kiba minzoku kokka*.
5. Terasawa Kaoru, *Ōken tanjō*.
6. Hōjō Yoshitaka, "Kyōdai zenpō kōenfun no sōshutsu."
7. Aston, *Nihongi*, 158–59.
8. Kumagai Kimio, *Ōkimi kara tennō e*.
9. Harada Masayuki, *Dogū*.
10. Ōba Iwao, "Kōkogaku-jō kara mita waga jōdaijin no takai kannen."
11. Okazaki Takashi, "Munakata chiiki no tenkai to Munakata Taisha."
12. Ōhira Shigeru, "Miwayama shutsudo no komochi magatama sashi to sono rekishiteki haikei."
13. Hōjō Yoshitaka, "'Yamato' genfūkei no tanjō."
14. Matsuki Takehiko, *Rettō sōseiki*.
15. Okada Seishi, "Kodai kokka ni okeru tennō saishi."
16. Hirose Kazuo, *Zenpō kōenfun kokka*.
17. Mitsuhashi Tadashi, "Kofun saishi kara ritsuryō saishi e."
18. Aston, *Nihongi*, II: 197–98
19. Nishimiya Hideki, "Jingi saishi."
20. Aston, *Nihongi* II: 96–97.
21. Toike Noboru, "Bunkyū no shūryō."

22. *Sendai-shi bunkazai chōsa hōkoku sho.*
23. Ishino Hironobu, *Yamatai-koku no kōhochi.*
24. Tsude Hiroshi, *Ōryō no kōkogaku.*
25. Tsude, *Ōryō no kōkogaku.*

CHAPTER 4

Between *Hitogami* and *Mononoke*

1. *Wei zhi,* as quoted in Ryusaku Tsunoda et al., *Sources of the Japanese Tradition,* Vol. I (New York: Columbia University Press, 1958), 4-5.
2. *Nihon kiryaku,* entry for Enryaku 19.7.23 (800).
3. Orikuchi Shinobu, "'Ho,' 'ura' kara 'hogahi' e."
4. Okada Shōji, "Onmyōdō saishi no seiritsu to tenkai."
5. Yamada Yūji, *Bakkō suru onryō.*
6. Toda Yoshimi, "Ritsuryōsei kara no kaihō."
7. Hayami Tasuku, "Kizoku shakai to himitsu shūhō."
8. Taniguchi Miki, "Heian kizoku no shippei ninshiki to chiryōhō."
9. Mark C. Funke, "Hitachi no Kuni Fudoki," *Monumenta Nipponica* 49:1 (Spring 1994), 1–29.
10. Sakurai Yoshirō, *Kamigami no henbō.*
11. Aston, *Nihongi,* I, 347.
12. Tr. Burton Watson, *Record of Miraculous Events in Japan* (New York: Columbia University Press, 2013), 13-14.
13. Watsuji Tetsurō, *Nihon rinri shisōshi,* vol. 1.
14. Ōtsu Tōru, *Kodai no tennōsei.*
15. Satō Hiroo, "Tatarigami no henshin."

CHAPTER 5

Escorts to the Other Shore

1. Satō Hiroo, *Kami, hotoke, ōken no chūsei.*
2. Nagaoka Ryūsaku, "Shinzō seiritsu ni kakawaru ichi kōsatsu."
3. Mitsuhashi Tadashi, "Kodai kara chūsei e no jingi shinkō no tenkai."
4. Satō, *Kami, hotoke, ōken no chūsei.*
5. Yamamoto Yōko, *Emaki ni okeru kami to tennō no hyōgen.*

6. Yoshihara Hiroto, "Kōgyoku Tennō no dajigoku tan."
7. Satō Hiroo, *Amaterasu no henbō.*
8. Satō, *Kami, hotoke, ōken no chūsei.*
9. Gorai Shigeru, *Zōho Kōya hijiri.*
10. Hosokawa Ryōichi, "Eison, Ninshō no jizen kyūsai."
11. Satō Hiroo, *Reijo no shisō.*
12. *Kōmyō shingon shijū shaku.*
13. Satō Masato, "Heian jidai kyūtei no shinbutsu kakuri."
14. Inoue Hiroshi, *Nihon chūsei kokka to shokoku ichinomiya-sei.*
15. Takahashi Miyuki, *Zōhoban Ise Shintō no seiritsu to tenkai.*
16. *Yuiitsu Shintō myōhō yōshū.*
17. Yamamoto Hiroko, "Shikōsha-tachi: Chūsei shingaku e mukete."
18. Ito Masayoshi, "Chūsei Nihongi no rinkaku."
19. Itō Satoshi, *Chūsei Amaterasu Ōmikami shinkō no kenkyū.*
20. Translation slightly modified from Mark Teeuwen and Hendrik van der Veere, *Nakatomi Harae Kunge: Purification and enlightenment in late-Heian Japan* (München: ludicium, 1998), 50–51.
21. Mark Teeuwen, "Jingi, jindō, soshite Shintō."

CHAPTER 6

The Undeparted Dead

1. Translation from Dennis Hirota, *No Abode: The Record of Ippen* (Honolulu: University of Hawaii Press, 1986), 29.
2. *Sasamegoto*, Tenri version.
3. For an English version of the story, see *The Lotus Sutra*, tr. Burton Watson (New York: Columbia University Press, 1993), 187–88.
4. "Kujō Michiie sō shobunjō."
5. *Bannaji Kabasaki engi narabi ni butsuji shidai.*
6. Katsuda Itaru, "Chūsei no yashikibo."
7. Irimada Nobuo, "Chūsonji Konjikidō no shisen."
8. Sasaki Tōru, "Kitakamigawa ryūiki ni hirogaru reijo."
9. Ihara Kesao, "Kamakura-ki no Suwa Jinja kankei shiryō ni miru Shintō to Butsudō."
10. Entry in *Azuma kagami* for Bunji 2.11.8 (1186).

11. More formally titled *Wakasa no Kuni chinju Ichi-Ni-no-miya shinjin ekeizu.*
12. Kuroda Hideo, "Kami to hito to."
13. Nakamura Ikuo, *Nihon no kami to ōken.*
14. From the *Genpei seisuiki.*
15. *Jingi seisō.*
16. Yamada Yūji, *Sutoku-in onryō no kenkyū.*

CHAPTER 7
The Ideology of Tōshō Daigongen

1. Satō Hiroo, *Nihon chūsei no kokka to Bukkyō.*
2. Fujii Yukiko, *Shōtoku Taishi no denshō*; Kuroda Toshio, *Ikkō ikki no seiji rinen.*
3. *Shūgi seihō ron.*
4. Asao Naohiro, "Shōgun kenryoku no sōshutsu."
5. *Iezusu-kai Nihon nenpō.*
6. Okada Shōji, "Kinsei no Shintō sōsai."
7. *Honkō Kokushi nikki.*
8. Sonehara Satoshi, *Shinkun Ieyasu no tanjō.*
9. Letter of Ieyasu to the viceroy of New Spain (Mexico), dated Keichō 17 (1612).
10. Mizutani Tagui, *Byōbo rantō to gense jōdo no shisō.*
11. Kishimoto Satoru, "Daimyō-ke sosen no shinkakuka o meguru ichi kōsatsu."
12. Katō Genchi, *Honpō seishi no kenkyū.*
13. Fujita Satoru, *Edo jidai no tennō.*
14. Ochiai Nobutaka, *Neko-e no tonosama.*
15. Watanabe Hiroshi, *Higashi Ajia no ōken to shisō.*

CHAPTER 8
The Heyday of Living Gods

1. Ichiro Hori, "Self-Mummified Buddhas in Japan."
2. Naitō Masatoshi, *Nihon no miira shinkō.*

3. *Mimibukuro*, Book 8.
4. Miyata Noboru, *Edo no chiisana kamigami*.
5. Yanagita, "Hito o kami ni matsuru fūshū."
6. *Shinran Shōnin eden*.
7. Kuroda Hideo, "Chūsei no tabisugata o megutte."
8. Katsurajima Nobuhiro, "Minshū shūkyō ni okeru kami shinkō to shinkō kyōdōtai."
9. *Konkō Daijin rikai*.
10. Kozawa Hiroshi, "Ikigami no shisōshi."
11. Murakami Shigeyoshi, "Bakumatsu ishin ki no minshū shūkyō ni tsuite."
12. Yasumaru Yoshio, "Nihon no kindaika to minshū shisō."
13. Maeda Tsutomu, *Kinsei Shintō to kokugaku*.
14. Suenaga Keiko, *Uden Shintō no kisoteki kenkyū*.
15. "Yamato ikusa akitsu sonae."
16. Cornelis Ouwehand, *Namazu-e and Their Themes*.

CHAPTER 9

The Road to Yasukuni Shrine

1. Anne Bouchy, *Kami to hito no hazama ni ikiru*.
2. Takahashi Akinori, *Edo no tenkinzoku*.

Bibliography

1. OTHER RELATED WORKS BY SATŌ HIROO

Amaterasu no henbō アマテラスの変貌. Hōzōkan, 2000.

"Changes in the Concept of Mountains in Japan." *Cahiers d'Extreme-Asie* 18 (2011).

"Chūsei ni okeru kami kannen no hen'yō 中世における神観念の変容." In Ito Satoshi 伊藤聡, ed., *Chūsei shinwa to jingi, Shintō sekai* 中世神話と神祇・神道世界. Chikurinsha, 2011.

"Higan ni kayou oto: Shinbutsu no koe ga noizu ni naru toki 彼岸に通う音: 神仏の声がノイズになるとき." *Bungaku* 11, no. 6 (2010).

"Higan ni sasou kami: Nihon no Jōdo shinkō ni okeru imēji to bijon 彼岸に誘う神: 日本の浄土信仰におけるイメージとヴィジョン." *Shiseigaku kenkyu* 16 (2011).

Kami, hotoke, ōken no chūsei 神・仏・王権の中世. Hōzōkan, 1998.

Kishōmon no seishinshi: Chūsei sekai no kami to hotoke 起請文の精神史. Kōdansha Sensho Mechie, 2006.

Nihon chūsei no kokka to Bukkyō 日本中世の国家と仏教. Yoshikawa Kōbunkan, 2010 (initial publication 1987).

"Ōto Nara no genzō 王都奈良の原像." In Matsuoka Seigō 松岡正剛, ed. *Narajia: Higashi Ajia no kyōdōtai: Ima narabon* ナラジア: 東アジアの共同体: イマナラボン. Maruzen, 2010.

Reijō no shisō 霊場の思想. Yoshikawa Kōbunkan, 2003.

"Reijō to junrei 霊場と巡礼." In Irumada Nobuo 入間田宣夫, ed. *Tsuwamono-tachi no gokuraku jōdo* 兵たちの極楽浄土. Kōshi Shoin, 2010.

"'Shinbutsu shugō' ron no keisei no shiteki haikei 「神仏集合」論の形成の史的背景." *Shūkyō kenkyū* 353 (2007).

Shisha no yukue 死者の行方. Iwata Shoin, 2008.

"Shisha wa yama ni sumu ka? 死者は山に棲むか" In Suwa Haruo 諏訪春雄 et al., ed., *Ajia yūgaku* 124: *Higashi Ajia no shisha no yukue to sōgi* アジア遊学 124: 東アジアの死者の行方と葬儀. Bensei Shuppan, 2009.

"Tatarigami no henshin: Tataru kami kara bassuru kami e 祟り神の変身." *Nihon shisō shigaku* 日本思想史学 31 (1999).

"Zenpō kōenfun ni yadoru mono 前方後円墳に宿るもの." In Kojita Yasunao 小路田泰直, ed., *Shi no kinō: Zenpō kōenfun to wa nani ka* 死の機能: 前方後円墳とは何か. Iwata Shoin, 2009.

2. Sources Cited

Abe Kin'ya 阿部謹也. *Chūsei senmin no uchū* 中世賤民の宇宙. Chikuma Shobō, 1978.

Aizawa Tadahiro 相沢忠洋. *"Iwajuku" no hakken: Maboroshi no kyūsekki o motomete* 「岩宿」の発見: 幻の旧石器を求めて. Kōdansha, 1969.

Amino Yoshihiko 網野善彦. *Muen, kugai, raku: Nihon chūsei no jiyū to heiwa* 無縁・公界・楽: 日本中世の自由と平和. Heibonsha, 1978.

Aritomi Jun'ya 有富純也. "Jinja shaden no seiritsu to ritsuryō kokka 神社社殿の成立と律令国家." *Kokuritsu Rekishi Minzoku Hakubutsukan kenkyū hōkoku* 国立歴史民俗博物館研究報告 148 (2008).

Asao Naohiro 朝尾直弘. "Shōgun kenryoku no sōshutsu 将軍権力の創出." In *Shōgun kenryoku no sōshutsu* 将軍権力の創出. Iwanami Shoten, 1994.

Aston, W. G., tr. from original Chinese and Japanese. *Nihongi: Chronicles of Japan from the Earliest Times to A.D. 697*. London: The Japan Society, 1896; Allen & Unwin [1956].

Bouchy, Anne. *Kami to hito no hazama ni ikiru* 神と人のはざまに生きる: 近代都市の女性巫者. Tokyo Daigaku Shuppankai, 2009. (original title: *Les oracles de Shirataka, ou, La sibylle d'Osaka: Vie d'une femme specialiste de la possession dans le Japon du XXe siecle*).

Cranston, Edwin A., tr. *A Waka Anthology, Volume I: The Gem-Glistening Cup*. Stanford: Stanford University Press, 1993.

Duthie, Torquil. *Man'yōshū and the Imperial Imagination in Early Japan*. Leiden: Brill, 2014.

Egami Namio 江上波夫. *Kiba minzoku kokka* 騎馬民族国家. Chūkō Shinsho, 1967.

Emura Hiroyuki 榎村寛之. *Ritsuryō tennōsei saishi no kenkyū* 律令天皇制祭祀の研究. Hanawa Shobō, 1996.

Frasier, James G. *The Golden Bough*. Translated into Japanese by Kikkawa Shin 吉川信 as *Kinshihen* 金枝篇. 2 vols. Chikuma Gakugei Bunko, 2003.

Fujii Manabu 藤井学. "Chūsei ni okeru kokkakan no ichi keitai: Nichiren no dōri to Shakuson goryō o chūshin ni 中世における国家観の一形態: 日蓮の道理と釈尊御領を中心に." In Dokushikai, eds., *Kokushi ronshū* 国史論集 1 (1959).

Fujii Yukiko 藤井由紀子. *Shōtoku Taishi no denshō* 聖徳太子の伝承. Yoshikawa Kōbunkan, 1999.

Fujita Satoru 藤田覚. *Edo jidai no tennō* 江戸時代の天皇. Kōdansha, 2011.

Funke, Mark C. "Hitachi no Kuni Fudoki 常陸国風土記," *Monumenta Nipponica* 49:1 (Spring 1994), 1–29.

Furuya Noriyuki 古屋紀之. *Kofun no seiritsu to sōsō saishi* 古墳の成立と葬送祭祀. Yūzankaku, 2007.

———. "Yayoi funbo kara kofun e: Sōsō girei ni miru henka 弥生墳墓から古墳へ: 葬送儀礼に見る変化." in *Haka kara saguru shakai* 墓から探る社会. Yūzankaku, 2009.

Gorai Shigeru 五来重. *Gankōji Gokurakubō: Chūsei shomin shinkō shiryō no kenkyū* 元興寺極楽坊: 中世庶民信仰資料の研究. Hōzōkan, 1964.

———. *Zōho Kōya hijiri* 増補高野聖. Kadokawa Sensho, 1975.

———. *Nihonjin no shiseikan* 日本人の死生観. Kadokawa Shoten, 1994.

Haga Shōji 羽賀祥二. *Meiji Ishin to shūkyō* 明治維新と宗教. Chikuma Shobō, 1994.

Hanazono Toshimaro 華園聡麿. "Nihon ni okeru reichi to reijō 日本における霊地と霊場." In *Iwanami kōza Nihon bungaku to Bukkyō* 岩波講座日本文学と仏教 7. Iwanami Shoten, 1995.

Harada Masayuki 原田昌幸. *Dogū* 土偶. *Nihon no Bijutsu* 日本の美術 345. Shibundō, 1995.

———. "Dogū saishi no kōzō 土偶祭祀の構造." *Kikan kōkogaku* 季刊考古学 107 (2009).

———. *Dogū to sono shūhen* 土偶とその周辺 I. *Nihon no Bijutsu* 日本の美術 526. Shibundō, 2010.

———. *Dogū to sono shūhen* 土偶とその周辺 II. *Nihon no Bijutsu* 日本の美術 527. Shibundō, 2010.

Hashimoto Hatsuko 橋本初子. *Chūsei Tōji to Kōbō Daishi shinkō* 中世東寺と弘法大師信仰. Shibunkaku Shuppan, 1990.

Hayami Tasuku 速水侑. "Kizoku shakai to himitsu shūhō 貴族社会と秘密修法." In *Heian kizoku shakai to Bukkyō* 平安貴族社会と仏教. Yoshikawa Kōbunkan, 1975.

Hayashi Makoto 林淳. "Shinbutsu shūgō kenkyūshi nōto 神仏習合研究史ノート." *Shintō shūkyō* 神道宗教 117 (1984).

Hayashi Mikiya 林幹弥. *Taishi shinkō no kenkyū* 太子信仰の研究. Yoshikawa Kōbunkan, 1980.

Hikino Kyōsuke 引野享輔. "Kinsei chūkōki ni okeru chiiki shinshoku hensei: 'Shinshū chitai' Aki o jirei to shite. 近世中後期における地域神職編成: 「真宗地帯」安芸を事例として" *Shigaku zasshi* 史学雑誌 111, no. 11 (2002).

———. "Kinsei kōki no chiiki shakai ni okeru hanshu shinkō to minshū ishiki 近世後期の地域社会における藩主信仰と民衆意識." *Rekishigaku kenkyū* 歴史学研究 820 (2006).

Hirose Kazuo 広瀬和雄. "Zenpō kōenfun to Yamato seiken 前方後円墳と大和政権." In *Nihon kodai ōken no seiritsu* 日本古代王権の成立. Aoki Shoten, 2002.

———. *Zenpō kōenfun kokka* 前方後円墳国家. Kadokawa Sensho, 2003.

Hirota, Dennis, tr. *No Abode: The Record of Ippen* 一遍の思想研究及び『一遍上人語録』の英訳と注釈. Honolulu: University of Hawaii Press, 1986.

Hōjō Katsutaka 北條勝貴. "Kodai Nihon no shinbutsu shinkō 古代日本の神仏信仰." *Kokuritsu Rekishi Minzoku Hakubutsukan kenkyū hōkoku* 国立歴史民俗博物館研究報告 148 (2008).

Hōjō Yoshitaka 北條芳隆. "Kyodai zenpō kōenfun no sōshutsu 巨大前方後円墳の創出." *Nihonshi no hōhō* 日本史の方法 5 (2007).

———. "Shuchō kara hitomi gokū e: Shiso tanjōsai to shite no zenpō kōenfun saishi. 首長から人身御供へ: 始祖誕生祭としての前方後円墳祭祀." *Nihonshi no hōhō* 日本史の方法 5 (2007).

———. "'Yamato' genfūkei no tanjō「大和」原風景の誕生." In *Shi no kinō: Zenpō kōenfun to wa nani ka* 死の機能: 前方後円墳とは何か. Iwata Shoin, 2009.

Hori Ichirō 堀一郎. "Man'yōshū ni arawareta sōsei to, takaikan, reikonkan ni tsuite 万葉集にあらわれた葬制と、他界観、霊魂観について." In *Shūkyō, shūzoku no seikatsu kisei* 宗教・習俗の生活規制. Miraisha, 1963.

———. *Minkan shinkōshi no sho mondai* 民間信仰史の諸問題. Miraisha, 1971.

———. "Self-Mummified Buddhas in Japan: An Aspect of the Shugen-Dō ("Mountain Asceticism") Sect 山嶽信仰の原初形態に関する一仮説." *History of Religions* 1:2 (Winter 1962). Published by University of Chicago Press.

Hosokawa Ryōichi 細川涼一. "Eison, Ninshō no jizen kyūsai: Hinin kyūsai o shujiku ni 叡尊・忍性の慈善救済: 非人救済を主軸に." *Ronkyū* 論究 (Chūō Daigaku Daigakuin) 11, no. 1 (2009).

Ihara Kesao 井原今朝男. "Kamakura-ki no Suwa Jinja kankei shiryō ni miru Shintō to Butsudō: Chūsei gokibun no jidaiteki tokushitsu ni tsuite 鎌倉期の諏訪神社関係資料にみる神道と仏道: 中世御記文の時代的特質について." *Kokuritsu Rekishi Minzoku Hakubutsukan kenkyū hōkoku* 国立歴史民族博物館研究報告 139 (2008).

Imahori Taitsu 今堀太逸. "Ekijin to jingi shinkō no tenkai 疫神と神祇信仰の展開." *Bukkyō shigaku kenkyū* 仏教史学研究 36, no. 2 (1992).

Imai Akihiko 今井昭彦. *Kindai Nihon to senshisha saishi* 近代日本と戦死者祭祀. Tōyō Shorin, 2005.

Imao Fumiaki 今尾文昭. "Hakkaku-fun no shutsugen to tenkai 八角墳の出現と展開." In *Kodai o kangaeru: Shūmatsuki kofun to kodai kokka* 古代を考える: 終末期古墳と古代国家. Yoshikawa Kōbunkan, 2005.

———. "Ritsuryō-ki ryōbo no jitsuzō 律令期陵墓の実像." In *Ritsuryō-ki ryōbo no seiritsu to tojō* 律令期陵墓の成立と都城. Aoki Shoten, 2008 (initial publication 2006).

Inoue Hiroshi 井上寛司. *Nihon no jinja to "Shintō"* 日本の神社と「神道」. Azekura Shobō, 2006.

———. *Nihon chūsei kokka to shokoku ichinomiya-sei* 日本中世国家と諸国一宮制. Iwata Shoin, 2009.

Inoue Mitsusada 井上光貞. *Nihon kodai no ōken to saishi* 日本古代の王権と祭祀. Tōkyō Daigaku Shuppankai, 1984.

Irimada Nobuo 入間田宣夫. "Chūsonji Konjikidō no shisen 中尊寺金色堂の視線." In *Chūsei chiiki shakai to kōryū* 中世地域社会と交流. Yoshikawa Kōbunkan, 1994.

Ishida Ichirō 石田一良. *Kami to Nihon bunka* カミと日本文化. Perikansha, 1983.

Ishii Susumu 石井進. *Insei jidai* 院政時代. Vol. 2 of *Kōza Nihonshi* 講座日本史. Tōkyō Daigaku Shuppankai, 1970.

Ishino Hironobu 石野博信. *Yamatai-koku no kōhochi: Makimuku iseki* 邪馬台国の候補地: 纏向遺跡. Shinsensha, 2008.

Isomae Jun'ichi 磯前順一. *Dogū to kamen: Jōmon shakai no shūkyō kōzō* 土偶と仮面: 縄文社会の宗教構造. Azekura Shobō, 1994.

Itō Masayoshi 伊藤正義. "Chūsei Nihongi no rinkaku: Taiheiki ni okeru Urabe Kanekazu setsu o megutte 中世日本紀の輪郭: 太平記における卜部兼員説をめぐって." *Bungaku* 文学 40, no. 10 (1972).

Itō Satoshi 伊藤聡. "Shinbutsu shūgō riron no hen'yō: Chūsei kara kinsei e 神仏習合理論の変容: 中世から近世へ." *Shūkyō kenkyū* 宗教研究 353 (2007).

——. *Chūsei Amaterasu Ōmikami shinkō no kenkyū* 中世天照大神信仰の研究. Hōzōkan, 2011.

Iwata Shigenori 岩田重則. *Senshisha reikon no yukue: Sensō to minzoku* 戦死者霊魂のゆくえ: 戦争と民俗. Yoshikawa Kōbunkan, 2002.

Kageyama Haruki 景山春樹. "Hieizan ni okeru Goeidō to byōbo 比叡山における御影堂と廟墓." In *Hieizan to Tendai Bukkyō no kenkyū* 比叡山と天台仏教の研究. Meicho Shuppan, 1975.

——. *Shinsōban: Shintaisan* 新装版: 神体山. Gakuseisha, 2001.

Kamikawa Michio 上川通夫. "Chūsei no sokui girei to Bukkyō 中世の即位儀礼と仏教." *Tennō daigawari gishiki no rekishiteki tenkai* 天皇代替り儀式の歴史的展開. Kashiwa Shobō, 1989 (initial publication 1987).

Kaneko Hiroyuki 金子裕之. "Kanmu shinwa to Fujiwarakyō 桓武神話と藤原京." *Nihonshi no hōhō* 日本史の方法 7 (2008).

Kaneko Shūichi 金子修一. "Kan-Tō kan ni okeru kōtei saishi no suii 漢唐間における皇帝祭祀の推移." *Ōken no kosumorojī* 王権のコスモロジー. Vol. 1 of *Hikaku rekishigaku taikei* 比較歴史学大系 1. Kōbundō, 1988.

Kataoka Kōhei 片岡耕平. "Chūsei no kegare kannen ni tsuite 中世の穢観念について." *Rekishi* 歴史 102 (2004).

Katō Genchi 加藤玄智. *Honpō seishi no kenkyū* 本邦生祠の研究. Meiji Seitoku Kinen Gakkai, 1931.

Katsuda Itaru 勝田至. "Chūsei no yashikibo 中世の屋敷墓." *Shirin* 史林 71, no. 3 (1988).

Katsurajima Nobuhiro 桂島宣弘. "Minshū shūkyō ni okeru kami shinkō to shinkō kyōdōtai 民衆宗教における神信仰と信仰共同体." In *Bakumatsu minshū shisō no kenkyū* 幕末民衆思想の研究. Bunrikaku, 2005 (initial publication 1984).

Kawamura Kunimitsu 川村邦光, ed. *Senshisha no yukue: Katari to hyōshō kara* 戦死者のゆくえ: 語りと表象から. Seikyūsha, 2003.

Kawane Yoshiyasu 河音能平. "Wakasa no Kuni chinju ichi-ni-no miya engi no seiritsu 若狭国鎮守一二宮縁起の成立." In *Chūsei hōkensei seiritsu shiron* 中世封建制成立史論. Tōkyō Daigaku Shuppankai, 1971.

Kidō Saizō 木藤才蔵. *Sasamegoto no kenkyū* ささめごとの研究. Rinsen Shoten, 1990.

Kishimoto Satoru 岸本覚. "Daimyō-ke sosen no shinkakuka o meguru ichi kōsatsu: Kumamoto-han o jirei to shite 大名家祖先の神格化をめぐる一考察: 熊本藩を事例として." In Sasaki Suguru 佐々木克 ed., *Meiji Ishin-ki no seiji bunka* 明治維新期の政治文化. Shibunkaku Shuppan, 2005.

———. "Kyū ryōshu no yuisho to nenki 旧領主の由緒と年忌." *Rekishi hyōron* 歴史評論 743 (2012).

Kita Yasuhiro 北康宏. "Ritsuryō ryōbo saishi no kenkyū 律令陵墓祭祀の研究." *Shigaku zasshi* 史学雑誌 108, no. 11 (1999).

Kojita Yasunao 小路田泰直. "Amino shigaku no koekata ni tsuite: Gendai mappō shisō kō. 網野史学の越え方について: 現代末法思想考" In Kojita Yasunao, ed., *Amino shigaku no koekata* 網野史学の越え方. Yumani Shobō, 2003.

———. "Hito, shakai, kami no tanjō ni tsuite no kasetsu: Izon riron no kakuritsu ni mukete 人・社会・神の誕生についての仮説: 依存理論の確立にむけて." *Nihonshi no hōhō* 日本史の方法 6 (2007).

Komatsu Kazuhiko 小松和彦. *Kami ni natta hitobito* 神になった人びと. Tankōsha, 2001.

Kondō Yoshirō 近藤義郎. *Zenpō kōenfun no jidai* 前方後円墳の時代. Iwanami Shoten, 1983.

———. *Zenpō kōenfun to Kibi, Yamato* 前方後円墳と吉備・大和. Kibibito Shuppan, 2001.

———. *Zenpō kōenfun no kigen o kangaeru* 前方後円墳の起源を考える. Aoki Shoten, 2005.

Kōnoshi Takamitsu 神野志隆光. "Kami to hito: Tennō sokushin no shisō to hyōgen 神と人: 天皇即神の思想と表現." *Kokugo to kokubungaku* 国語と国文学 67, no. 11 (November 1990 special issue).

Kozawa Hiroshi 小沢浩. "Ikigami no shisōshi 生き神の思想史." In *Ikigami no shisōshi* 生き神の思想史. Iwanami Shoten, 2010 (initial publication 1987).

Kumagai Kimio 熊谷公男. "Kodai ōken to tama 古代王権とタマ(霊)." *Nihonshi kenkyū* 日本史研究 308 (1988).

———. *Ōkimi kara tennō e* 大王から天皇へ. Vol. 3 of *Nihon no rekishi* 日本の歴史. Kōdansha, 2001.

———. "Jitō no sokuigi to 'chitenka Ōkimi' no sokui girei 持統の即位儀と「治天下大王」の即位儀礼." *Nihonshi kenkyū* 日本史研究 474 (2002).

Kuno Takeshi 久能健. *Tōhoku kodai chōkoku shi no kenkyū* 東北古代彫刻史の研究. Chūō Kōron Bijutsu Shuppan, 1971.

Kuroda Hideo 黒田日出男. "Chūsei no tabisugata o megutte 中世の旅姿をめぐって." In *Sugata to shigusa no chūseishi* 姿としぐさの中世史. Heibonsha, 1986.

———. "Kami to hito to: 'Wakasa no kuni chinju shinjin-e keizu' o yomu 神と人と:「若狭国鎮守神人絵系図」を読む." In *Ō no shintai, Ō no shōzō* 王の身体、王の肖像. Heibonsha, 1993.

———. "Shōzōga to shite no Go-Daigo Tennō 肖像画としての後醍醐天皇." In *Ō no shintai, Ō no shōzō* 王の身体、王の肖像. Heibonsha, 1993.

Kuroda Satoshi 黒田智. *Chūsei shōzō no bunkashi* 中世肖像の文化史. Perikansha, 2007.

Kuroda Toshio 黒田俊雄. "Ikkō ikki no seiji rinen: 'Buppōryō' ni tsuite 一向一揆の政治理念:「仏法領」について." In *Nihon chūsei no kokka to shūkyō* 日本中世の国家と宗教. Iwanami Shoten, 1975 (initial publication 1959).

———. "Chūsei shūkyōshi ni okeru Shintō no ichi 中世宗教史における神道の位置." In *Nihon chūsei no shakai to shūkyō* 日本中世の社会と宗教. Iwanami Shoten, 1990 (initial publication 1979).

Maeda Tsutomu 前田勉. *Kinsei Shintō to Kokugaku* 近世神道と国学. Perikansha, 2002.

Maruyama Shigeru 丸山茂. "Jinja kenchiku no keisei katei ni okeru kanshasei no igi ni tsuite 神社建築の形成過程における官社制の意義について." *Kenchiku shigaku* 建築史学 33 (1999).

Matsuki Takehiko 松木武彦. *Rettō sōseiki* 列島創世記. Nihon no rekishi 日本の歴史 1. Shōgakukan, 2007.

———. *Shinka kōkogaku no daibōken* 進化考古学の大冒険. Shinchō Sensho, 2009.

Matsumoto Naoko 松本直子. *Jōmon no mura to shakai* 縄文の村と社会. Iwanami Shoten, 2005

———, Nakazono Satoru 中園聡, and Tokitsu Yūko 時津裕子 eds. *Ninchi kōkogaku to wa nani ka* 認知考古学とは何か. Aoki Shoten, 2003.

Mithen, Steven J. *The Prehistory of the Mind: A Search for the Origins of Art, Religion, and Science*. London: Thames and Hudson, 1996.

Mitsuhashi Tadashi 三橋正. "Kodai kara chūsei e no jingi shinkō no tenkai 古代から中世への神祇信仰の展開." In *Heian jidai no shinkō to shūkyō girei* 平安時代の信仰と宗教儀礼. Zoku Gunsho Ruijū Kanseikai, 2000.

———. "Kofun saishi kara ritsuryō saishi e 古墳祭祀から律令祭祀へ." In *Nihon kodai jingi seido no keisei to tenkai* 日本古代神祇制度の形成と展開. Hōzōkan, 2010.

Miura Sukeyuki 三浦佑之. "Ningen tekkotsu ron 人間鉄骨論." In Nakamura Ikuo 中村生雄, Miura Sukeyuki 三浦佑之, and Akasaka Norio 赤坂憲雄 eds. *Shuryō to kugi no bunkashi* 狩猟と供犠の文化誌. Shinwasha, 2007.

Miyake Hitoshi 宮家準. *Reizan to Nihonjin* 霊山と日本人. Nihon Hōsō Shuppan Kyōkai, 2004.

Miyata Noboru 宮田登. *Ikigami shinkō: Hito o kami ni matsuru shūzoku* 生き神信仰: 人を神に祀る習俗. Hanawa Shobō, 1970.

——. "Nōson no fukkō undō to minshū shūkyō no tenkai 農村の復興運動と民衆宗教の展開." In *Hayarigami to minshū shūkyō* はやり神と民衆宗教. Yoshikawa Kōbunkan, 2006.

——. *Edo no chiisana kamigami* 江戸の小さな神々. Seidosha, 1989.

Mizutani Tagui 水谷類. *Byōbo rantō to gense jōdo no shisō* 廟墓ラントウと現世浄土の思想. Yūzankaku, 2009.

——. *Bozen saishi to seisho no toporojī* 墓前祭祀と聖所のトポロジー. Yūzankaku, 2009.

Mori Kōichi 森浩一. "Nihon no kodai bunka 日本の古代文化." In Ishimoda Shō 石母田正 et al., eds. *Kodaishi kōza* 古代史講座 3: *Kodai bunmei no keisei* 古代文明の形成. Gakuseisha, 1962.

Motoyasu Hiroshi 本康宏史. *Gunto no irei kūkan: Kokumin tōgō to senshisha-tachi* 軍都の慰霊空間: 国民統合と戦死者たち. Yoshikawa Kōbunkan, 2002.

Muguruma Yumi 六車由美. *Kami, hito o kuu: Hitomi gokū no minzokugaku* 神、人を喰う: 人身御供の民俗学. Shin'yōsha, 2003.

——. "Hitobashira no shisō, joron 人柱の思想・序論." In *Shuryō to kugi no bunkashi* 狩猟と供犠の文化誌. Shinwasha, 2007.

Murakami Shigeyoshi 村上重良. "Bakumatsu Ishin ki no minshū shūkyō ni tsuite 幕末維新期の民衆宗教について." In *Nihon shisō taikei: Minshū shūkyō no shisō* 日本思想大系: 民衆宗教の思想. Iwanami Shoten, 1971.

——. *Irei to shōkon: Yasukuni no shisō* 慰霊と招魂: 靖国の思想. Iwanami Shinsho, 1974.

Nagaoka Ryūsaku 長岡龍作. "Shinzō seiritsu ni kakawaru ichi kōsatsu: Kodai Nihon no Hachimanjin 神像成立に関わる一考察: 古代日本の八幡神." *Za Gurēto Budda Shimpojiumu Ronshū* ザ・グレイトブッダ・シンポジウム論集 3. *Kami to hotoke: Shūkyō bunka to sono rekishiteki kiban* カミと仏: 宗教文化とその歴史的基盤. Tōdaiji, 2005.

——. "Kodai Nihon no 'shōjin' kan to zōzō 古代日本の「生人」観と造像." *Bijutsu shigaku* 美術史学 29 (2008).

Naitō Masatoshi 内藤正敏. *Nihon no miira shinkō* 日本のミイラ信仰. Hōzōkan, 1999.

Nakamura Ikuo 中村生雄. *Nihon no kami to ōken* 日本の神と王権. Hōzōkan, 1994.

——. "Sesshō zaigōkan to sōmoku jōbutsu shisō 殺生罪業観と草木成仏思想." In *Shuryō to kugi no bunkashi* 狩猟と供犠の文化誌. Shinwasha, 2007.

Nakano Yasuhide 中野豈任. *Wasurerareta reijō: Chūsei shinseishi no kokoromi* 忘れられた霊場: 中世心性史の試み. Heibonsha Sensho, 1988.

Nakazawa Shin'ichi 中沢新一. *Kuma kara Ō e* 熊から王へ. Kōdansha Sensho Mechie, 2002.

———. *Kami no hatsumei* 神の発明. Kōdansha Sensho Mechie, 2003.

Namihira Emiko 波平恵美子. *Nihonjin no shi no katachi: Dentō girei kara Yasukuni made* 日本人の死のかたち: 伝統儀礼から靖国まで. Asahi Sensho, 2004.

Naumann, Nelly. *Yama no kami* 山の神. Translated into Japanese by Nomura Shin'ichi 野村伸一 and Hieda Yōichirō 檜枝陽一郎. Gensōsha, 1994.

Nishimiya Hideki 西宮秀紀. "Jingi saishi 神祇祭祀." In *Rettō no kodaishi* 列島の古代史 7: *Shinkō to sekaikan* 信仰と世界観. Iwanami Shoten, 2006.

Nishimiya Kazutami 西宮一民. "Yashiro kō: Kotoba to moji ヤシロ(社)考: 言葉と文字." In *Jōdai saishi to gengo* 上代祭祀と言語. Ōfūsha, 1990.

Ōba Iwao 大場磐雄. "Kōkogaku-jō kara mita waga jōdaijin no takai kannen 考古学上から見た我が上代人の他界観念." In Akata Mitsuo 赤田光雄 ed. *Sorei shinkō* 祖霊信仰. Minshū shūkyōshi sōsho 民衆宗教史叢書 26. Yūzankaku, 1991 (initial publication 1950).

Ochiai Nobutaka 落合延孝. *Neko-e no tonosama: Ryōshu no fōkuroa* 猫絵の殿様領主のフォークロア. Yoshikawa Kōbunkan, 1996.

Ōe Shinobu 大江志乃夫. *Yasukuni Jinja* 靖国神社. Iwanami Shinsho, 1984.

Ōhira Shigeru 大平茂. "Miwayama shutsudo no komochi magatama saishi to sono rekishiteki haikei 三輪山出土の子持勾玉祭祀とその歴史的背景." In Sugiyama Shigetsugu 椙山林継 and Yamagishi Ryōji 山岸良二 eds. *Genshi, Kodai Nihon no saishi* 原始・古代日本の祭祀. Dōseisha, 2007.

Okada Seishi 岡田精司. "Kodai kokka ni okeru tennō saishi 古代国家における天皇祭祀." In *Kodai saishi no shiteki kenkyū* 古代祭祀の史的研究. Hanawa Shobō, 1992.

———. "Kofun-jō no keishō girei setsu ni tsuite 古墳上の継承儀礼説について." *Kokuritsu Rekishi Minzoku Hakubutsukan kenkyū hōkoku* 国立歴史民俗博物館研究報告 80 (1999).

Okada Shōji 岡田荘司. "Kinsei no Shintō sōsai 近世の神道葬祭." In Ōkura Seishin Bunka Kenkyūjo, eds. *Kinsei no seishin seikatsu* 近世の精神生活. Zoku Gunsho Ruijū Kanseikai, 1996.

———. "Onmyōdō saishi no seiritsu to tenkai 陰陽道祭祀の成立と展開." In Murayama Shūichi 村山修一 et al., eds. *Onmyōdō sōsho* 陰陽道叢書 1: *Kodai* 古代. Meicho Shuppan, 1991 (initial publication 1987).

———, ed. *Nihon Shintō shi* 日本神道史. Yoshikawa Kōbunkan, 2010.

Okamura Michio 岡村道雄. *Jōmon no seikatsushi* 縄文の生活誌, rev. ed. Kodansha, 2002.

Okazaki Takashi 岡崎敬, "Munakata chiiki no tenkai to Munakata Taisha 宗像地域の展開と宗像大社." In *Munakata Okinoshima* 宗像沖ノ島. Munakata Taisha Fukkō Kiseikai, 1961.

Ōkubo Tetsuya 大久保徹也. "Kami kannen to zenpō kōenfun saishi カミ観念と前方後円墳祭祀." In *Nihon kodai ōken no seiritsu* 日本古代王権の成立. Aoki Shoten, 2002.

———. "Kofun ron: 'Ō' o fukusei suru kokoromi 古墳論: <王>を複製する試み." *Nihonshi no hōhō* 日本史の方法 3 (2006).

———. "Kofun zōei o unagashita shi no imēji 古墳造営を促した死のイメージ." In Kojita Yaunao 小路田泰直 et al., eds. *Shi no kinō: Zenpō kōenfun to wa nani ka* 死の機能: 前方後円墳とは何か. Iwata Shoin, 2009.

Ono Kazuyuki 小野一之. "Shōtoku Taishibo no tenkai to Eifukuji no seiritsu 聖徳太子墓の展開と叡福寺の成立." *Nihonshi kenkyū* 日本史研究 342 (1991).

Oppenheimer, Stephen. *Out of Eden: The Peopling of the World*. Edinburgh: Constable & Robinson, 2004. Translated into Japanese by Nakamura Akiko 仲村明子 as *Jinrui no sokuseki 10-man'nen zenshi* 人類の足跡10万年全史. Sōshisha, 2007.

Orikuchi Shinobu 折口信夫. "Daijōsai no hongi 大嘗祭の本義." In *Orikuchi Shinobu zenshū* 折口信夫全集 3. Chūō Kōronsha, 1995 (initial publication 1928).

———. "'Ho,' 'ura' kara 'hogahi' e 「ほ」・「うら」から「ほがひ」へ." In *Orikuchi Shinobu zenshū* 折口信夫全集 4. Chūō Kōronsha, 1995.

Ōtsu Tōru 大津透. *Kodai no tennōsei* 古代の天皇制. Iwanami Shinsho, 1999.

Ouwehand, Cornelis. *Namazu-e and Their Themes*. Leiden: E. J. Brill, 1964.

Ponsonby-Fane, R.A.B. *Studies in Shinto and Shrines*. London: Routledge, 2014 (initial publication 1942).

Saitō Hideki 斉藤英喜. "Tataru kami to takusen suru kami 祟る神と託宣する神." In *Nihon no kami* 日本の神, vol. 1. Heibonsha, 1995.

Sakamoto Koremaru 坂本是丸. "'Nihon fashizumu' to jinja, Shintō ni kansuru sobyō 「日本ファッシズム」と神社・神道に関する素描." *Kokugakin Daigaku Kenkyū Kaihatsu Suishin Sentā kenkyū kiyō* 国学院大学研究開発推進センター研究紀要 6 (2012).

Sakurai Kentarō 桜井徳太郎. *Nihon minzoku shūkyō ron* 日本民俗宗教論. Shunjūsha, 1982.

Sakurai Yoshirō 桜井好朗. *Kamigami no henbō: Shaji engi no sekai kara* 神々の変貌: 社寺縁起の世界から. Tōkyō Daigaku Shuppankai, 1976.

Sasaki Fujio 佐々木藤雄. "Kanjō resseki to Jōmon-shiki kaisō shakai 環状列石と縄文式階層社会." In *Jōmon shakai ron* 縄文社会論, vol. 2. Dōseisha, 2002.

———. "Tōhoku no kanjō resseki: Sono nazo ni semaru 東北の環状列石: その謎に迫る." *Kikan Tōhokugaku* 季刊東北学 15 (2008).

Sasaki Kōkan 佐々木宏幹. *Shamanizumu: Ekusutashī to hyōrei no bunka* シャーマニズム: エクスタシーと憑霊の文化. Chuokoron-Shinsha, 1980.

Sasaki Kōmei 佐々木高明. *Yama no kami to Nihonjin: Yama no kami shinkō kara saguru Nihon no kisō bunka* 山の神と日本人: 山の神信仰から探る日本の基層文化. Yōsensha, 2006.

Sasaki Tōru 佐々木徹. "Kitakamigawa ryūiki ni hirogaru reijō 北上川流域に広がる霊場." In Tōhoku Chūsei Kōko gakkai 東北中世考古学会 ed. *Chūsei no seichi, reijō* 中世の聖地・霊場. Kōshi Shoin, 2006.

Satō Masato 佐藤眞人. "Heian jidai kyūtei no shinbutsu kakuri: 'Jōgan-shiki' no kitei o megutte 平安時代宮廷の神仏隔離:「貞観式」の規定をめぐって." In Nijyūnisha Kenkyūkai 二十二社研究会 eds. *Heian jidai no jinja to saishi* 平安時代の神社と祭祀. Kokusho Kankōkai, 1986.

Shibata Minoru 柴田実. "Sosen sūhai no genryū 祖先崇拝の源流." In Akata Mitsuo 赤田光男, ed. *Sorei shinkō* 祖霊信仰. Minshū Shūkyōshi Sōsho 民衆宗教史叢書 26. Yūzankaku, 1991 (initial publication 1959).

Shimazono Susumu 島薗進. "Ikigami shisōron 生神思想論." In Shūkyō Shigaku Kenkyūkai 宗教史学研究会, ed. *Gendai shūkyō e no shikaku* 現代宗教への視角. Yūzankaku, 1978.

——. "19-seiki Nihon no shūkyō kōzō no hen'yō 一九世紀日本の宗教構造の変容." In *Kosumorojī no "kinsei"* コスモロジーの「近世」. Iwanami Kōza Kindai Nihon no Bunkashi 岩波講座近代日本の文化史. Iwanami Shoten, 2001.

——. *Kokka Shintō to Nihonjin* 国家神道と日本人. Iwanami Shinsho, 2010.

Shintani Takanori 新谷尚紀. *Nihonjin no sōgi* 日本人の葬儀. Kinokuniya Shoten, 1992.

——. *Ososhiki: Shi to irei no Nihonshi* お葬式: 死と慰霊の日本史. Yoshikawa Kōbunkan, 2009.

Shiraishi Taichirō 白石太一郎. "Yayoi, kofun bunkaron 弥生・古墳文化論." In *Kodai*, vol 1. Iwanami Kōza Nihon Tsūshi 岩波講座日本通史. Iwanami Shoten, 1993.

——. "Haka to takaikan 墓と他界観." In Uehara Mahito 上原真人 et al., eds. *Shinkō to sekaikan. Rettō no kodaishi* 7: *Hito, mono, koto* 信仰と世界観: 列島の古代史: ひと、もの、こと. Iwanami Shoten, 2006.

——. "Haniwa gunzō o kangaeru: Jinbutsu haniwa gunzō wa nani o kataru ka 埴輪群像を考える: 人物埴輪群像は何を語るか." In Ōsaka Furitsu Chikatsu Asuka Hakubutsukan 大阪府立近つ飛鳥博物館 eds. *Haniwa gunzō no kōkogaku* 埴輪群像の考古学. Aoki Shoten, 2008.

Sonehara Satoshi 曽根原理. *Tokugawa Ieyasu shinkakuka e no michi* 徳川家康神格化への道. Yoshikawa Kōbunkan, 1996.

——. *Shinkun Ieyasu no tanjō: Tōshōgū to gongensama* 神君家康の誕生: 東照宮と権現様. Yoshikawa Kōbunkan, 2008.

Sueki Fumihiko 末木文美士. *Nihon Bukkyō shi: Shisōshi to shite no apurōchi* 日本仏教史: 思想史としてのアプローチ. Shinchōsha, 1992.

Suenaga Keiko 末長恵子. *Uden Shintō no kisoteki kenkyū* 烏伝神道の基礎的研究. Iwata Shoin, 2001.

Suga Miho 須賀みほ. *Tenjin engi no keifu: Kenkyū shiryō hen; Zuhan hen* 天神縁起の系譜: 研究資料編; 図版篇. Chūō Kōron Bijutsu Shuppan, 2004.

Sugiyama Shigetsugu 椙山林継 and Yamagishi Ryōji 山岸良二 eds. *Genshi, kodai Nihon no saishi* 原始・古代日本の祭祀. Dōseisha, 2007.

Suzuki Masataka 鈴木正崇. *Yama to kami to hito: Sangaku shinkō to Shugendō no sekai* 山と神と人: 山岳信仰と修験道の世界. Tankōsha, 1991.

Takagi Hiroshi 高木博志 and Yamada Kunikazu 山田邦和, eds. *Rekishi no naka no ten'nōryō* 歴史の中の天皇陵. Shibunkaku Shuppan, 2010.

Takagi Yutaka 高木豊. "Nichiren no shisō no keishō to hen'yō 日蓮の思想の継承と変容." In *Nichiren* 日蓮. Nihon shisō taikei 日本思想体系. Iwanami Shoten, 1970.

Takahashi Akinori 高橋章則. *Edo no tenkinzoku: Daikansho tedai no sekai* 江戸の転勤族: 代官所手代の世界. Heibonsha Sensho, 2007.

Takahashi Miyuki 高橋美由紀. *Zōhoban: Ise Shintō no seiritsu to tenkai* 増補版伊勢神道の成立と展開. Perikansha, 2010 (initial publication 1994).

Takahashi Wataru 高橋渉. "'Sangaku shinkō' no gainen「山岳信仰」の概念." *Miyagi Gakuin Joshi Daigaku kenkyū ronbunshū* 宮城学院女子大学研究論文集 62 (1985).

Takatori Masao 高取正男. *Shintō no seiritsu* 神道の成立. Heibonsha Sensho, 1979.

Tanaka Fumihide 田中文英. "Jūichi, jūni seiki ni okeru Jōdokyō no tenkai 十一・十二世紀における浄土教の展開." In Ōsaka Rekishi Gakkai 大阪歴史学会, eds. *Historia* ヒストリア 54 (1969).

Tanaka Satoru 田中悟. *Aizu to iu shinwa* 会津という神話. Minerva Shobō, 2010.

Taniguchi Miki 谷口美樹. "Heian kizoku no shippei ninshiki to chiryōhō 平安貴族の疾病認識と治療法." *Nihonshi kenkyū* 日本史研究 364 (1992).

Tatsumi Kazuhiro 辰巳和弘. *Haniwa to kaiga no kodaigaku* 埴輪と絵画の古代学. Hakusuisha, 1992.

———. *Seinaru mizu no matsuri to kodai ōken: Tenpaku Iwakura iseki* 聖なる水の祭りと古代王権: 天白磐座遺跡. Shinsensha, 2006.

———. *Seiju to kodai Yamato no ōkyū* 聖樹と古代大和の王宮. Chūō Kōronsha, 2009.

Teeuwen, Mark. "Jingi, jindō, soshite Shintō 神祇、神道、そして神道." *Bungaku* 文学 9, no. 2 (2008).

———, and Hendrik van der Veere, *Nakatomi Harae Kunge: Purification and Enlightenment in Late-Heian Japan*. In *Buddhismus-Studien* 1 (1998) München: Iudicium verlag 1998.

Terasawa Kaoru 寺沢薫. *Ōken tanjō* 王権誕生. In *Nihon no Rekishi* 日本の歴史 2. Kōdansha, 2000.

Toda Yoshimi 戸田芳実. "Ritsuryōsei kara no kaihō 律令制からの解放." In *Nihon chūsei no minshū to ryōshu* 日本中世の民衆と領主. Azekura Shobō, 1994 (initial publication 1975).

Toike Noboru 外池昇. *Bakumatsu, Meiji-ki no ryōbo* 幕末・明治期の陵墓. Yoshikawa Kōbunkan, 1997.

———. "Bunkyū no shūryō 文久の修陵." *Bessatsu rekishi dokuhon* 別冊歴史読本 78: *Rekishi kenshō tennōryō* 歴史検証天皇陵. Shin Jinbutsu Ōraisha, 2001.

Tsuda Sōkichi 津田左右吉. "Nihon no Shintō. 日本の神道" In *Tsuda Sōkichi zenshū* 津田左右吉全集, vol. 9. Iwanami Shoten, 1964.

Tsude Hiroshi 都出比呂志. *Ōryō no kōkogaku* 王陵の考古学. Iwanami Shinsho, 2000.

Tsuji Zennosuke 辻善之助. "Honji suijaku 本地垂迹." In *Nihon Bukkyōshi* 日本仏教史, vol. 1 *Jōseihen* 上世編. Iwanami Shoten, 1934.

Tsunematsu Mikio 常松幹雄. *Saiko no ōbo: Yoshitake Takagi iseki* 最古の王墓: 吉武高木遺跡. Shinsensha, 2006.

Tsunoda Ryusaku, et al., *Sources of the Japanese Tradition*, vol. I. New York: Columbia University Press, 1958.

Umehara Takeshi 梅原猛. *Nihon no shinsō: Jōmon, Ezo bunka o saguru* 日本の深層: 縄文・蝦夷文化を探る. Shūeisha Bunko, 1994.

Umezawa Isezō 梅沢伊勢三. *Ki Ki hihan: Kojiki oyobi nihon shoki no seiritsu ni kansuru kenkyū* 記紀批判: 古事記及び日本書紀の成立に関する研究. Sōbunsha, 1962.

Watanabe Hiroshi 渡辺浩. *Higashi Ajia no ōken to shisō* 東アジアの王権と思想. Tokyo Daigaku Shuppankai, 1997.

Watson, Burton, tr. *The Lotus Sutra*. New York: Columbia University Press, 1993.

———, tr. *Record of Miraculous Events in Japan*. New York: Columbia University Press, 2013.

Watsuji Tetsurō 和辻哲郎. *Nihon rinri shisōshi* 日本倫理思想史, vol. 1. Iwanami Shoten, 1952.

Yamada Yūji 山田雄司. *Sutoku-in onryō no kenkyū* 崇徳院怨霊の研究. Shibunkaku Shuppan, 2001.

———. *Bakko suru onryō: Tatari to chinkon no Nihonshi* 跋扈する怨霊: 祟りと鎮魂の日本史. Yoshikawa Kōbunkan, 2007.

Yamamoto Hiroko 山本ひろ子. "Shikōsha-tachi: Chūsei shingaku e mukete 至高者たち: 中世神学へ向けて." In *Nihon no kami* 日本の神, vol. 1. Heibonsha, 1995.

———. *Chūsei shinwa* 中世神話. Iwanami Shoten, 1998.

Yamamoto Yōko 山本陽子. *Emaki ni okeru kami to tennō no hyōgen* 絵巻における神と天皇の表現. Chūō Kōron Bijutsu Shuppan, 2006.

Yamaori Tetsuo 山折哲雄. "Kodai Nihon ni okeru kami to hotoke no kankei 古代日本における神と仏の関係." *Tōhoku Daigaku Bungakubu kenkyū nenpō* 東北大学文学部研究年報 29 (1980).

Yanagita Kunio 柳田国男. "Yamamiya kō 山宮考." In *Teihon Yanagita Kunio shū* 定本柳田国男集, vol. 11. Chikuma Shobō, 1963 (initial publication 1947).

———. "Senzo no hanashi 先祖の話." In *Yanagita Kunio zenshū* 柳田国男全集, vol. 13. Chikuma Shobō, 1990 (initial publication 1946).

———. "Hito o kami ni matsuru fūshū 人を神に祀る風習." In *Yanagita Kunio zen-shū* 柳田国男全集, vol. 13. Chikuma Shobō, 1990 (initial publication 1926).

Yasumaru Yoshio 安丸良夫. "Nihon no kindaika to minshū shisō 日本の近代化と民衆思想." In *Nihon no kindaika to minshū shisō* 日本の近代化と民衆思想. Aoki Shoten, 1974 (initial publication 1965).

———. *Kindai tennōzō no keisei* 近代天皇像の形成. Iwanami Shoten, 1992.

———, and Isomae Jun'ichi 磯前順一, eds. *Yasumaru shisōshi e no tairon* 安丸思想史への対論. Perikansha, 2010.

Yoshihara Hiroto 吉原浩人. "Kōgyoku tennō no dajigoku tan 皇極天皇の堕地獄譚." *Kokubungaku kaishaku to kanshō* 国文学解釈と鑑賞 711 (1990).

3. Special Journal Issues and Essay Collections

"Jōmon jidai no matsuri 縄文時代の祭り." *Kikan kōkogaku* 季刊考古学 107 (2009).

Kashihara Kōkogaku Kenkyūjo, eds. *Mizu to saishi no kōkogaku* 水と祭祀の考古学. Gakuseisha, 2005.

"Kofun jidai no matsuri 古墳時代の祀り." *Kikan kōkogaku* 季刊考古学 96 (2006).

"Nihon no stōn sākuru 日本のストーンサークル." *Kikan kōkogaku* 季刊考古学 101 (2007).

Nihonshi Kenkyūkai: Kyoto Minka Rekishi Bukai, eds. *"Ryōbo" kara mita Nihonshi* 「陵墓」からみた日本史. Aoki Shoten, 1995.

Ōsaka Furitsu Chikatsu Asuka Hakubutsukan, eds. *Haniwa gunzō no kōkogaku* 埴輪群像の考古学. Aoki Shoten, 2008.

"Rekishi kenshō: Tennōryō 歴史検証天皇陵." *Bessatsu rekishi dokuhon* 別冊歴史読本 78. Shin Jinbutsu Ōraisha, 2001.

4. Local Histories, Archaeological Reports, Catalogues

"Dainenjiyama yokoana bogun hakkutsu chōsa hōkokusho 大念寺山横穴墓群発掘調査報告書." *Sendai-shi bunkazai chōsa hōkokusho* 仙台市文化財調査報告書 311 (2007).

"Kōko shiryō 考古資料." *Sendai-shishi: Tokubetsuhen* 仙台市史: 特別編 2 (1995).

Kokuhō dogū ten 国宝土偶展. Tokyo Kokuritsu Hakubutsukan, 2009.

"Mogasaki yokoanabo-gun 茂ヶ崎横穴墓群." *Sendai-shi bunkazai chōsa hōkokusho* 仙台市文化財調査報告書 130 (1989).

"Mutsu no kuni to Sendai heiya 陸奥国と仙台平野." *Sendai-shishi: tsūshihen* 仙台市史: 通史編 2 (2000).

"Shiseki: Tōmizuka kofun 史跡遠見塚古墳." *Sendai-shi bunkazai chōsa hōkokusho* 仙台市文化財調査報告書 15 (1979).

5. Primary Sources

GR	*Gunsho ruijū* 群書類従
KST	*Shintei zōho kokushi taikei* 新訂増補国史大系
NKBT	*Nihon koten bungaku taikei* 日本古典文学大系
NKBZ	*Nihon koten bungaku zenshū* 日本古典文学全集
NST	*Nihon shisō taikei* 日本思想体系
SNKBT	*Shin Nihon koten bungaku taikei* 新日本古典文学大系
SNKBZ	*Shinpen Nihon koten bungaku zenshū* 新篇日本古典文学全集
STJH	*Shintō taikei: jinja hen* 神道大系: 神社編
STRH	*Shintō taikei: ronsetsu hen* 神道大系: 論説篇
ZGR	*Zoku gunsho ruijū* 続群書類従

"Ari no omoi 蟻の念." In *Uden Shintō* 烏伝神道 1, vol. 45 of *Zoku Shintō taikei* 続神道大系. Shintō Taikei Hensankai, 2001.

Azuma kagami 吾妻鏡. 4 vols. KST. Yoshikawa Kōbunkan, 1968.

Ban'naji Kabasaki engi narabi ni butsuji shidai 鑁阿寺樺崎縁起并仏事次第. In *Tochigi kenshi, shiryō hen, Chūsei* 栃木県史: 資料編、中世 1. Tochigi ken, 1973.

Bashō 芭蕉. In *Yōkyokushū* 謡曲集 1, NKBZ 33. Shōgakukan, 1973.

"Byōkutsu-ge 廟崛偈." In *Teihon Shinran shōnin zenshū* 定本親鸞上人全集 6. Kyoto: Hōzōkan, 1970.

Daijingū sankeiki 大神宮参詣記. In GR 27 Shingi bu 神祇部. Gunsho Ruijū Kanseikai, 1969.

"Dōjōji engi 道成寺縁起." In *Kuwanomidera engi, Dōjōji engi* 桑実寺縁起、道成寺縁起, vol. 24 of *Zoku Nihon no emaki* 続日本の絵巻. Chūō Kōronsha, 1992.

Eiga monogatari 栄華物語. 2 vols. NKBT 75–76. Iwanami Shoten, 1964–65.

Engishiki 延喜式. KST 26. Yoshikawa Kōbunkan, 1972.

Fudoki 風土記. SNKBT 5. Shōgakukan, 1997.

Fujisan ki 富士山記. In *Honchō monzui* 本朝文粋. KST 29-2.

Fusō ryakuki 扶桑略記. In *Teiō hennenki; Fusō ryakuki* 帝王編年記; 扶桑略記. KST 12.

Genji monogatari 源氏物語. 5 vols. NKBT 19–23. Iwanami Shoten, 1958–63.

Genpei seisuiki 源平盛衰記. 7 vols. Chūsei no bungaku 中世の文学. Miyai Shoten, 1994–2015.

"Gishi wajinden 魏志倭人伝." In Wada Kiyoshi 和田清 and Ishihara Michihiro 石原道博, eds. *Gishi wajinden* 魏志倭人伝. Iwanami Shoten, 1951.

"Gochinza hongi 御鎮座本記." In *Ise Shintō* 伊勢神道 1, STRH 5. Shintō Taikei Hensankai, 1993.

"Go-Fushimi tennō zō sō Eison bosatsu-gō choku 後伏見天皇贈僧叡尊菩薩号勅." In *Honchō bunshū* 本朝文集, KST 30. Yoahikawa Kōbunkan, 2000.

"Gokurakuji-dono goshōsoku 極楽寺殿御消息." In Ozawa Fumio 小澤富夫, ed., *Zōho kaitei buke kakun; ikun shūsei* 増補改訂武家家訓; 遺訓集成. Perikansha, 2003.

Gukanshō 愚管抄. NKBT 86. Iwanami Shoten, 1967.

Gyokuzui 玉蘂. Shibunkaku Shuppan, 1992.

"Hai Kurishitan bun 排切支丹文." In *Kirishitan sho; Hai-Ya sho* キリシタン書; 排耶書. NST 25. Iwanami Shoten, 1970.

Heike monogatari 平家物語. 2 vols. NKBT32–33. Iwanami Shoten, 1959–60.

Himitsu nenbutsu shō 秘密念仏抄. In *Shingon-shū anjin zensho* 真言宗安心全書 2. Kyoto: Shuchiin Daigaku, 1973.

"Hōki hongi 宝基本記. In *Ise Shintō* 伊勢神道 1, STRH 5. Shintō Taikei Hensankai, 1993.

Hokke genki 法華験記. In *Ōjōden; Hokke genki* 往生伝; 法華験記. NST 7. Iwanami Shoten, 1974.

Hokkekyō 法華経. 3 vols. Iwanami Bunko, 1962–67.

Honchō seiki 本朝世紀. KST 9. Yoshikawa Kōbunkan, 2003.

Hosshinshū 発心集. In *Hōjōki; Hosshinshū* 方丈記; 発心集. Shinchō Nihon koten shūsei. Shinchōsha, 1976.

Ichigon hōdan 一言芳談. In *Kana hōgoshū* 仮名法語集. NKBT 83. Iwanami Shoten, 1964.

Iezusu-kai Nihon nenpō イエズス会日本年報. In Iezusu-kai Nihon nenpō イエズス会日本年報, vol. 1 of 2. Shin ikoku sōsho. Yūshōdō Shoten, 1969.

Imakagami 今鏡. In *Imakagami; Masukagami* 今鏡; 増鏡. KST 21-2. Yoahikawa Kōbunkan, 2007.

Ippen hijiri e 一遍聖絵. In *Nihon emakimono zenshū* 日本絵巻物全集, vol. 10. Kadokawa Shoten, 1960.

Ippen Shōnin goroku 一遍上人語録. In *Hōnen; Ippen* 法然; 一遍. NST 10. Iwanami Shoten, 1971.

Ishiyamadera engi 石山寺縁起. In *Nihon no emaki* 日本の絵巻 16. Chūō Kōronsha, 1988.

Izumi Shikibu shū 和泉式部集. In *Heian Kamakura shikashū* 平安鎌倉私家集. NKBT 80. Iwanami Shoten, 1964.

Jikkunshō 十訓抄. In *Ujishūi Monogatari; Kojidan; Jikkunshō* 宇治拾遺物語; 古事談; 十訓抄. KST 18. Yohikawa Kōbunkan, 2007.

Jingi seisō 神祇正宗. ZGR 3a. Zoku Gunsho Ruijū Kanseikai, 1959.

Kaidōki 海道記. In *Chūsei nikki kikō shū* 中世日記紀行集. SNKBZ 48. Shōgakukan, 1964.

Kankyo no tomo 閑居の友. In *Hōbutsushū; Kankyo no tomo, Hirasan kojin reitaku* 宝物集; 閑居友; 比良山個人霊託. SNKBT 40. Iwanami Shoten, 2005.

Kii no kuni meisho zue 紀伊国名所図会. Edo-period printed book in the Kanō Collection, Tōhoku University Library, Sendai.

Kitano Tenjin engi 北野天神縁起. In *Jisha engi* 寺社縁起, NST 20. Iwanami Shoten, 1975.

Kōfukuji sōjō 興福寺奏状. In *Kamakura kyū Bukkyō* 鎌倉旧仏教, NST 15. Iwanami Shoten, 1971.

Kojidan 古事談. In *Kojidan; Zoku kojidan* 古事談; 続古事談. SNKBT 41. Iwanami Shoten, 1993.

Kojiki 古事記. In *Kojiki; Jōdai kayō* 古事記; 上代歌謡. NKBZ 1. Shogakukan, 1973.

Kojikiden 古事記伝. In *Motoori Norinaga zenshū* 本居宣長全集 9. Chikuma Shobō, 1968.

Kokawadera engi emaki 粉河寺縁起絵巻. In *Jisha engi* 寺社縁起. NST 20. Iwanami Shoten, 1975.

Kōmyō shingon shijū shaku 光明真言四重釈. In *Shingon-shū anjin zensho* 真言宗安心全書 2. Kyoto: Shuchiin Daigaku, 1973.

Konjaku monogatari shū 今昔物語集. 5 vols. NKBT 22–26. Iwanami Shoten, 1959–63.

Konkō Daijin rikai 金光大神理解. In *Minshū shūkyō no shisō* 民衆宗教の思想. NST 67. Iwanami Shoten, 1971.

Kōyasan ki 高野山記. ZGR 28 a. Zoku Gunsho Ruijū Kanseikai, 1959.

"Kujō Michiie sō shobunjō 九条道家惣処分状." In Kamakura ibun 鎌倉遺文 10. Tōkyōdō Shuppan, 1972.

Kurozuka 黒塚. In *Yōkyokushū* 謡曲集 2. NKBZ 34. Shōgakukan, 1975.

Man'yōshū 万葉集. 4 vols. SNKBT 1–4. Iwanami Shoten, 1999–2003.

"Mekishiko sōtoku ate Tokugawa Ieyasu shokan メキシコ総督宛徳川家康書簡." In Dai Nihon shiryō 大日本史料 12:9. Tokyo Daigaku Shiryō Hensanjo, 1971.

Mimibukuro 耳嚢. 3 vols. Iwanami Shoten, 1991.

Mizukagami 水鏡. In *Ōkagami; Mizukagami* 大鏡; 水鏡, KST 21-a. Yoshikawa Kōbunkan, 2003.

Motomezuka 求塚. In *Yōkyokushū* 謡曲集 2. NKBZ 34. Shōgakukan, 1975.

Myōkōnin den 妙好人伝. In *Kinsei Bukkyō no shisō* 近世仏教の思想. NST 57. Iwanami Shoten, 1973.

Nakatomi no harae kunge 中臣祓訓解. In *Chusei Shintō ron* 中世神道論, NST 10. Iwanami Shoten, 1977.

Nihon kiryaku 日本紀略. KST 10–11. Yoshikawa Kōbunkan, 1965.

Nihon Ōjō gokuraku ki 日本往生極楽記. In *Ōjōden; Hokke genki* 往生伝法華験記. NST 7. Iwanami Shoten, 1974.

Nihon ryōiki 日本霊異記. SNKBT 70. Iwanami Shoten, 1967.

Nihon sandai jitsuroku 日本三大実録. KST 4. Yoshikawa Kōbunkan, 1973.

Nihongi Miwa-ryū 日本紀三輪流. In *Chūsei Nihongi shū* 中世日本紀集, vol. 7 of *Shinpukuji zenbon sōkan: Shingi-bu*. Kyoto: Rinsen Shoten, 1999.

"Ōhōri Suwa Nobushige gejō utsushi 大祝諏訪信重解状写." In *Suwa shishi* 諏訪市史, vol. 1. Suwa Shishi Hensan Iinkai, 1995.

Ōjōyōshū 往生要集. In *Genshin* 源信, NST 6. Iwanami Shoten, 1970.

Ritsuryō 律令. NST 3. Iwanami Shoten, 1976.

Saigoku sanjūsansho meisho zue 西国三十三所名所図会. Kyoto: Rinsen Shoten, 1991.

San'ikun 三彝訓. In *Kinsei Bukkyō no shisō* 近世仏教の思想. NST 57. Iwanami Shoten, 1973.

Sanjūichi-nichi no onmaki 三十一日の御巻. In *Minshū shūkyō no shisō* 民衆宗教の思想. NST 67. Iwanami Shoten, 1971.

Sarashina nikki 更級日記. In *Tosa nikki; Kagerō nikki; Murasaki Shikibu nikki; Sarashina nikki* 土佐日記; 蜻蛉日記; 紫式部日記; 更級日記. SNKBT 24. Iwanaami Shoten, 1989.

Sasamegoto ささめごと. Tenri edition, in Kidō Saizō 木藤才蔵, *Sasamegoto no kenkyū* ささめごとの研究. Kyoto: Rinsen Shoten, 1990.

Shasekishū 沙石集. NKBT 85. Iwanami Shoten, 1966.

Shintō taii 神道大意 (Wakabayashi Kyōsai 若林強斎). In *Suika Shintō* 垂加神道 2, STRH 100.

Shintō taii 神道大意 (Yoshida Kaneo 吉田兼雄). In *Urabe Shintō* ト部神道 1, STRH 95.

Shintōshū 神道集, Tōyō Bunko edition. Kadokawa Shoten, 1959.

Shoku Nihon kōki 続日本後紀. KST 3. Yoshikawa Kōbunkan, 1971.

Shoku Nihongi 続日本紀. 5 vols. SNKBT 12–16. Iwanami Shoten, 1989–98.

Shoshin honkai shū 諸神本懐集. In *Shinshū shiryō shūsei* 真宗史料集成 1. Kyoto: Dōhōsha, 2007.

Shūgi seihō ron 宗義制法論. In *Bandai kikyō roku* 万代亀鏡録 3. Shuppan Kagaku Sōgō Kenkyūjo, 1982.

Shūi Ōjōden 拾遺往生伝. In *Ōjōden; Hokke genki* 法華験記, NST 7. Iwanami Shoten, 1974.

Sōkonshū 草根集. In *Sōkonshū; Gondai sōzu shinkeishū; Saishō* 草根集; 権大僧都心敬集; 再昌. Waka bungaku taikei 66. Meiji Shoin, 2005.

Sumidagawa 隅田川. In *Yōkyokushū* 謡曲集 2, NKBZ 34.

Taiheiki 太平記. 3 vols. NKBT 34–36. Iwanami Shoten, 1960–62.

Tendai Hokkeshū gozu hōmon yōsan 天台法華宗牛頭法門要纂. In *Tendai honkaku ron* 天台本覚論, NST 9. Iwanami Shoten, 1973.

Tengu no sōshi 天狗草子. In *Tsuchigumo no sōshi; Tengu no sōshi; Ōeyama eko-toba* 土蜘蛛草子; 天狗草子; 大江山絵詞. Zoku Nihon no emaki taisei 19. Chūō Kōronsha, 1975.

Tenjin engi 天神縁起. In Suga Miho 須賀みほ, *Tenjin engi no keifu* 天神縁起の系譜. Chūō Kōron Bijutsu Shuppan, 2004.

Tōshōsha engi: kana engi 東照社縁起; 仮名縁起. In *Kōzuke no kuni; Shimotsuke no kuni* 上野; 下野国. STJH 25. Shintō Taikei Hensankai, 1992.

Tōshōsha engi: mana engi 東照社縁起; 真名縁起. In *Kōzuke no kuni; Shimotsuke no kuni* 上野; 下野国. STJH 25. Shintō Taikei Hensankai, 1992.

Toyo-ashihara jinpū waki 豊葦原神風和記. In *Tendai Shintō* 天台神道 1, STRH 3. Shintō Taikei Hensankai, 1990.

Tōyūki 東遊記. In Tachibana Nankei 橘南谿, *Tōzai yūki* 東西遊記 1. Heibonsha, 1974.

Tsugaro no ochi 都介路廼遠地. In Sugae Masami zenshū 菅江真澄全集 3. Miraisha, 1972.

Uji shūi monogatari 宇治拾遺物語. In *Uji shūi monogatari; Kohon setsuwashū* 宇治拾遺物語; 古本説話集. SNKBT 42. Iwanami Shoten, 2016.

Uneme 采女. In *Yōkyokushū* 謡曲集 1, NKBZ 33. Iwanami Shoten, 1973.

Wakasa no Kuni chinju Ichi-Ni-no-miya engi 若狭国鎮守一二宮縁起. in Kawane Yoshiyasu 河音能平, "Wakasa no Kuni chinju Ichi-Ni-no-miya engi no seiritsu," *Chūsei hōkensei seiritsu shiron* 中世封建制成立史論. Tokyo Daigaku Shuppankai, 1971.

Wakasa no Kuni chinju Ichi-Ni-no-miya shinjin ekeizu 若狭国鎮守一二宮神人絵系図. In *Wakasa; Echizen; Kaga; Noto no Kuni* 若狭; 越前; 加賀; 能登国. STJH 33. Shintō Taikei Hensankai, 1987.

Yamato ikusa akitsu sonae 和軍蜻蛉備. In *Uden Shintō* 烏伝神道 4, vol. 48 of *Zoku shintō taikei* 続神道大系. Shintō Taikei Hensankai, 2003.

Yuiitsu Shintō myōhō yōshū 唯一神道妙法要集. In *Chūsei Shintō ron* 中世神道論, NST 19. Iwanami Shoten, 1977.

Zenkōji engi 善光寺縁起. In ZGR 28a. Zoku Gunsho Ruijū Kanseikai, 1926.

Image credits

All uncredited photographs were taken by the author.

Chapter 1
Tamonten zō 多聞天像 (Image of Tamonten). From the exhibition catalogue *Horyūji Shōwa shizai chōsa kansei kinen: Kokuhō Horyūji ten* 法隆寺昭和資材帳調査完成記念 国宝法隆寺展 (Nara Kokuritsu Hakubutsukan, 1994).

Chapter 2
Gasshō dogū 合掌土偶 (Praying earthenware figurine). From the exhibition catalogue *Bunkachō kaigai ten Daiei Hakubutsukan kikoku kinen: Kokuhō dogū ten* 文化庁海外展大英博物館帰国記念 国宝土偶展 (Bunkachō, 2009).

Chapter 4
Shinzō 神像 (Image of a God). From the exhibition catalogue *Kamigami no bi no sekai: Kyoto no Shintō bijutsu* 神々の美の世界 京都の神道美術(Kyoto Kokuritsu Hakubutsukan, 2004).

Kitano-sha ezu 北野社絵図 (Painting of Kitano Shrine). From the exhibition catalogue *Shinbutsu shūgō* 図録 神仏習合 (Nara Kokuritsu Hakubutsukan, 2007).

Yuzū Nenbutsu engi 融通念仏縁起 (Origins of the Yuzū Nenbutsu sect). From *Yuzū Nenbutsu engi*, vol. 21 in *Zoku Nihon no emaki* 続日本の絵巻 (Chūō Kōronsha, 1992).

Chapter 5

Yamagoshi Amida zu 山越阿弥陀図 (Amida Coming Over the Mountains). From the exhibition catalogue *Shinbutsu shūgō* 図録 神仏習合 (Nara Kokuritsu Hakubutsukan, 2007).

Kasuga no miya mandara (Mandala of the Kasuga Shrine). From the exhibition catalogue *Shinbutsu shūgō* 図録 神仏習合 (Nara Kokuritsu Hakubutsukan, 2007).

Chapter 6

Yūreizu 幽霊図 (Portrait of a Ghost). From *Bessatsu Taiyō* 98: *Yūrei no shōtai* 別冊太陽 98: 幽霊の正体 (Heibonsha, 1997).

Dōjōji engi 道成寺縁起 (Origins of Dōjōji Temple). From *Kuwanomidera engi*; *Dōjōji engi*, vol. 21 in *Zoku Nihon no emaki* 続日本の絵巻 (Chūō Kōronsha, 1992).

Index

About the Author

SATŌ HIROO was born in 1953 in Miyagi Prefecture. He earned his M.A. in the Graduate School of Arts and Letters at Tōhoku University in 1978. After serving as an instructor at Morioka University beginning in 1985, he was appointed assistant professor in the Faculty of Arts and Letters at Tōhoku University in 1992. He received his Ph.D. in 2000, and was named professor in the Graduate School of Arts and Letters in 2001, where he was appointed dean in 2014. He specializes in intellectual history focused on the religious traditions of Japan.

He has published numerous scholarly articles and books, including *Shisha no hanayome* (Brides of the Dead; Genki Shobō, 2015); *Kamakura Bukkyō* (Kamakura Buddhism; Chikuma Gakugei Bunko, 2014); *Shisha no yukue* (Whither the Dead?; Iwata Shoin, 2008); *Shinkoku Nihon* (Japan: Land of the Gods; Chikuma Shinsho, 2006); and *Amaterasu no henbō* (The Changing Face of Amaterasu; Hōzōkan, 2000).